NASD ARBITRATION SOLUTION:

FIVE BLACK-BELT PRINCIPLES TO PROTECT AND GROW YOUR FINANCIAL SERVICES PRACTICE

Thomas J. Hine, CFP®, CFS, MBA, and
John K. Brubaker

John Wiley & Sons, Inc.

Published by John Wiley & Sons, Inc., Hoboken, New Jersey.
Published simultaneously in Canada.

Wiley Bicentennial Logo: Richard J. Pacifico

For general information on our other products and services or for technical support, please contact our Customer Care Department within the United States at (800) 762-2974, outside the United States at (317) 572-3993, or fax (317) 572-4002.

Wiley also publishes its books in a variety of electronic formats. Some content that appears in print may not be available in electronic books. For more information about Wiley products, visit our web site at www.wiley.com.

Library of Congress Cataloging-in-Publication Data:

Hine, Thomas J. 1961-
  NASD arbitration solution : five black belt principles to protect and grow your financial services practice / Thomas J. Hine and John K. Brubaker.
    p. cm.
  Includes bibliographical references.
  ISBN 978-0-470-12632-5 (cloth)
  1. National Association of Securities Dealers.   2. Securities—United States.   3. Arbitration and award—United States.   I. Brubaker, John K., 1953- II. Title.
  KF1070.H56 2007
  346.73'09220269--dc22

                                                          2007007065

Printed in the United States of America.

10 9 8 7 6 5 4 3 2 1

To Henry H. Hine, my wonderful father,
who died February 18, 2006: soldier, statesman,
leader, and mentor. I am grateful for all the great
years we had together. If I can become half the
father for my children that you were for me, that
would be the accomplishment of a lifetime.

As you taught me, "When you aim high, you hit high."

Thomas J. Hine

In loving memory of my parents,
John and Joyce Brubaker,
this is dedicated to Angel, Eric, Mark,
Meg, Melissa, Crystal, and the future
generations of our family.

John K. Brubaker

CONTENTS

Why I Wrote This Book   vii

Acknowledgments   xi

Introduction   xv

Part One   My NASD Arbitration from Start to Finish

Chapter 1   Sweating Bullets   3

Chapter 2   24: The Day That Almost Never Ended   25

Chapter 3   Expert Witness Unmasked: An Offer to Settle—
             I Finally Get to Testify   53

Chapter 4   Cross-Examination—It Was War   81

Chapter 5   Closing Arguments—And a Decision   105

**Part Two   Five Black-Belt Principles to Protect and
             Grow Your Financial Services Practice**

Chapter 6   The Cycle of Life   131

Chapter 7   To Protect and Grow   141

Chapter 8   Humility: The White-Belt Attitude   147

Chapter 9   Integrity: Look in the Mirror   157

Chapter 10   Duality: Yin and Yang   165

Chapter 11   Awareness: The Third Eye   177

Chapter 12   Dedication: Kaizen   189

Part Three How to Prevail in an NASD Arbitration Hearing

Chapter 13   What's the Cost?   199

Chapter 14   Case Studies   207

Chapter 15   The Lawyer's Perspective: How to Prepare
             and Try an NASD Arbitration Case—
             by James W. Weller, Esq.   219

Chapter 16   How to Prepare for NASD Arbitration   251

Chapter 17   Preparing to Testify and Managing Your
             Case to Conclusion   267

Appendices

Appendix A   NASD Arbitration Case Flow   283

Appendix B   NASD Arbitration Trends   291

Appendix C   Errors-and-Omissions Insurance   295

Appendix D   Technology Tools   299

Index   303

About the Authors   309

WHY I WROTE THIS BOOK

After more than 10 years as a registered representative, without warning, in September 2002, I became the subject of an investor complaint to the NASD. Over the following 21 months, I went through an NASD arbitration to resolve this dispute. It was one of the most powerful experiences of my professional life. The story of the dispute and its resolution is described in detail in Part One.

After my NASD process was completed, I went to work strengthening my practice, based on the knowledge I had gained. I learned that many reps who have been through NASD arbitration used their experience in a similar, positive manner. I began sharing some of my experiences with fellow registered representatives and found that they were fascinated by many of the details I shared about the process. I started to realize that NASD arbitration is, to a great extent, shrouded in mystery for many reps. Those who go through it are reluctant to discuss it, preferring to put the experience behind them and move on.

I accepted some speaking opportunities and spoke about it some more, to increasingly enthusiastic response. It was clear that this topic hit a chord with many reps. In the summer of 2004, I gave an address at a national broker-dealer convention on NASD compliance, sharing what I had learned from my experience. The response was fantastic. At least a dozen people told me that it was the best talk they had ever heard on the subject. After some more thought, I decided to try and write a book.

This was a dilemma for me, as I did not possess the writing background, knowledge of the publishing industry, or time necessary. I began to tap into my network to see if I could find a collaborator. I was fortunate to be introduced to John Brubaker, who became my co-author.

To the best of my knowledge, this represents the first time that an entire NASD arbitration process has been described in print at this level of detail by a registered representative. I made the decision to subject myself to this level of scrutiny because I strongly believe that the information the story contains will be of use to my fellow registered representatives, as well as to anyone who has interest in the securities industry.

Despite the fact that NASD arbitration can become a career-defining event, many reps are woefully ignorant about how the system actually works. As part of the work on this book, we interviewed a number of reps who have been through the process. One constant refrain was the lack of solid, clear, and helpful information by which the rep can guide him- or herself through the process. By providing this never-before-seen glimpse into NASD arbitration, we offer a teaching tool to anyone who is interested.

No system of dispute resolution will be perfect. My experience has taught me that balance is necessary. There must be a forum so that investors who are the victims of the unethical or prohibited business practices of registered representatives can have their claims examined, and can receive compensation for provable economic loss. Registered representatives who themselves are the victim of baseless charges should not have their careers damaged. The current system lacks a clear method for filtering out those claims with merit from those that do not. This book is aimed at providing the registered representative with certain tools to help defend against those claims that he or she believes are unfounded.

I look to the future in the hopes that the current system can evolve into one that provides investors with the forum they deserve, but minimizes the involvement of registered representatives who are not guilty of improper business practices.

The overwhelming majority of reps are hardworking, dedicated, and ethical. Increased attention to client service, through portfolio reviews, constant communication, and a high level of documentation, benefits everyone. If registered representatives who read this book come away with a better knowledge of NASD arbitration, and an increased motivation to continuously improve their financial services practices, this book will have accomplished its objective. The end result would be a small contribution toward improving the quality of the securities industry and a mutual benefit for the investor client and registered representative.

ACKNOWLEDGMENTS

This book was made possible by the contributions of many people. We want to thank, first and foremost, our families—immediate and extended. They represent all that is truly important in the world, and their support is sustaining and inspiring.

We owe a great deal to Debra Englander, our editor. To work with an executive editor of the preeminent publisher of business books in the world is a dream come true for any aspiring author. She can say more in two sentences than most people do in 20 pages. Our thanks to Greg Friedman and all the fine people at John Wiley & Sons, Inc. We are honored and thrilled to be part of the company's 200th year in business.

To refer to Don Gastwirth as merely our "literary agent" is a bit of a misnomer. He is so much more than that. Don's willingness to represent the project at its inception gave us the impetus to prepare the proposal. It was on Don's recommendation that we made John Wiley & Sons, Inc. our first, and hopefully, only choice to publish this book. Thanks to his effective advocacy, this dream came to pass. Don is a brilliant strategist, skilled attorney, shadow editor, irrepressible kibitzer, needed humorist, motivator of the best within us, and treasured friend.

Chris Gryzen, a compliance professional, was incredibly helpful in many aspects of this work. He provided us with great research and valuable insight, often on short notice. He was a delight to work with in every way. Bill Thomas did a wonderful job in creating the initial cycle. Kim Riendeau took that and our ideas and created the "Protect and Grow" logo, a perfect graphical representation of what was in our minds.

We want to thank all of the people whom we have trained with in the martial arts over the years. Tom owes the deepest respect and gratitude to Sensei Robert Jacobs, who is Tom's instructor, and Master M. Mori, who is instructor to both of them. Tom is grateful for Master Mori's true commitment to the spirit of karate-do. John is forever grateful for the wisdom, encouragement, and living example of Master Michael Romano and Grandmaster Ho Soo Hwang, who were John's master and grandmaster.

Tom would like to thank Ron Carson, Steve Sanduski, and Lee Brower, who have been a positive influence through their coaching programs. He would also like to thank Khouree Gale-Lemay, Kristy Klein, and the rest of his staff at Capital Wealth Management, LLC. David Spinar, the chief compliance officer of Securities America, provided valuable insight.

The authors would like to thank Gail Lebert, who introduced them to each other, and to Chris Brubaker, who provided a serene and supporting setting in Tampa, Florida, where the core of the book concept and proposal was drafted. John would like to thank John Bermon, Faith Manierre, Christine Pallotti, David Roncari, and Jim Sullivan for their invaluable coaching and mentoring.

Jim Weller, Esq., and Joan Herman of Nixon, Peabody, LLP, played a prominent role in the events described in Part One, and Jim did a great chapter in Part Three. Both were extremely helpful throughout the process of writing the manuscript, in a number of ways. Peter Evans of Rogin Nassau was especially helpful in Part Three, and gave additional perspective that helped complement Jim Weller's material.

A number of people read various drafts of the manuscript and gave us extremely helpful feedback. These include Beatrice Abigail, Mark Blake, Fritz Brauner, Eric Brubaker, Jason Brubaker, Carolyn Hine, John L. Carlson, Camille Gagliardi, Margaret

(Peg) Hine, John Horan, Jeff Lang, Scott LeClaire, Rochana Norby, Don Patrick, JoAnne Riley, and Mallory Selfridge. Mitch Zuckoff was tremendously helpful with his insights on our original book proposal, as well as sharing his publishing experience.

If there is value in this book, these people share the credit. Any mistakes are our own.

Thomas J. Hine
John K. Brubaker

INTRODUCTION

Welcome to the right-brain guide to NASD compliance. The idea of writing a book to present a National Association of Securities Dealers (NASD) arbitration solution presents a dilemma. It is a topic of intense interest, provoking deep fear among the registered representative community. Yet there is no subject about which reps have greater denial than that of NASD compliance. Reps comfort themselves with the rationalization that only a small percentage will be affected, but also know that the downside of an investor claim against themselves could be a career-defining, or even career-ending experience.

The concerns are quite real. High-profile cases are publicized in the trade press, and reps buzz among themselves to discuss the latest stories and their implications. Top producers, past champions of national conventions, have had to surrender their licenses and leave the business forever, with a multimillion-dollar award against them as their final career legacy. Nightmare stories circulate about plaintiff attorneys systematically targeting reps, invading their practices by recruiting not one but multiple clients as claimants. At a recent plaintiffs bar convention, a presentation was made on successful strategies for suing financial advisers over the coming decade.

Some reps are shocked when they learn that former clients, with whom they felt they had a good relationship, have filed claims against them in the multimillions of dollars range. In some cases, the claim exceeds the upper limit of a rep's errors-and-omissions (E&O) insurance, leaving them exposed to a judgment that has the potential to bankrupt them. Rumors float about broker-dealer firms becoming uninsurable, and having to consider self-insuring.

Registered representatives see NASD arbitration as a system that, however well intentioned, is increasingly hostile to them. Some have bitterly referred to the system as a form of legalized extortion. Out-of-pocket expenses paid by the registered representative, derived from the deductible for E&O insurance coverage, can be as high as $40,000 for a single claim. Some representatives have been hit with multiple claims requiring multiple deductibles, as attorneys use a type of affinity marketing to find claimants. NASD is putting more pressure on broker-dealer firms to deal harshly when representatives are found to have committed a violation of any kind.

Despite the intense interest in the subject, ironically there is also no topic about which there is a higher level of resistance by registered representatives than that of compliance. Mandatory classes are referred to darkly among the rep community as "sales prevention training." Eyes glaze over as a well-meaning compliance officer goes over the latest set of policies, forms, procedures, and best practices. Reps joke about preferring a trip to the dentist, without novocaine, over one more compliance class, and keeping their broker-dealer's compliance manual by their bedside so it is there to read in case they need something to help them get to sleep.

It is time to break this deadlock, to try a different approach. Registered representatives are by and large entrepreneurs and salespeople by nature. A majority are classic "right-brain" types—relatively high on creativity and strong on interpersonal skills, typically weaker on accounting, forms, procedures, and follow-through.

To date, compliance training, with its emphasis on forms, details, and legalities, has been taught using a left-brain approach to a predominantly right-brain audience. For many registered representatives, compliance is not taught in a manner that connects well with their personality or learning style. Furthermore, with a heavy emphasis on "how" to do it, and less on "why," some reps expose themselves to the risk of an investor complaint through laxity, perhaps driven by a sense of denial that it could happen to them.

Part One, "My NASD Arbitration from Start to Finish," is the story of Tom Hine's NASD arbitration case. It covers the period from September 2002, in which Tom received a Statement of Claim from a former client, through June 2004, in which he received the final decision of the arbitration panel. It details the process from beginning to end, including Tom's extensive pre-hearing preparation and the drama of four days of hearings in New York City spread out over seven months before a three-person NASD arbitration panel. It includes the legal strategies, the ebbs and flows, testifying under oath, cross-examination, and closing arguments. Part One includes actual word-for-word testimony transcribed from audiotapes of the hearings.

Readers will watch the process unfold through Tom's eyes, and feel the strong emotions that accompany an experience of this professional magnitude. Registered representatives will learn dozens of little details about the process that previously was possible only through the crucible of actual experience.

Because of the shame associated with being subjected to arbitration, the issue is nearly taboo among registered representatives—spoken about in hushed tones, if at all. Reps who have been through the process fear that among their peers there may be an unspoken but powerful assumption that anyone accused must have done something wrong. Like an IRS audit, even if an individual survived one with no negative consequence, it would not likely make for good cocktail party conversation. Representatives who go through NASD arbitration and lose rarely wish to discuss it. Those who come out with no award given against them generally want to go back to work and forget the ordeal.

We believe that this is the first time that an NASD arbitration hearing has been described from beginning to end at this level of detail by a registered representative. It should prove to be an invaluable instructional and motivational tool for anyone who needs to know about the NASD arbitration process. Registered representatives who read Part One will, through the power of narrative, find it educational and, hopefully, motivational.

This particular story will make it clear that, contrary to the comfortable myth by which some reps may feel nearly invulnerable, no registered representative is immune from the threat of an investor complaint. For many reps, improved compliance is a matter more of motivation than knowledge. As Chris Gryzen, vice president of compliance at BancWest Investment Services and special faculty member at Creighton University, said, "In the next five years, investment firms will spend over a billion dollars and spend countless hours in exhaustive, defensive preparation in response to customer complaints and arbitration cases. What is so exasperating is that many of the complaints are completely avoidable. It's not a matter of a registered representative's not knowing what to do. Rather, it is a case of their not doing what they already know."

Statistics demonstrate that on average a little less than 1 percent of all registered representatives will be taken to NASD arbitration each year. However, for the rep who is planning a career of 20 or more years, the cumulative risk is significant. The downside of having a formal Statement of Claim is enormous. The cost for a rep to defend himself or herself through an entire NASD arbitration process in time, money, emotional stress, and lost opportunity typically involves tens of thousands of dollars, and can be in excess of $100,000. Any award or settlement of $10,000 or more becomes a permanent part of a rep's record, with far-reaching negative career consequences.

Part Two is "Five Black-Belt Principles to Protect and Grow Your Financial Services Practice."

Interwoven into Part One is the story of how Tom, under the

greatest pressure of his professional life, found himself guided by five simple but powerful principles that are an important part of his more than 20 years of martial arts training. These concepts—humility, integrity, duality, awareness, and dedication—are described as "black-belt" principles. They are properly thought of not as being exclusively associated with martial arts, but instead are universal in nature. Tom describes how his martial arts training had the effect of deepening and strengthening in him these principles that had been originally taught to him by his parents.

Both of the co-authors of this book are martial arts practitioners, with a combination of more than 30 years of experience between them. Each has been profoundly and positively influenced by the training, and especially by the inspiration and wisdom of their instructors. However, readers do not need any background or interest in martial arts to apply the five black-belt principles in this book, which are properly thought of as universal principles.

In martial arts, *black belt* represents a level of attainment through years of practice. The holder of a black belt should exemplify a combination of ability, humility, and strength of character. *Black belt* is also used as a term in business to represent a high level of excellence, as in General Electric's Six Sigma program of quality management. As used in this book, black belt can be thought of as a combination of these ideals—exemplifying a standard of continuously improving excellence in business performance, the efficient delivery of service excellence, and a registered representative who grows throughout his or her career in self-knowledge, wisdom, and serenity.

Part Two integrates these principles into a cycle, defining a system of self-improvement that could apply to any human endeavor. This system is then enhanced into the Cycle of Life, which provides the registered representative with a single visual image that integrates all of the fundamental ideas necessary to protect and grow a financial services practice.

Part Two then clarifies each principle and demonstrates how it can be applied to the development of a prosperous, ethically sound, client-focused financial services practice. The approach of Part Two blends philosophy with practical suggestions and illustrative anecdotes. The result is an easy-to-remember formula for balanced business and character development.

Part Three, "How to Prevail in an NASD Arbitration Hearing," provides the registered representative a comprehensive, detailed operations manual and game plan for NASD arbitration. The title of Part Three requires a little explanation. NASD arbitration provides investors who believe they may have been victimized by unethical sales practices with a forum to present their case in a quasi-legal setting, and recover damages through settlement or award. NASD arbitration identifies representatives who have engaged in such practices, and their broker-dealer firms, and provides compensation to investors through an agreement to settle or the decision of NASD arbitrator(s) after a hearing. Awards can be in the millions of dollars and can include punitive damages.

In cases of provably egregious behavior, some registered representatives have been forced to surrender their licenses and leave the profession. When the facts warrant it, every reasonable person is in favor of such action—the essence of what it means to be a self-regulatory organization (SRO). The purpose of Part Three is not to provide the rep who has acted irresponsibly or unethically from the consequences of his or her behavior. It is, however, to provide those many reps who, although in their opinion they have done no wrong, are brought into NASD arbitration, with the knowledge and tools to defend themselves honestly in this system.

Due in part to a system that makes it easy to file a complaint, and that offers potentially large payouts for attorneys who try cases in which claimants win awards, it is inarguable that many representatives who have genuinely done nothing improper become ensnared in the process. Many representatives who have been through NASD arbitration bitterly complain that they were forced to settle or that an award was given in circumstances in which they didn't do anything wrong.

There is a debate within the industry as to what percentage of claimants have legitimate grievances. Robin S. Mills, president of the Financial Advisor's Legal Association, said, "Sadly over 80 percent of all claims are GROUNDLESS" (emphasis supplied in original e-mail text, 2006). Coming from an advocate, this estimate has to be considered on the high side. To try and develop a genuinely accurate estimate is virtually impossible.

The important point is that many representatives (the authors believe it is a majority) who are drawn into NASD arbitration are individuals who have not committed acts of gross malfeasance or negligence against their clients. In our view, it is tragic for an honest, hardworking registered representative to suffer the lifetime of professional consequences that come from an award or settlement of $10,000 or more if that rep has not engaged in any genuinely inappropriate conduct.

Settlements driven by the desire of E&O carriers to engage in litigation risk management or awards by arbitrators that seem more driven by sympathy for the plight of a specific investor than an actual violation of a rule or standard by a registered representative are the inevitable collateral damage of the system. It is our belief and hope that honest reps who find themselves caught up in the NASD arbitration system will find the knowledge and encouragement to effectively prepare and successfully assist their attorney in presenting their case.

Part Three begins with a chapter of four case studies, each with its own unique set of circumstances and lessons. It follows with a breakdown of actual cost of NASD arbitration to the registered representative, with 10 major categories and 13 subcategories.

Chapter 15, "How to Prepare and Try an NASD Arbitration Case," is written by James W. Weller, Esq., an attorney at Nixon, Peabody, LLC. Mr. Weller has a distinguished career of academic excellence and professional distinction. He provides the reader with the attorney's view of an arbitration case, from beginning to end. Mr. Weller provides numerous tips for the registered representative on how to work with an attorney to achieve the best possible outcome in NASD arbitration. The next two chapters are written from the registered representative's view, and provide insight and specific ideas to use in every phase of the NASD arbitration process.

In this volume, there are several "voices." Part One is in a narrative, written in the voice of Tom Hine. Part Two is written in the combined voice of the co-authors. Part Three begins with a chapter with four voices of registered representatives who have experienced NASD arbitration. The chapter by James Weller is written in his voice. The rest of the information is in the combined voices of the co-authors. Throughout the book, the terms *Registered Representatives, registered reps,* and *reps* are used interchangeably, much as the terms are used in conversation between, well, the reps.

Inspirational speakers often make the point that the Chinese symbol for *problem* is a combination of the symbols for *crisis* and *opportunity*. Registered representatives in the twenty-first century find themselves at a crossroads. Increasingly complex products, stricter regulations, real-time business, and a competitive global environment create more challenge than ever before. However, technological tools for research, communication, and record keeping allow for dramatically improved operational efficiency, client tracking, and record keeping.

We live in a real-time business world, the post-Enron, Sarbanes-Oxley "flat" world of globalized business. It is an age in which transparency, ethics, doing the right thing, and an audit trail are not merely commendable, self-protective business practices. They are becoming a necessity.

A high standard of ethics, transparency, running a clean and tight ship—these are and will be the standards now and into the future.

As this book is being written, Baby Boomers are retiring at a record rate, with 1,000 people turning 60 every day. The greatest wealth transfer in civilized history is now taking place. There is an increasing complexity of financial products and services, making it virtually impossible for individual representatives to be completely on top of the information curve. Counterintuitively, the solution may be a return to simplicity, clarity, and adherence to the universal principles of humility, integrity, duality, awareness, and dedication. This book is designed to encourage registered representatives to reset their sights higher than ever, clean their house where appropriate, and help this generation retire in comfort.

Financial advisers who embrace this challenge and build professional practices on the soundest of foundations, will serve their clients, personally prosper, experience deep satisfaction, and help lead themselves, their clients, and the financial services industry into a limitless future. We hope that this book is a small contribution in that direction.

Thomas J. Hine
John K. Brubaker

March 12, 2007

MY NASD ARBITRATION— FROM START TO FINISH

Humility

Dedication

Integrity

Awareness

Duality

Sweating Bullets

How Did I End Up Here?

1 Liberty Plaza, 27th Floor
New York, New York
November 3, 2003

Sometimes life's big moments are not the ones you choose in advance, but rather those that events force upon you. This, for me, was going to be one of those moments. After months of preparation and anticipation, I was finally going to face my former client, my accuser in the final dispute arena of our profession—an NASD (National Association of Securities Dealers) arbitration. This event is sometimes innocuously referred to as an "arbitration hearing." I didn't think about it that way. As far as I was concerned, it was both a "trial" and a "battle," and in my preparation I had come to picture this moment in those terms. Despite the very heavy dose of reality I was experiencing regarding what was about to take place, in the back of my mind I couldn't help but think: How did I end up here?

A Million-Dollar Producer

I love the investment advisory business. It is, for me, a dream career. It requires me to give everything that I have every day of my career. I am an analyst, a strategist, a sales professional, a chief executive of my practice, a leader and motivator of my staff, a user of technology tools, a voracious consumer of ideas and information, and sometimes a little bit of a personal and family counselor. I love to work with clients and, using all my experience and every resource at my disposal, understand the specifics of their financial needs and goals and to help guide them through the perilous shoals of investing to secure the future for themselves, their families, and future generations.

Beginning with my first day in the business, I set my sights high. I had worked for the first 11 years in the business with other firms. In 2001, I went out and started my own firm. In 2003, my practice reached the magical million-dollar mark in terms of annual revenue generated, and I became what is known as a "million-dollar producer." Reaching this level is understood as a significant accomplishment in the business.

I admit to having a streak of idealism about our profession. From time to time, I am jokingly accused of being a "Boy Scout" by my colleagues. I am the rep who arrives 15 minutes early and sits in the front row of the training classes, taking notes as if my life depended on it. I have always been an organizer and a documentor. There are times when I exasperate my staff, calling back to check on a detail that might seem minor, but I can't rest until I have a sense of completion. For more than 10 years working with clients, I had a spotless U-4, the standard in our industry for a clean bill of health.

A Statement of Claim Appears—Out of Nowhere

It was a complete surprise when on September 17, 2002, I received a faxed NASD Statement of Claim at my office, notifying me that a former client had filed for arbitration with the NASD asking for $85,000 in damages, alleging, among other things, that I had put him into investments that were "unsuitable." I couldn't believe it.

I later found that it is typical for clients to first forward through attorneys a "letter of demand," which is a claim of losses or damages and an attempt to negotiate a settlement of those demands. In this approach, the threat of going to the NASD arbitration process is part of the lever the claimant has. In this case, the client had skipped that step entirely and filed for NASD arbitration.

I was stunned to read that my former client was claiming "losses" of $85,000. As I read it, I felt as though I were having an out-of-body experience. Reading this document with my name on it felt like a nightmare into a surreal, make-believe world being described in legal language.

The chronology that my former client and his attorney had sketched out in the complaint was filled with blatant mischaracterizations. To me, it read like a work of fiction. Had the document not had my name on it, the entire episode might have had a comic tinge to it. People have often thought of me as the clean-cut, wide-eyed *Mr. Smith Goes to Washington* character. The rep described in this document seemed like the financial equivalent of Darth Vader.

But there wasn't anything humorous about it. This was serious business. As my mind raced to try and recall details of our working relationship, I didn't recall anything whatsoever that would have justified a complaint.

Notify Everyone and Anyone

I put the document down and tried to think everything through. I realized that there were some immediate actions I had to take. I had the clarity to place a call to a private attorney who had some experience in securities litigation. I have always believed in getting the best expert advice possible, and my strong Rolodex came through with this resource. She quickly returned my call, heard the details of the situation, and informed me that I had an obligation to notify everyone and anyone who might be affected by this.

Having already swallowed this bitter pill, I wasn't particularly in the mood to start announcing my news to the world. But I knew my attorney was right, so I made the calls. This claim involved a period of time in which I was working with two broker-dealer firms.

After calling the home office of both firms, I called the errors-and-omissions insurance carrier, a step I have since found out is one that many reps don't take, either out of ignorance or not wanting to face reality. By the end of the day, I had a little life in me, and I was able to go home, tell my wife, and begin thinking practically and strategically about what to do next.

Researching the Facts of the Case

After hearing back from the broker-dealer's home office and finding out that they were going to contact the errors-and-omissions insurer, who would assign me an attorney, I sat down again with a new level of seriousness. Like a first-year law student, I rolled up my sleeves and made a thorough review of the facts of my relationship and the documentation I had to support it.

In a simple sentence, this was the story of an individual who got started investing with me in 1997, rode the stock boom to a nice portfolio increase, and had his portfolio return to its original size as a result of the tech correction. That was the essence of it.

He came to me in the fall of 1997 as a result of a referral. He was in his early 60s, anticipating retirement, and at that point in time had approximately $850,000 of investable assets. He started his relationship with me cautiously, investing approximately $220,000 in October 1997. I served as a broker, not a fiduciary or trustee. I had no discretion on his accounts. At the time he came to see me, his portfolio was earning 5 to 6 percent. He wanted more growth and to be able to withdraw an income stream. He expressed clearly the intention to invest for a period of at least 7 to 10 years, to ride out market fluctuations.

Although we had agreed at the beginning of the relationship that his risk tolerance classified him as a growth investor, I put his initial $220,000 in investments that were more appropriately classified as "growth and income," one level more conservative, as was my practice with new clients. We met regularly and reviewed his portfolio. He was pleased with his progress and wanted to increase his investable assets with me and become more aggressive.

He incrementally opened four additional accounts over a 27-month period. After he opened the last of these accounts, his holdings consisted of three non-qualified variable annuities, one qualified brokerage account (consisting of stock and bond mutual funds), and one non-qualified brokerage account (consisting primarily of utility stocks he had owned before he met me and some exposure to mutual funds). By January 2000, he had invested a total of $857,000, which represented the majority of his portfolio.

This client saw his portfolio achieve significant growth. Along with that growth, he expressed on a number of occasions the desire to become incrementally more aggressive in his posture. At one point, he called me expressing a desire to make a specific investment in a technology growth fund. By March 2000, his portfolio was worth nearly $1.1 million.

Over the next year, his portfolio experienced a decrease in value, as the market was in a period of correction. By March 2001, his portfolio was worth $798,000. Suddenly, and without any warning, in April 2001, he informed our firm that he was closing his accounts with us. When accounting for the $64,000 income he had withdrawn, his portfolio had a net gain of $5,000 over the 42-month period.

As would come out in the hearing, this client received a level of service that was well beyond the required standard of care, and arguably was in the top tier of the financial services profession. There were regular meetings and extensive communication. He had signed more than a dozen prospectus receipts that identified him as a growth investor. All in all, this was the story of an individual who had been disappointed by his investment results over a 42-month period of time—less than half of the 7 to 10 years he had initially said was his time horizon—but no real cause for complaint beyond that.

Investors who have their portfolio rise and then fall tend to regard any decrease in value as a "loss." Financial analysts look at it a little differently. If you start with a portfolio of a certain asset size, and end up after a period at that same size, analysts consider that "breaking even." Arguably, there has been some opportunity cost (the time value of money), but no real net asset loss. One could understand my former client's disappointment, but he was one of hundreds of thousands, if not millions, who had experienced the late 1990s and early 2000 market roller coaster. My view was that if the NASD was going to start covering this type of loss, it would change the meaning of the word *risk* dramatically. It would mean, in effect, that errors-and-omissions insurance carriers were now underwriting individual investor risks.

Martial Arts Training—A Place of Peace

I returned to my normal schedule, which in addition to a fairly intense pace of professional responsibilities, also included martial arts training, which I had been doing regularly for more than 20 years. What had started at age 12 as an interest and revived again at age 19 as a hobby had literally become a way of life. I started training, as many do, for increased mental and physical discipline and to learn self-defense. I became absorbed in the majesty of the training and its ability to help me shape a working philosophy of life.

The training became an essential, integrated part of my day-to-day existence. I considered my training time as an invaluable investment in my own development. While it may sound strange to the uninitiated, martial artists sometimes spend hours in a class repeating a single technique, until exhaustion overcomes them. In the latter stages of this type of workout, the body's natural fatigue relaxes the muscles, concentrates the attention on minor adjustments of the body, improves the strength of the stances, and almost naturally leads toward the elusive moment of perfection that martial artists seek.

I love the structure of martial arts, and the etiquette—bowing with respect, learning the fine points of the different ways to bow, and the purpose and meaning of each. You finish each workout with a silent, reflective meditation. After completing every belt test or tournament, I examined every aspect of the event to see how I could have done better. I relished pressing on to the next challenge, the next technique, and the next level of skill and awareness.

After four years of training, I received my first-degree black belt certification in Shotokan karate, and I was quite humbled by the experience. While many students level off or even quit at this stage, I continued to set my sights higher. By my twentieth year of training, I had earned the rank of fourth-degree black belt, and I had competed in national and international tournaments.

The serious practice of martial arts almost inevitably transforms other parts of your life in a positive way. To the true martial artist, the concepts of honor and integrity are so deeply ingrained that it is incongruous and inconceivable to engage in intentional deceit—personal or professional. You understand at a deep, intuitive level the meaning of the quotation "When you seek perfection, the difficult becomes easy." The training becomes a natural counterbalance to the stresses of modern life—a place where you go on a regular basis to be at peace, to push yourself to higher levels, and to be a good and faithful member of your dojo, or school. It becomes a place of peace, reflection, and certainty in an increasingly complex and fast-paced world.

The Case Begins—Talking to the Attorney

I got a call informing me that I would be represented in the NASD arbitration by Jim Weller of Nixon, Peabody LLP. I did a little research and found out that their firm is highly respected. Any good news was welcome at this point.

I called Jim to set up a meeting and told him about the research I had done. He seemed pleasantly surprised by my aggressive attitude, telling me that in many cases he had to convince the reps he represented to come in and meet with him. With all that was at stake, I couldn't imagine being so lax.

I asked him what I could do between then and our meeting to prepare. He told me that it would be helpful to him if I could organize the client relationship in chronological order and prepare a document that would help him respond to the Statement of Claim. Although I had researched the facts, I had not actually sat down to write out the narrative. It turned out that it might have been a blessing, as Jim explained to me that from this point forward all such documents would be considered as work product, and therefore would be protected under attorney-client privilege.

He also gave me a list of items he would need. I had many of them, but not all. I was all over it. We went through the allegations from the Statement of Claim and I briefly told him the facts related to each. My confidence began to rise a little bit, as I really felt I could answer every single one of them, but Jim cautioned me that there are always bumps in the road that you can't see ahead of time.

It was a relief just to be working with someone on this. I got off the phone with a clear road map of what I needed to do between then and my meeting with him. My competitive nature had begun to kick in. I was determined to do everything I could to win the case.

I was also determined not to let this distraction take away any time from my normal business activities. I was disciplined in not taking normal work time to do my NASD arbitration "homework." Over the next couple of weeks, using Weller's list, I went through my case again, first from the perspective of the Statement of Claim, and then in a chronological fashion. I wrote up a summary of what had happened with this client, so Jim could see in his mind the sequence of events, backed by the documents. I organized the files so that he could follow the narrative clearly. During this time, I hit one of those bumps in the road. Although I had a lot of documents and records about this client, unfortunately there were some notes I had taken in meetings with him that I was unable to locate. I hoped it wouldn't be a big deal.

No Alternative to Victory

I was soon fully invested in the process, and it was no longer a fight over money, or even avoiding a "ding" on my record. I looked at it as a matter of personal honor and professional integrity. I was committed to myself, my family, and even my clients, to get my day in court and to prevail. I believed deeply that if it could be proven before industry experts that I did something wrong with this client, then a sacred wall had been breached in my practice and in my character, and the consequences of that were too devastating for me to contemplate. It would mean that the very foundations of my professional practice were weak.

The unthinkable result would be that my practice, and my sense of myself as a professional, would be forever wounded. It couldn't have been clearer in my mind. There simply was no alternative to victory.

The Doctrine of Overwhelming Documentation

Once I had mentally joined the battle, I threw myself into preparation with a sense of commitment and even joy. I knew I had the facts on my side, and I wanted to be sure that the arbitrators knew this as well. I used what I call the Doctrine of Overwhelming Documentation. I made it a major mission to organize all of the information I had on this client and be able to present it at a moment's notice during the hearing. I wanted to go completely beyond the standard of "sufficient" documentation. I wanted to overwhelm. If we were going to go into battle, I wanted every bit of information, every scrap of relevant paper, every bit of electronic documentation, and I wanted it completely organized and accessible. After going through this process to a level at which I was satisfied, I traveled to New York to meet Jim Weller.

Meeting My Attorney—And Getting a Passing Grade

Somehow, I had expected to meet an older attorney, a veteran of legal wars. But, in fact, Jim Weller was probably a little younger than I. His relaxed, open manner put me at ease immediately. But beneath that relaxed, next-door neighbor demeanor was someone you would want next to you in a foxhole with mortar rounds exploding overhead. He was a legal professional with a steel-trap mind, bulldog tenacity, and a real genius for legal strategy and timing.

Although there was, strictly speaking, nothing on the line when I went in for my appointment, I had butterflies in my stomach. I felt as if Jim were actually my first judge—a trial run, but my first test. I wanted to lay out the case to him and see if he could find any flaws. I fully expected him to be a tough critic and an acute questioner.

I walked into his office with a large container full of files and charts. To the extent that I could, I had absorbed the role of imagining that I was my own attorney, and I went through my case. I had been mentally rehearsing during the whole drive down. My heart was pumping, and I launched into the narrative.

At this point, a lot of the information was very sharp and clear in my mind. I went through the Statement of Claim point by point, and showed Jim how I could refute each one. It had alleged that I had taken "de facto control" over the client's accounts. The truth was that I was acting for the first 41 of the 42 months in question as a broker, not as a fiduciary, so there was no way I could have taken control of the accounts. He claimed to have desired a "very conservative investment strategy." The truth was that he had filled out an initial questionnaire, which was also known as an investor scorecard, and had signed disclosure forms throughout our relationship that identified him as, variously, a "growth" or "growth and income" client. I had recommended specific funds consistent with this profile, sent prospectus receipts to the client, and had signed receipts that indicated he had reviewed them. I had signed disclosure forms that clearly showed this. He claimed that I had "misrepresented the risks of investments" recommended, but those same disclosure forms clearly indicated this was not the case. I had copies of the monthly statements he had consistently received from my clearing firm.

I continued. My former client's Statement of Claim alleged that I had purchased individual "junk bond securities" when no such securities had been purchased. He stated that I was "churning" his accounts, which meant buying and selling primarily in order to generate transaction revenue. The truth was that the large majority of his investments were in financial products that did not generate transaction revenue. What I was doing, and any rep will be familiar with this, was simply rebalancing his variable annuity subaccounts, with his permission.

The other side claimed that there was a nearly three-month delay between his request and our office's execution of a technology fund trade that had cost him money. The truth was that this was held up because he had not returned a form that he needed to sign to allow us to make the trade.

The Statement of Claim suggested that I had instigated much of the trading without my client's knowledge. I had regular portfolio review meetings with him, one of which included his accountant, a CPA. I had printouts of the pie charts I had shown my client indicating his asset allocation and Morningstar ratings on his funds, virtually all of which were highly rated.

I delivered all of this information with seriousness and intensity. I remember thinking to myself that this was how I would feel when the time came to testify. When I was finished with the presentation and the follow-up questions, I learned that I had gotten a passing grade.

Jim cautioned me that this was just a preliminary review. He needed to study all the documents I had brought him, and he was sure he would have additional questions for me. He outlined for me my next assignment, which was to take this initial preparation and go to a much greater level of detail. He suggested that I put together charts about the client's actual portfolio performance over time. He also told me that I needed to begin "thinking like a lawyer," which meant to try and look at my own case from the claimant's point of view. He wanted me to examine all of the documents with a skeptical eye and see if I could find anything that the other side could put in a negative light. He said, "I want us to have a list of the worst questions they could possibly ask you." It all made sense to me.

"Arbitration Cases Take on a Life of Their Own"

Jim complimented me on my documentation, which he said was beyond what most reps have in cases like this. But he also warned me that arbitrations by their nature are a roll of the dice. You have almost no control over who will be judging the case. The arbitrators may have little real experience in this. You just don't know once testimony starts how it is going to work out. You don't know if you catch an arbitrator on a bad day. There is often an underlying sympathy for the accuser. Once initiated, arbitrations take on a life and character all their own. Evidence that supports your side of the case and may seem clear sitting in a comfortable office may not seem as clear to the arbitration panel. In any adversarial proceeding, there is risk of an undesirable outcome.

Jim's hopeful but sobering analysis was well taken. As I drove back from New York, I felt that I had done as well as could be expected, but I knew there was a lot more work ahead. I found out after the entire process was over that Jim was impressed by the level of my conviction about my innocence. He said that in the NASD arbitration cases he had tried while most reps at first claim complete innocence, their conviction breaks down as the facts of their case come out.

He also told me that it was at this session that he got the idea that I would testify well in a hearing, if the case got that far. One of the hidden factors in NASD arbitration is the confidence that the defendant's attorney has in his client's ability to present himself in the unique crucible of testimony and cross-examination. Some registered representatives may be very good at their profession, highly persuasive when it comes to facing clients, innocent of the wrongdoing for which they are charged, and very knowledgeable about the facts of the case. But for any of a number of reasons they may not pass the test of being a good witness on their own behalf. This ultimately will factor into an attorney's judgment in terms of settlement and whether to push for continuing a case.

I deeply believe that this is just another example of the benefits of my years of martial arts training and competition. In a belt test or in a tournament, you have to be able to bring all of your concentration, focus, and energy to bear and act fearlessly and react instinctively and effectively under combat or conditions of uncertainty. Like an actor or actress who has been on the stage, these hours of preparation, along with my rock-solid conviction, all went into helping me prepare to present myself to the NASD arbitrators.

Finding Some Holes in My Case

Jim and I communicated regularly as the process went forward. The paperwork seemed to bolster my case. I had 17 signed prospectus receipts or new account forms, most of which checked "growth" as an objective. There were pie charts that had been shown to the client in portfolio reviews. There had been ongoing communication with me and with the staff. He had provided us with a referral, indicating he was happy with the service he was getting.

Nevertheless, as Jim Weller had asked, I faithfully tried to go through the documents and find something wrong in my argument—to try the case against me. Jim helped in that he tried to do the same with the documents I had sent him. Between the two of us, we had identified five potential problems.

First, the initial document that had been filled out for this client was known as an investor scorecard. Reps are familiar with this type of document. It contained a series of questions in three categories: risk tolerance, investment objective, and time horizon. Each question had a multiple-choice answer. Point totals are given for answers and added up on the last page of the category. Each potential client was given a score for each of those three areas, and also an aggregate score totaling all three areas (see Table 1.1).

My former client had scored a 93. Based on the ranges given, he could have been placed into any of three asset allocation model portfolios: income with moderate growth, growth with income, or growth. I had placed him as "growth." It was clear that the other side was going to argue that this was too aggres-

TABLE 1.1   Investor Scorecard

Adjusted Total Range	Score	Asset Allocation Model Portfolios
39–72		Income with Capital Preservation
60–95		Income with Moderate Growth
85–115		Growth with Income
90–120	**93**	**Growth**
105–125		Aggressive Growth

sive a classification, that I should have put him into a lower risk tolerance category.

I had made this recommendation based on a variety of factors. He had been in the market for years. He had stated unequivocally that he was a long-term investor, and planned to keep this portfolio for at least 7 to 10 years. On a number of other forms, he had indicated a desired annual rate of return of 10 to 15 percent. Jim felt that this issue would be a key to the case.

Second, I had also uncovered a form known as a "financial fact-finding questionnaire," which we used at the time to review a client's personal and financial circumstances. This form was incompletely filled out. There were some handwritten notes in it that included some useful information. I explained to Jim that this particular form was to be used if you were charging a client a fee to prepare a financial plan. I did not perform that particular service for this client, thus the form was not filled out. Jim made the point that the other side would almost certainly argue that I had performed imperfect due diligence on this client, leading to a misdiagnosis of his risk tolerance.

Third, although there were numerous signed prospectus receipts indicating a desire for "growth," I had located one survey in which the client had conspicuously characterized his investment philosophy as "conservative with income—50/50." This contradicted virtually all of the other paperwork (signed prospectus receipts and new account forms), but Jim warned that he and his attorney would try and make a big point of this, underscoring their argument of unsuitability.

Fourth, unfortunately, I had been unable to locate some of my contemporaneous, handwritten notes from some of our portfolio reviews. Although I could reconstruct what we had talked about from his pie charts and the other signed paperwork from that time period, Jim told me that the notes would have been much better received by the arbitrators.

Fifth, I had dug a little further into researching the trade in which my former client had claimed he had lost value due to a delay in executing the trade. It turned out that he had sent in a check that arrived at our office a few days after our firm had switched broker-dealer firms. The office had apparently sent him new forms to fill out, but in the mix a couple of weeks had passed, and they were going to argue that he lost money because of it.

Setting My Goals

Jim tried to allay my concerns, explaining while each of these issues was a potential problem, overall, I had much better documentation than the typical rep. In addition, the patterns of the client relationship would enable him to argue that the client had ratified the work I had done on his behalf.

Personally, I had set my goals, and I didn't want to back off. First, I did not want to negotiate a settlement of the case, and I had told Jim that. I genuinely hoped I could prove that I had provided the appropriate level of care for this client. My thinking was that I would contest every point and fight it to the finish. I had set the standard of "no award" at the end of my case as the desired outcome.

I was also extremely conscious of "Plan B," which was a settlement or award of less than $10,000. All registered representatives know that any settlement of $10,000 or more becomes a permanent part of your U-4, the record that follows you throughout your career. This information is accessible by anyone at any time over the Internet through NASD BrokerCheck. It could someday make the difference that causes a potential client not to work with you and cause all kinds of additional professional complications. As much as I didn't want to consider the possibility of anything less than a total vindication, I was aware of this secondary, but really critical, objective.

Humility in Martial Arts

I had come to realize that this case was going to be one of the really big tests in my career to that point. So, I again was very grateful for the clarity I felt while training, and from what I had learned that I felt I might be able to apply to survive the test.

One of the first and most lasting lessons received by a beginning martial artist is that of humility. In attending your first martial arts class, humility is something that comes naturally to many students. Everyone in class knows more than you do, so you automatically respect them and listen to what they tell you.

Over time, humility becomes an important part of your growth as a martial artist, and it is derived from a number of sources. You have humility from respect for those more experienced and accomplished than you, respect for an opponent in a contest, respect for other students of all experience and skill levels, respect for your school, and respect for the entire system you are learning.

One of the most compelling aspects of martial arts is that as you develop technique and improve in every area, you come to realize that the more you know, the more there is to learn. As you improve, the instructor gets more demanding. Execution of technique can improve indefinitely. Just because you might perform a particular move or strike perfectly, or nearly perfectly, one time means almost nothing. It could have been a coincidence. Can you do it again and again? Can you increase the power with which you execute? Can you select and employ the proper technique at the proper moment? Can you perform at your best at a moment of truth, under maximum pressure, when your life might be in danger?

Over years of training and literally thousands of classes, in what is referred to by masters of martial arts as "the sweat of perfection," a martial artist becomes grounded in an attitude of genuine humility. Contrary to the Western approach to competitive athletics, in which so much of athletic prowess is centered around a concept of pride, it is almost universally true that the greatest practitioners of martial arts are individuals of profound humility. They walk into a room and radiate calmness, integrity, and purpose. They bow with perfect balance and reverence.

Through their demeanor and their character, they inspire others to improve themselves, as martial artists and as human beings.

The Power of the White-Belt Attitude

Early in my martial arts training, I became very committed to developing what is known as a white-belt attitude. Years ago in Korea and Japan at the founding of martial arts, there were only two belt colors—white and black. White belts were worn by beginners, and they remained at that belt level until they became black belts, a process that often took many years.

In today's "Americanized" version of martial arts, virtually every school and every system starts at white and progresses to black through a series of four or five colors, often including yellow, green, blue, and red or brown. In a mixed class that includes all belt levels, it is easy to pick out the white belts, the beginners.

I was taught as a white belt the importance of developing and always maintaining a white-belt attitude. This has also been referred to as "the beginner's mind." It means being in maximum learning mode in every class. It means asking questions of your instructors and their assistants until you really know a technique or principle. It means having tremendous enthusiasm for every aspect of the training—the warm-up; the kicks and punches; the *kata,* or forms; the self-defense techniques; and *kumite,* or sparring. I was taught that each class was an opportunity to learn and the goal was to finish the class learning as much as possible. A true white belt is a literal sponge, soaking up every bit of knowledge and insight from every moment of training. A white belt is someone committed to maximum self-development.

Applying the Humility Principle
in NASD Arbitration

Humility and the white-belt attitude were absolutely critical to my ability to participate effectively in every part of the process.

Humility helped me prepare as if the entire outcome depended on me. It kept my emotions in check during the NASD arbitration. I was able to minimize my distress at obstacles or setbacks. And I also kept the balance, not getting overconfident when it looked like I was doing well.

An attitude of humility meant that my lawyer and I arrived an hour early every day of the trial, completely organized and well dressed, ready for anything. It helped me to have the proper etiquette, which meant showing unfailing courtesy to the panel of arbitrators. It meant always disagreeing with my opponent and his attorney with complete professionalism, though at times it seemed nearly impossible to do so. It meant having an attitude that exemplified respect for the process and all of the participants. It meant going back over the case constantly, looking for ways to improve, and for new insights.

The white-belt attitude was a hidden weapon throughout the entire process. It gave me the impetus. As a self-described arbitration rookie, I wanted to learn everything I could about the process. It caused me to do extra work in preparing the documentation and the narrative. It required me to go and meet the lawyer, going eye to eye with the person who would represent me.

I insisted on personally going over every exhibit we were going to use. Normally, that is a job strictly for the lawyer and the paralegals. I made it my job. I didn't want to be susceptible to being confused at a moment of truth. I fully expected to go up against a top-gun attorney, and I didn't want to leave anything to chance.

During my preparation, without even asking Jim, I took it upon myself to invest some time researching my opponent's background through public records. As a result, I uncovered the fact that he owned $500,000 in real estate, which he had not disclosed in his filings. This revelation was significant because claimants often posture themselves as being both financially unsophisticated and, ironically, having as few assets as possible.

This makes the actions of the representative appear to be even more damaging

The Attorney Switch

Two weeks before the hearing date, we received a bit of unexpected news. Jim informed me that the other side had switched attorneys. The law firm representing the complainant had handed the case from a junior attorney to one of the partners. When I first heard that, I was worried that the case had somehow been escalated. Jim Weller explained to me that this likely meant that the junior attorney had been assigned to try and go out and push for a settlement, hoping the case would not go to an actual hearing.

When it became apparent that we were not going to settle, the case had been kicked up to a more senior attorney. Jim said that, although this new attorney would have a higher level of legal skill, his lack of familiarity with the details of the case would set their side back. He would be going into the trial somewhat cold.

Sweating Bullets

On Sunday night, November 2, 2003, I drove to New York and stayed over in a Manhattan hotel near where the hearing would be held. A momentous drive.

I remember with crystal clarity the meal I ate the night before—chicken fried rice and wonton soup—hoping it would bring me good luck. I slept very lightly that night, subconsciously fearing missing the alarm and backup wake-up call I had left with the front desk of the hotel. I recall carefully putting on the tie I had chosen for this momentous personal occasion. I had my shoes shined to a high gloss. Although from an external perspective I probably looked like any of hundreds of middle-aged executives walking around Wall Street, in my own mind I was dressed for battle. I was in a battle not only for my career, but for vindication of my character and the foundation of the way I provided service to my clients. It is amazing how clear and concentrated the mind can become at a time of maximum danger. My senses and thought patterns were on high alert. My heart was palpitating, my mouth was dry, my stomach was grinding, and I was sweating bullets.

Humility

Dedication

Integrity

Awareness

Duality

"24"—The Day That Almost Never Ended

NASD Hearing Day One— November 3, 2003

Into the Hearing Room

The cab ride to the NASD building was very dramatic. I felt the weight of the moment. This sense of seriousness was made even more intense by the setting—1 Liberty Plaza is in the heart of the financial district in southern Manhattan. Although it was more than two years since September 11, 2001, the increased security of the post-9/11 world was apparent. There were police cars, other government vehicles, and uniformed individuals every-where. It seemed that every half block there was a fire truck or police vehicle with a siren on, racing through the traffic. The ten-sion was palpable.

I had arrived early and I was pacing back and forth over the steel grating outside the entrance to the building, rehearsing in my mind anything and everything I could think of that would help me make my case. It was a huge lift to see Jim and his paralegal, Joan Herman, arrive.

Jim had a big, bulging briefcase. Joan came in wheeling a huge, rolling file with all our backup documentation and exhibits. I remember feeling amazed at how much preparation had been done for what was, in the context of Jim's legal practice with NASD arbitration hearings, a fairly small case, though it meant everything to me.

This was a quasi-legal proceeding. It had begun with the filing of a legal document. There were lawyers for each side, rules of admissibility of evidence, direct testimony, cross-examination, and a panel of arbitrators who could be thought of as judges. Because of all these factors, I had painted in my mind a picture of a large courtroom setting, with the polished marble floor, a formal stand for testimony, and the judges towering above the proceedings from their Olympian heights.

I was a little disappointed when I got to the room and saw what it was—the equivalent of a small, modern corporate conference room. The participants were sitting around a table. We were really in close quarters. It struck me that this was going to increase the intensity, as I was going to be nearly "up close and personal" with my former client and his attorney. I adjusted myself to the reality of the situation and got ready for the proceedings to begin. My emotions were running at a high pitch. Go time.

All Dressed Up and Nowhere to Go— Where Is the Claimant?

Jim and I went through our checklist, and it was apparent to both of us that we were ready to go. At about 8:45 A.M. the arbitrators came into the conference room. As I looked at each of them and politely said hello, I ran through in my mind what I knew about each. Once again, I thought of them as my jury, the people who would decide my fate. I kept checking my watch as 9:00 A.M. approached. I wondered where our opponents were.

Nine o'clock came and went and there was no sign of them. I couldn't believe it. For months, this date and time had been burned into my mind. To not have my accuser here seemed almost unreal. For all of my preparation, one possibility I had never anticipated was that my accuser would be late to the trial. I kept checking my watch. Every couple of minutes seemed like half an hour. The arbitrators were sitting calmly, acting as if nothing were wrong. But the atmosphere in the room kept getting thicker.

As the minutes burned away and there was no sign of them, I had a momentary sense of elation. I asked Jim if they didn't show up by a certain time, was there any chance that the case could be dismissed? He assured me that the answer was "No." It seemed unfair, even outrageous to me. Was there no penalty for this type of behavior? What kind of results would you get if you showed up 30 minutes late to a job interview? Wasn't this many times more important? Was the system completely stacked on the side of the accuser?

At about 9:45 A.M. my former client and his attorney came rolling into the hearing room. Looking back now, the scene had an almost comic aspect and, truthfully, it had to play to our advantage. They burst into the room like the Keystone Cops on roller skates on their way to a bank robbery. Both the accuser and his attorney were completely disheveled and disorganized. Both of them had a distracted, unkempt appearance—visibly sweating, hair blown around, neckties loose, and papers sticking out of their briefcases. These were the people who had taken such a vicious shot at me, and whose accusations threatened to damage my career. I couldn't wait to hear what they were going to say.

The Dog Ate Their Homework

Their excuse was that they had taken the 6:30 A.M. train out of New Haven and gotten delayed.

I wondered how, for an event of this magnitude, requiring the attendance of half a dozen other extremely busy people, could you possibly base your transportation plan on taking a train that, if everything went perfectly, would get you to your destination barely in time? I was really steamed. My accuser had gone to great lengths to claim he had been wronged. He had accused me of violations of all kinds of laws and reckless disregard for his well-being. All these resources had been assembled for him to have his proverbial "day in court." But he couldn't show up on time!

I was waiting for the arbitrators to somehow admonish them and was stunned when they didn't. I wanted action and I wanted vindication. Jim told me to take a deep breath and get control of myself. We had a long day ahead of us. The marathon was about to begin.

The Solemn Echoes of September 11, 2001

As our opponents took a few minutes to get prepared, I walked over to a window in the hearing room that looked out onto Ground Zero and the ruins of the World Trade Center Twin Towers. I felt a little selfish, almost ashamed, as I thought of all the families who had experienced losses of which I couldn't even conceive. Wouldn't any of them gladly trade places with me? I pulled myself together, walked away from the window, took a couple of minutes to gather my energy, got my focus and attitude in the proper place, and sat down.

Meeting the Arbitration Panel

The process started in a very formal manner. The arbitration chairperson read some carefully worded instructions and introduced himself and his two fellow panel members. He was Albert G. Besser, Esq., and his record was extremely impressive. A Phi Beta Kappa graduate of Yale University and Yale Law School, where he was on the *Yale Law Journal*, Mr. Besser had served with the Office of Strategic Services in China during World War II. He was an assistant U.S. attorney and had a long and distinguished record in private legal practice, which included a landmark antitrust case that was decided by the United States Supreme Court. Mr. Besser had an extensive background with securities-related issues. He introduced Ms. Barbara Weisman, Esq., who was an arbitration expert with more than 1,000 cases heard (though no securities experience) and Ms. Mary Dubas, the identified securities industry expert. I realized that these three people were going to be the ones to decide my fate at the end of this hearing. I looked at them as the jury for this case.

Before he began the formal hearings, Mr. Besser noted for the record that the "respondent and his legal representatives" (Jim Weller, Joan Herman, and I) had "arrived before the claimant and his legal representation," but made assurances that beyond a discussion of the weather, no discussions of substance took place. I thought it was a curious way to say that my accuser and his team arrived almost an hour late, but so be it.

The Opening Statements

My former client's attorney gave his opening statement first. Although I was not at all surprised to hear what he said, it almost immediately got a little bit under my skin. It was a follow-up to the Statement of Claim, a soap opera tale of woe, portraying my former client as a simple, hardworking, unsuspecting salt-of-the-earth type of guy who had put his trust in me and had his retirement ruined.

He started right out of the gate with two whoppers, claiming first that the client desired only a 5 percent rate of return and the claim that "Mr. Hine promised him that a 10 percent rate of return was a sure thing—nothing to worry about." I did no such thing, with him or with anyone—ever.

He played the violin a little bit, talking about his client's desire to leave money to his children, and mentioning some problems one of his children had experienced, something clearly designed to elicit sympathy, not inform about the facts of the case. Although Jim Weller had prepared me for this type of talk, it was frustrating to listen to. I thought to myself, "This is what you have to stoop to in order to try and win a lawsuit?"

Jim Weller rose to deliver the first words of my defense. It was short, information filled, calmly delivered, and to the point. He previewed some of the facts. The claimant had opened not one account but five over a period of more than two years. He came to me on the recommendation of his wife, who had been a long-term client of mine. He pointed out that the client had told me he was a long-term investor, intending to keep these accounts for at least 7 to 10 years, that he would ride out any short-term market declines, was comfortable with risks, and sought growth investments with a high rate of return—10 percent or more. I had designed and managed a portfolio completely consistent in every way with these objectives—one that was very well diversified and achieved significant growth during the first two years of our relationship, but that had suffered a decline in value at a time when the equity markets were in one of the biggest bear markets since the Great Depression.

He closed his statement with the ringing words, "I ask that the panel at the conclusion of the evidence dismiss all counts of the Statement of Claim and also expunge this proceeding from Mr. Hine's records." I got a little charge when Jim sat down, but didn't have any time to enjoy it. The opposing attorney was to begin the direct examination of my former client.

Direct Testimony—The Claimant Goes on the Record

The hearing started with direct examination of my former client by his attorney. As they had initiated the claim, this gave them the opportunity to get their case on the record to start things off. Although I should have expected it, it sickened me to see the way he and his attorney portrayed him. This man was a shrewd and sophisticated individual who had been successful in business and real estate and very aware of his investments. He was an individual I found to be quite competent and capable of making decisions. Yet listening to the testimony, one would have concluded that he was a simplistic, "unsophisticated" (to use a term used in the Statement of Claim) individual who was putty in the hands of the evil, scheming, manipulative broker. They positioned my former client as Mr. Magoo and me as Snidely Whiplash.

In the direct examination, my accuser and his attorney welcomed the panel into their alternate universe by hammering five clear themes:

1. That he was a conservative investor and wanted only a 5 percent annual rate of return
2. That I had repeatedly, and in a number of different ways, guaranteed him an annual rate of return of 10 percent or higher
3. That he didn't know or understand much about investments
4. That he put everything in my hands, and I made all decisions
5. That I had seized control of his investments and did what I wanted

These were the foundations of their case. The attorney asked him question after question. Often, one question would be a mere rephrasing of the previous question. All of this gave my former client the opportunity to hit one of these points, again and again. He must have said some form of, "I told Tom all I wanted was 5 percent growth" eight or nine times. At one point, he actually said "5 percent growth or 3 percent growth." Of course, at the time he came to see me, his portfolio was generating between a 5 percent and 6 percent annual return, so why did he see me in the first place?

The presentation of the alternate universe theory had several problems. Chief among them was the fact that my former client had filled out a number of forms that clearly contradicted this story. On his investor profile, the document that began our relationship, and on a number of other documents throughout the relationship, he identified his desired annual rate of return at "10 percent to 15 percent." This totally undercut the entire strategic thrust of their theory—and they couldn't let it stand.

They figured out a fairly clever, though to me transparently silly, story to cover this. Under carefully scripted leading questions from his attorney, I sat there and listened as my former client claimed that when he was filling out his initial investor profile, he wrote down "10 percent," but that an associate of mine who was in the room at the time told him that he should put in a range, not a single number. So he put a "dash and then 15 percent" in. Then, he testified he just blindly used this on other documents going forward. I thought this was ridiculously weak as a story. The idea of an associate kind of hanging around in the dark corners of the office (no doubt in a trench coat and hat pulled over his head) while we had this type of meeting was simply not something we did. Further, if the former client was going to put a range and all he wanted was 5 percent, why was the range not 5 percent to 10 percent instead of 10 percent to 15 percent? This single issue was the persistent and central dispute that was the foundation of the entire case.

Another little riff was that I had guaranteed him a minimum of a 10 percent annual portfolio growth. He said this a number of different ways. He claimed that I said "10 percent was no problem" and "10 percent, that was the minimum" and "10 percent, that was the base." Any rep who has actually practiced in our profession knows that one would simply never say these things. I obviously told him that, historically, the equities markets, *over a long period of time,* averaged an 8 to 10 percent annual rate of return, combining capital appreciation and dividend reinvestment. I am sure that I showed him the Ibbotson chart that shows the growth in the various U.S. markets over the past 65 years. But to my consternation, he was allowed to claim that this became Tom Hine's personal guarantee to him.

The other two points were also related: "I didn't understand what I was doing" and "I left everything in Tom's hands." These also were said in multiple ways. He said, **"**I put everything in his hands," "I relied on him to make all the decisions," "Tom sent the forms and I just signed them," "I trusted him to take care of my money," and "He was the expert—so whatever he said, I did." All of this conveyed the alternate universe self-description of the client as an uninformed, passive individual who did little in our relationship but say "yes" and sign forms.

Their side also cleverly snuck in another major misrepresentation. The client had, over a 27-month period of time, invested $850,000 through my former firm. For some reason they didn't seem to have done the math, and rounded this down to $800,000, an amount they referred to frequently throughout the entire hearing process. But they spoke as if the $800,000 was all turned over in one lump sum at the beginning. The mental image one got listening to this is that he walked into my office with a grocery bag full of cash, plunked it on my desk, and said "You invest this." Under direct testimony, he said, "I turned over all $800,000 to Tom" and "I gave him everything I had—$800,000." The truth was that he initially invested about $220,000, and over the course of more than two years opened four additional accounts, because he was happy with my performance and service level. This to me was significant information, but it was not helpful to the case they were trying to make. So, they just blithely ignored it, plowed through, and weaved their tale.

The hearing had some breaks, which was a big relief. The intensity was very high, and it was great to get out of the room and away from the pressure cooker. Early in the trial, I would use these breaks to plead with Jim and Joan about the unfairness of what was being presented. They both tried to calm me down, explaining that this was standard procedure, and that we would get our turn. They also told me to channel my energy into taking notes during the testimony and to give Jim any points he could use on cross-examination—a great assignment for me. I got into this little project, writing things down, making notes for Jim, and referencing exhibits that would help him make the points. My head was really in the game.

At one point, something very interesting happened. Ms. Weisman, one of the panel members, interrupted the direct examination. The attorney was asking my former client if I had ever discussed a number of investments with him, corporate high-yield bonds and high-yield municipal bonds among them. Ms. Weisman blurted out, "I don't understand what this means." She made it clear that she had no idea what these various investment products were and the impact of the questions and testimony on the claimant's case. When we got to a break, Jim and I both expressed surprise at this. We expected that each panel member would have a working knowledge of the basics of the investment field. But she was clearly indicating that she did not. We came to realize that with 1,100 arbitrations in her background, she was a real expert in process.

This knowledge affected our strategy throughout the trial. From this point forward, we went out of our way to make sure that all of the potentially technical aspects of the business were explained in the clearest possible way. At the time, though, we realized that we had to make a major effort to explain the meaning of "nondiscretionary" client relationship, which is what this was (for 41 of the 42 months of the relationship). We needed to be sure that she understood that I could *not* have "taken over" my client's accounts, that trades could be conducted *only* with his written or verbal approval.

When the direct examination was done, I thought to myself, "Thank God for cross-examination." I kept my calm as the day wore on. I felt quite confident that our side would have its good moments. There were a lot of holes in this man's story, and I had given Jim a lot of facts to dismantle their claims.

Exposing the Accuser on Cross-Examination

When Jim Weller went up to cross-examine my accuser, it was fantastic to watch how it unfolded. I saw all of my diligence and preparation come to fruition. Throughout the rest of the morning and early afternoon, through highly pointed and effective cross-examination, Jim literally exposed my accuser with the facts, the truth, and the right questions, which he had beautifully prepared. It was like watching a dream script come to pass before my eyes.

One of the items he covered was the "real estate card" I had given him. He made the accuser admit under oath that he had not reported half a million dollars of real estate assets, representing approximately one third of his net worth. It was clear to me that this was a conscious decision on his part and a ploy to make himself seem less powerful and more of a victim. Although we had this information well before the trial, Jim had decided not to reveal it as part of the pretrial skirmish. He felt it would be effective to confront the accuser with this information face to face, when he was under oath. Jim referred to this as—and I love this phrase—"poisoning the well."

Although my accuser tried to pretend that it was no big deal, nothing more than a clerical-level oversight, I felt it was really telling. I tried to put myself in the shoes of the arbitrators and really believed that this undercut the credibility of my accuser. If he omitted something this big, how could they believe him on the small things? In my own mind, I didn't see how he could be taken seriously throughout the rest of the trial. Why not just shut it down then and there? But, obviously, this was not about to happen.

Early in the cross-examination, Jim got right to the investor scorecard. Out of well over 1,000 pages of exhibits, it was perhaps the most crucial document we had. Reps will recognize this. Rather than analyzing his score and my subsequent classifications, Jim went to the answers my former client had given to specific questions. For the question "Which of the following investments would you feel most comfortable owning?," he had checked "stocks with new growth companies." Under cross-examination he stated, "I should have checked blue-chip stocks." Interesting.

For the question "Which of the following investments would you least like to own?," he had checked "certificates of deposit"—ironically, the very kind of "safe" investment he and his attorney had been suggesting would have been the most appropriate, or suitable, for him. In a revealing answer, he said, "To me, that was like investing money at 4 percent or something," which was a mere 1 percent lower than the 5 percent he claimed to have told me was his goal. I saw all of this as clear as day. I only hoped that the panel members saw what I was seeing.

I was amazed at how, even when confronted with unambiguous proof, he would try to obfuscate and wiggle out. But he couldn't. Jim Weller was a total pro, hitting each point cleanly and clearly and moving on to the next. He had explained to me that he needed to walk a fine line in his approach. Because of the unspoken rules that govern this type of proceeding, although the accuser's attorney had free rein to attack me as vigorously as possible, Jim felt that he needed to watch his own tone in cross-examining the accuser. He needed to make his points strongly, but without sarcasm or drama, for fear of alienating the arbitrators. He did it perfectly, and I enjoyed watching this part of the hearing. This was working just the way I had hoped it would. Jim calmly but methodically dismantled the underpinnings of their case: risk tolerance.

Q: "You did write it in on this form that your anticipated return on investment was 10 percent to 15 percent, is that correct?"

A: "That's correct."

Q: "Now before you came to Mr. Hine, you had an annuity that was generating approximately 5 percent, is that correct?"

A: "Probably—5 to 6."

Q: "Now, did you understand that in order to go from 5 percent return to a 10 to 15 percent return that you were going to have to take on more risk?"

A: "Absolutely."

Q: "So you realized that you were going to have to get into

riskier investments in order to achieve the kind of investment objective that you sought?"

A: "Over what I had, yeah."

I was mesmerized watching this. To the credit of my accuser,
though he and his attorney had carefully sculpted the facts in
their Statement of Claim, opening statement, and in his direct examination, it did seem to me that he was answering Jim's questions truthfully.

He would often try to spin an answer in a way that was favorable to him, not directly answering the question and attempting
to get back to one of his talking points. At times, my former client
answered as if he were under duress, and at times almost regret-
fully. But he did answer truthfully.

Arbitration Chair Besser was clearly in control of these proceedings, and he was quite impressive. He was astute—never
letting either side get away with that type of sloppiness. What
was so fascinating is that the chairman showed both great insight into the process and an almost photographic recall of existing testimony, yet at the same time obviously did not understand
some of the technical aspects of the investment business. I made
note of this. But he really kept things on track during the trial.

Jim walked my former client through the specifics of our relationship. Jim got him to admit not only that we talked on the
phone, and that he received regular statements from my clearing
firm, but that we actually met face to face several times to review
his accounts. He asked several questions about a meeting with
the client and his former accountant. Any rep will recognize that
having a meeting of this type is going above and beyond what is
necessary.

To me, the questions and answers just demonstrated that I had
rigorously adhered to the fundamentals of sound, ethical business practices. But I was glad that the panel was hearing this.

Q: "Isn't it a fact that at these meetings Mr. Hine would talk to

you about the mutual funds that you held in these accounts?"

A: "Yes."

Q: "As a matter of fact, he would tell you, would he not, about
the sectors which those mutual funds were invested in, isn't
that also correct?"

A: "I believe he would show me pie charts."

Q: "Pie charts? He would show you pie charts, which would
show how the accounts were distributed into different sectors, correct? That's correct."

A: "Yes."

Q: "Did he ever refuse to answer any questions about those pie
charts?"

A: "No."

Q: "He was very cooperative, happy to talk with you about
them?"

A: "Yes, yes."

Q: "In addition to showing you these pie charts that broke
down how your accounts were allocated, he would also talk
to you about the Morningstar ratings for these accounts, is
that correct?"

A: "Yes."

Q: "So he would talk to you about whether or not a particular
account had three stars or four stars or five stars with Morningstar, is that correct?"

A: "Yes."

I was thrilled that all of this truth was coming out. The grand
finale of this part of the day came when Jim asked my former
client the final question. I thought the exchange was particularly
devastating to his case. Jim nailed down what the whole complaint, in our view, was about.

Q: "Would it be fair to say that the reason you closed the account with Mr. Hine was because there was a decline in the
value of your holdings during 2001?"

A: "That was the major reason."

In my own admittedly partisan mind, I felt the hearing should be over. My accuser's entire case had come apart before their eyes because of the truth that came out under the calm, deliberate cross-examination by my attorney. To me it should be all over, the equivalent of a mistrial. Everybody goes home.

But Joan explained to me that this was actually very typical, business as usual. For us, good so far, but far from over. Joan was very nice, very understanding, and extremely well organized. She and Jim Weller had obviously worked together for years. Their communication was smooth. She often anticipated what he wanted or needed next. The two of them were like a finely tuned machine.

I later found out that Joan had amazing credentials in her own right. She had worked on two really big cases—the MGM Grand balcony collapse and the Exxon *Valdez* oil spill. What was wonderful was that she never wore her credentials on her sleeve. She was on an even keel, down to earth, and very focused.

After Jim finished his cross-examination, the next item on the agenda was known as redirect. This gave my accuser's attorney an opportunity to rehabilitate his testimony by asking him additional questions. I felt that his effort was especially weak. He tried to undermine the testimony about the client review meetings by asking, "Did he explain the meaning of those pie charts?" and similar-type questions. The essence of his argument seemed to be that I was at fault for not providing my former client with a personal tutorial service that would give him the equivalent of an MBA education in finance, along with tests, term papers, and grading. I felt it did virtually nothing to reverse what had been shown in cross-examination—that, in working with this client, I had in fact far exceeded the standards for a nondiscretionary account, and likely even had it been a discretionary account. Next up, the expert witness.

The Inexpert Expert Witness

As part of the preparation for the hearing, Jim Weller had informed me that the opposing attorney had notified him that they intended to call an expert witness. When we saw in advance the credentials of this individual, we were not impressed, to say the least. He was a CPA who had earned his stock broker's license just two years ago. While we didn't want to be overconfident, it was hard for either of us to see what real expertise or value he would bring to the proceedings.

Little did we know that, with an intensity perhaps born of desperation, they were ready and willing to throw everything imaginable at us, in the hopes that the law of averages would prevail and they would find something that would "stick." In a rambling and lengthy direct examination that took the rest of the day, their side made apparent that in their opinion the damages (which were listed as $85,000 in the Statement of Claim) had mysteriously nearly tripled.

As I had come to understand more and more the realities of NASD arbitration and how the game is played, I understood exactly what was going on. A term used by those involved is *loosey-goosey*, which means that testimony is allowed without as firm a foundation of evidence as would be required in criminal or even civil litigation.

It was my belief that they were playing by the rules of "legal lottery" and simply picking a number that was approximately double what they were hoping to settle for, given the tendency of many arbitration panels to settle cases by "splitting the difference." So, if you want $50,000, just ask for $100,000. Under this theory, I felt that with their Statement of Claim they were hoping to get $42,500.

Imagine my surprise when I heard the expert witness claim that the actual damages were not $85,000, but rather $220,000 at one moment, $200,000 at another, and $190,000 in a third. The initial claim, which had never been justified in any logical way, had magically nearly tripled. The opposing team had rubbed Aladdin's lamp during lunch and out popped a genie with a $200,000+ invoice, but an invoice apparently still without an exact amount.

They also came up with additional new lines of argument that had nothing whatsoever to do with the original pleading. It seemed that they were admitting that the fundamentals of their case weren't valid, so they thought they would try out some new theories to see if they could get a winner. In the one-armed bandit of NASD arbitration, they were hoping the money machine would spit out some dollars before they ran out of time or arguments to make. To me, this was unbelievable—theater of the absurd.

The 5 Percent Theory

The major theory of the "expert" witness was that the client's risk profile had been misdiagnosed to begin with and that this "original sin" eventually resulted in large dollar losses over the course of the relationship during the time in question. It is easy to see where he was going with this. The expert witness had a be-ginning point and an end point and he could do math. He fig-ured out that if $850,000 had been invested at 5 percent annual rate of return, the portfolio would have been worth more than $1 million after three and a half years. In this scenario, in alternate universe dollars, my client was owed more than $150,000. How convenient.

He had two main goals during his testimony: first, to convince the panel that I had misdiagnosed the client to begin with as a growth client, and second, to present a seemingly factually grounded smoke-and-mirror act to try and give credibility to the now magical "5 percent theory."

Obviously, given what had already come out in direct and cross-examination, the "expert" had a steep hill to climb on the first point—the diagnosis. The accuser had agreed that he had filled out multiple questionnaires and forms indicating that he was a growth investor, and indicating a desired rate of return between 10 and 15 percent. He had testified to a lot of follow-up meetings and opportunities to object to my recommendations. His wife, who was financially knowledgeable, had been at these meetings. One meeting had been with an accountant. Until the termination of the relationship, no objections had been raised by the former client, his wife, or his accountant.

When in Doubt, Throw It Out

The expert came up with a brilliant way to achieve this objective: simply ignore all the information that contradicted his pre-arranged conclusion. I am not kidding. He very smoothly started out by saying that he had conducted his "expert analysis" by interviewing the former client, finding out about his life circumstances, and reviewing his tax returns. He had elicited from the client the fact that the client wanted to pull out $2,200 per month for his retirement income needs (which was true).

Beyond this $26,400 annually (which represented, how convenient, a 3 percent return on an $850,000 portfolio), he proclaimed confidently that the client didn't need asset appreciation. He ignored the $15,000 of annual income the client received from his real estate limited partnerships (admitted to under oath during cross-examination). His expert conclusion was that this client had "a low to moderate scale of risk tolerance, and he didn't really need growth of principle to achieve his life goals, and he was looking for income preservation"—flying in the face of all testimony and exhibits. The expert made no mention whatsoever of the numerous forms that the former client had filled out indicating his interest in "growth" or his desire for a 10 to 15 percent rate of return. I was just about ready to jump out of my seat.

Mythical Models Appear from Nowhere

The second major point of his testimony was that he had done "industry research" to come up with "models" that, if followed, would have resulted in the happy ending that had served as his starting point. This was, if anything, even more beyond the pale than his first claim. With a very authoritative voice, in response to the questions of my accuser's attorney, he explained how he had done some research through his firm's broker-dealer.

He took his flawed initial diagnosis and validated it by going online to the broker-dealer's web site. By a strange and unsettling coincidence, his broker-dealer happened to be the same one I was working with for the majority of time I had worked with this client. The expert knew what he was looking for. After some work, he found some asset allocation models that had no relevance whatsoever to this case, but that affirmed his prearranged conclusion. Then he presented them as "official recommendations of the broker-dealer firm."

They were nothing of the sort, but the fact that they came from the same broker-dealer firm that I represented gave them a superficial credibility as he presented them to the panel. I wasn't even sure that the industry expert on the arbitration panel understood that not only the underlying assumption of his testimony (the asset allocation diagnosis) was bogus, but so was this whole presentation.

Stunning Gall

The conclusion of the expert's research was that instead of the highly diversified set of investments that I had recommended to him, I should have developed a portfolio comprised of 60 percent equities and 40 percent fixed income and cash.

He then made a truly astonishing suggestion—that each of these major components should have been invested in a single vehicle. The equities, according to him, should have been entirely comprised of the Russell 3000 Index. The fixed income component, by this theory, should have all been invested in the Lehman Aggregate Bond Index. Under this scenario, the client would have realized approximately $220,000 in increased value over the time period in contention, though they couldn't even be pinned down on that.

The expert and the attorney presented a legal precedent that supposedly bolstered this theory. They cited the famous "Berkshire Life" case, in which an institution was required to pay a large settlement despite the fact that the client had lost no money. This precedent became a standard cited by NASD arbitration plaintiff attorneys, especially in cases such as this.

To anyone who knows the slightest thing about investing, the idea of putting a client's equity or fixed portion of a portfolio entirely into a single fund or index is obviously patently ridiculous. Even if directly instructed by a client to do so, it would be the height of irresponsibility for any financial adviser to, in effect, bet the stack on one fund or index. If it didn't turn out well for the client, it would be a clear case of irresponsibility, and the adviser would (and should) be brought into arbitration and lose.

It was the absolute height of "Monday morning quarterbacking" for anyone to say, now looking back and knowing what we know, if you had done this, it would have resulted in that—along the lines of a lottery player walking into a bank to apply for a loan and telling the lending officer, "I have assets. I played the lottery yesterday and if I had just picked these numbers, I would be a multimillionaire today."

The gall was stunning, but I could see how it might be effective. The coincidence that he was using information from the same broker-dealer firm through which I had handled my former client's accounts for most of this relationship was especially troubling to me. It was pure expert witness spin, but could the arbitrators recognize the smoke and mirrors?

Did I Assassinate Pope John Paul?

This was obvious to me and to Jim Weller. But, strangely, the arbitrators seemed to be taking the notion seriously. One could tell from the types of questions they were asking and the tone of those questions that they were giving credence to his theory.

Naturally, the expert claimed that it was, of course, "possible" to do this. To me, it was about as credible as someone asking if it were "possible" that I had been the one to try and assassinate Pope John Paul II in 1980. I can just imagine the sequence of questions:

Q: "How old were you in 1980?"
A: "I was 19 years old."
Q: "Were you physically able to shoot a gun at that time?"
A: "Yes."
Q: "Do you have a passport?"
A: "Yes."
Q: "Can you prove that you were not in Vatican Square on that day?"
A: "No."

The expert witness's entire line of wildly speculative testimony was a nightmare scenario as far as I was concerned. I was urgently whispering to Jim, telling him "You've got to stop this! You can't let this continue. This is becoming a kangaroo court." (I am not even sure today what a kangaroo court is, but it sounded right at the time.)

As of Now, This Testimony Stands

For the first time in the entire trial, I felt as though I were on the outside looking in, and I could feel my winning case beginning to slip away. It bothered me that Jim didn't seem to be as upset about this as I was. He tried to explain to me that he had heard this type of argument in other cases he was trying and that things like this are part of the system. On every break, Jim was telling me to calm down. But I couldn't sit by dispassionately while our case crumbled before our eyes.

At one point in the middle of this, Chairman Besser turned to Jim and stated, "Mr. Weller, you are going to have to tell us tomorrow if you agree with these calculations. You will have to tell us tomorrow. We can't figure it out. As of now, unless it is refuted, this testimony stands." When I heard that, I got a knot in my stomach. And for his generally cool demeanor, I had the feeling that it upset Jim, too. This thought terrified me. I realized that however bizarre and unfounded this theory had been, if we didn't clearly refute it, I might lose.

The attorney then had the expert witness give his analysis of an issue that my former client had brought up on direct testimony. He had called my office at one point and wanted to invest some funds in a risky technology fund. He sent me a check, which was invested for him in this fund. However, there was a delay between our receipt of the check and its investment in this fund, due to a procedural issue.

The technology fund issue presented two problems for the former client and their side, but one for me as well. One problem for their side was that this undercut their "Rain Man" theory—that this individual was a financially unsophisticated individual who didn't know much about investing. If that was the case, then how was it that he happened to be reading an article in which this fund was mentioned, requested some information about it, and felt confident enough to decide, on his own, to invest in it? Second, with all of the talk about his desire for a "conservative" strategy, a 5 percent return (despite writing "10 to 15 percent" on several forms as his investment objective), what was he doing investing in this type of product? They had tried to address this in his direct testimony by having him say that he had decided that this would be his "one flyer." The expert witness reinforced that by making the analogy of someone taking a chunk of money and going to Foxwoods Casino, which is located about half an hour from his house in Connecticut.

The story of this trade did create a problem for me, though a fairly minor one. By a coincidence, the check he sent to our office for this investment arrived on the second day of our switchover from our former broker-dealer firm to a new broker-dealer firm. Because of that, we couldn't execute the trade immediately. There was an exchange involving sending some papers to the client to fill out, which he didn't get back to our office immediately. Eventually, the fund was bought approximately six weeks after the money arrived, causing an arguable loss to the client. This one issue was, as it turns out, the only legitimate claim the former client had in his entire case—and it was one with a lot of gray area, not really a black-and-white issue. At the end of the day, the panel spent some time asking about the details of this trade and trying to figure out what had happened and how much they were claiming he lost as a result.

Lots of Work Left to Do

As I listened to the testimony and observed the questions, voice inflections, and body language of the arbitrators, the simmering confidence I had felt earlier in the day had nearly evaporated. When we broke at around 5:00 P.M., it was obvious to me that there were a lot of issues on the table and I realized that my side had some serious work to do.

Jim asked me some questions that spurred me to do the work that proved to supply what we later both felt were the turning points of the entire hearing. During the discussion of the Russell 3000 strategy, Jim asked me if there were any guidelines supplied by my former broker-dealer firm that would have invalidated this claim.

I said yes, of course, every quarter of every year the company provided us with models that represented guidelines of how a registered representative could allocate the assets of a client, based on his or her risk category. He asked me, "Did you follow those models?" I said, "Yes, of course. And it really was not that big a deal; the models merely represent guidelines that the rep is free to follow or not follow. They essentially represent a consensus opinion of standard industry practices."

He then asked me the big question: "Can you get your hands on those models before tomorrow?" Of course, I immediately thought, and said, "Yes." But it proved to be a lot tougher than I had at first considered. Our hearing was taking place in 2003. We wanted the asset allocation models for 1997 and 1998, and we needed them tomorrow. It was 5:00 P.M. I had caught a huge break in that the firm's headquarters was on the West Coast, three hours earlier in the day.

A Quick Mental Trip to Martial Arts World—The Integrity Principle

As I walked back to the hotel to jump on the phone and get those models, I reflected back again on my martial arts background. I had lived and trained in New York City for a number of years, and part of me wished I could go back to that simpler time. For a martial artist, at the heart of the ability to make progress is a type of deep personal integrity, which becomes both a goal and a pathway to the future. In this sense, integrity does not refer merely to simple surface issues such as telling the truth and speaking to others with honor and respect. It is a type of searching of one's soul to constantly ask the question: "Am I doing my best?" A martial artist who is being true to himself or herself is often said to be living "the way."

Every martial artist who has trained for several years will recognize that it is possible to glide through a class, or even a week of classes, in a type of cruise control. You are there physically going through the motions, but not mentally, spiritually, or emotionally. You are not committed to each moment of the class. Integrity is developed from a minute-by-minute, day-by-day, and week-by-week commitment to personal effort to doing one's best.

For the martial artist, constant self-examination, self-scrutiny, is one of the prices paid in order to progress, in order to fulfill your potential. Among people who train regularly, integrity as represented by personal commitment to doing one's best creates the highest respect. Naturally, there is a type of unspoken pecking order among martial artists in terms of speed, size, strength, ability to kick and punch, and so on. But at the deepest level, martial artists respect commitment. Those students who are always doing their best, and treating each moment of each class as if it is the most important moment ever, inculcate in others the highest admiration.

Many training centers, known as *dojos*, have the walls covered with floor-to-ceiling mirrors. There is both a practical and metaphorical reason for this. Many exercises are conducted with the student looking at the mirror. By being faced literally with yourself, you can follow the instructors and see how closely you are following their teaching. Does your punch finish precisely where it is supposed to? Are you following the patterns in precise sequence? Training in front of a mirror is one of the best ways to assess yourself and to improve.

I felt the loneliness of the moment as I got to my hotel. I was fatigued. It had been a long day already. If the pressure hadn't been so great, I might have wanted to forget going after those asset allocation models. Let Jim Weller work his magic somehow on cross-examination. Vince Lombardi used to say that "fatigue makes cowards of us all." But I like to believe that those years of training kicked in and gave me that little extra jolt of electrical energy to get started. I got to my room and got on the phone.

Racing the Clock to Get the Models

Even though there were a few business hours left on the West Coast, I began to realize it would take a minor miracle for me to produce those models. But Jim was really certain that if we could somehow get our hands on those models and show I had followed them, the other side would not have a leg to stand on. If it was going to take a minor miracle, then it was a minor miracle I was determined to produce. My day was only half over. I went to my room, ordered Chinese food to be delivered so as not to waste a moment, and began my work on the "second shift."

I got on the phone with a tremendous sense of urgency. The time differential meant that it was late afternoon and there were people working with whom I could speak. Normally, I am an extremely calm and courteous individual. That day, I know that I was not my normal self. People who were polite, but essentially unhelpful, got a dose of my desperation.

I kept working my way from one person to another, hoping to find that helpful person who would understand what I needed and realize the importance of getting it done immediately. The truth was that, although my name was the lead in the complaint, the broker-dealer was also exposed to risk. Our fates were tied together in the arbitration. They were funding my efforts, and if I lost, it would reflect negatively on them and, eventually, on the rating for their errors-and-omission insurance rates.

The challenge was that this was November 2003 and I needed the asset allocation models for 1997 and 1998. They *must* be somewhere that someone could get to them. It felt like a scene out of a movie. As the clock approached 8:00 P.M. on the East Coast, it approached 5:00 P.M. on the West Coast. Those models were of no value to me in 24 or 48 hours. I needed them faxed to me tonight. The clock was ticking.

The Triumph of Tenacity

Amazingly, my obsessiveness, tenacity, and persuasive communication skills were rewarded. A woman I will always be grateful to offered to help. She told me that she had access to the models, but would need to secure permission from a company compliance officer to release them to me.

Finally, after much churning in my stomach and a sense of near panic, my guardian angel came back to me with the great news. She had gotten the permission she needed and could fax me the models. Originally, I had mentioned the 1997 and 1998 models for the "growth" and "growth and income" categories. Realizing that the other side would probably try and make something sinister if we didn't produce *all* the categories, I quickly thought to ask her to send all of them to me by fax. And she agreed. I had an enormous sense of relief in hearing this, but not total relief. That wouldn't come until I had them physically in my hands.

Finally, at 11:00 P.M., I got a phone call from the front desk telling me that a fax for me had just arrived. I had in my possession the proof we needed to combat today's expert testimony on asset allocation. Though I knew by now never to be overconfident, in my heart of hearts I thought to myself "Game. Set. Match."

At last, I felt the relief of what had been relentless pressure. I hadn't even testified, and I was absolutely drained. It was a day of wild emotions. At one point, I thought we had won the case. When I left the hearing, I was sure we were in big trouble if I couldn't get those models. I got to sleep quickly, but not too deeply. No REM sleep for me on this night.

Tomorrow would be critically important. The day that I thought would never end finally did.

Humility

Dedication

Integrity

Awareness

Duality

Expert Witness Unmasked: An Offer to Settle—I Finally Get to Testify

NASD Hearing Day Two— November 4, 2003

Is Every Case Like This?

As I walked into the hearing room a good half hour before the scheduled start, my mind went back to all of the drama and events of the prior day. It was a day in which, as the saying goes, it felt as though my professional life were flashing before me.

I remember turning to Jim and Joan and asking them, "Is every case like this?" When they told me "yes," I said, "I could never do what you do for a living." It seemed as though my entire fate had rested on my ability to successfully execute an almost unimaginable sequence of events in a compressed time frame and show up at court with those asset allocation models in hand. It could so easily have worked out that I didn't get them.

Had that happened our case would have been in real trouble. Yesterday's expert testimony, as bogus as it was, would "stand." As it turned out, it would be many hours before the asset allocation models would even come into play.

The Chairman Begins the Unmasking

The day started out on what, to me, was a very encouraging note. Chairman Besser demonstrated his acute sense of the case by starting off the official part of the day by asking the expert witness some simple questions. In his inability to give straight answers, the expert's façade began to crumble.

The expert had loftily rolled out the Russell 3000 Theory, making it seem as if my former broker-dealer firm was instructing its registered representatives to invest 100 percent of a "moderate conservative" investor's portfolio in the Russell 3000 Index. Chairman Besser started out the day by asking the expert to clarify whether the Russell 3000 and the Lehman Brothers Aggregate Bond Index were "benchmarks," indexes, or actual funds. The reality was that they were indexes. It was also true that an investor could have essentially made an investment in a financial product that mirrored each of these indexes. But the expert didn't know this. He had spun his golden theory without even bothering to check something as basic as "could the client actually have made these investments?" It was beautiful to watch this exchange.

Q: "Is it a fund—if I wanted to, could I invest in the Russell 3000?"

A: "Yes you could … The Russell 3000—I am not sure if there is an actual fund for it."

Jim Weller had asked me the day before this same question—could you buy this fund? I told him that the answer was qualified "yes," but, to my amusement and enjoyment, the expert didn't know the answer—so he tap danced. Besser wasn't going to let this ambiguity stand, so he simply rephrased the question.

He wanted an answer, and the expert didn't want to say the magic words "I don't know."

Q: "The question is: If I wanted to, could I call up my broker and invest $10,000 in what you have called the Russell 3000?"

A: "I believe so, but I am not certain."

Chairman Besser decided to continue to test the expert and ask him about another one of the key terms he had used the day before. The expert had testified that instead of the investments that were made, had I properly diagnosed my former client, then the broker-dealer firm would have told me to put his money in what he referred to as the "Russell 3000 Fund" and the "Lehman Brothers Aggregate Bond Index." He obviously didn't know if the Russell 3000 Index was actually a purchasable investment. So, Chairman Besser decided to continue the questioning.

Q: "Could I invest $10,000 in the Lehman Brothers Aggregate Bond Index?"

A: "It might not be exactly the Lehman Brothers Aggregate Bond Index, but it would be something very, very similar to it."

Q: "Like what?"

A: "An index fund for the bond market."

It is a classic bit of wisdom that when your opponent is in the midst of destroying himself, just stand back and watch. I was really enjoying this. Although he maintained a very neutral, judicial tone throughout the hearing, I had to believe that Chairman Besser was very unimpressed that this expert didn't even possess this very basic information. How worthwhile could his advice be?

$25,000—Lost and Found

The client and his attorney were claiming they had "lost" $25,000 as a result of what is known in the industry as a 1035 exchange or, simply put, the surrender of a life insurance policy. The policy had a paid-up cash surrender value of $125,000, with a death benefit of $150,000. The policy was transferred over to an annuity, in large part because the client no longer needed the insurance. The "expert" was claiming that the client "lost" $25,000 as a result of the transfer of the policy.

This was another example of either ignorance on the part of the expert or cynicism on the part of my accuser and his team. To anyone who knew the slightest thing about how this type of transaction works, they understood that the client lost no money. He had accepted the cash surrender value, which was $25,000 less than the face value of the policy. One could claim a loss only if the assumption was that the client was planning to die shortly after the transaction occurred. It would be easy enough to refute, but I was itching to get the chance to set the record straight and a little frustrated that this type of error would even be permitted as testimony in a hearing of this magnitude.

A hole had been blown in their case already. But if the expert felt rebuffed by Chairman Besser's pointed questions, it was nothing compared to what he must have felt like after Jim Weller got done with a few hours of cross-examination. After listening to yesterday's high-blown rhetoric, it was a lot of fun to watch.

Pay No Attention to the Man Behind the Curtain

I realize that as a party to the proceedings, I looked at everything through the prism of my case and how it was proceeding. But years later, after listening to the actual tapes, I can now say that Jim Weller's tone, demeanor, and delivery were very professional. It was, in my mind, a contrast to the opposing attorney, who at times was highly effective and at other times was distracted, distracting, and annoying to listen to.

The next several hours were devoted to a brilliant, and even excruciating, prolonged cross-examination of the expert witness by Jim Weller. Once again, I marveled at his nuanced grasp of the most complex, sophisticated issues, his tremendous preparation, and his skill at asking questions that get at the truth.

He began by calmly but professionally demonstrating that this individual had virtually no relevant credentials to substantiate the title "expert" or to give weight to any of the analysis he had given the day before. I savored watching Jim calmly and surgically shine the light of truth on yesterday's star witness.

He started out by asking some simple but very revealing questions about the expert's claim of expertise.

Q: "Have you ever managed any money for a client?"
A: "No."
Q: "Have you ever allocated any money for a client?"
A: "No."
Q: "Have you ever purchased any annuities for a client?"
A: "No."
Q: "Have you ever purchased any mutual funds for a client?"
A: "No."
Q: "Have you ever written in the area of suitability?"
A: "No."
Q: "Have you ever testified before in the area of suitability?"
A: "No."

It went on like that—and on and on and on. But unlike Barry Scheck in his browbeating of Dennis Fung in the O. J. Simpson case, Jim was not gratuitous in the way he did this. Every single question—and many of them were nice and short and simple—got at some relevant information.

"Bring Me the Holy Grail"

We took a mid-morning break and I was feely pretty good at this point. But Jim didn't allow me to relax—he had had another brainstorm. In classic Weller fashion, he had come up with a great strategy and had another request for me to fulfill. Jim asked me during lunch break, when it would be the start of business on the West Coast, to call back to the broker-dealer firm and talk with someone in the research department and see if I could get someone to agree to testify by telephone in the afternoon. He explained to me that NASD arbitration hearings allowed for sworn testimony via the telephone.

This seemed like a fantastic idea to me—get an actual officer to testify live to what we were saying. One of the exposed weaknesses of the expert's direct testimony that had come out due to questioning by the panel members is that although he was liberally using terms such as *the broker-dealer recommendations* and *the broker-dealer recommends this*, he hadn't actually talked with anyone at the broker-dealer corporate home office. I realized what a coup it would be to get this. Before the break ended, I called the broker-dealer and left a voice mail for the director of research about the situation, telling him I would call him back just after 9:00 A.M. his time.

Debunking the Mythology

The foundation of the expert's theory was that I had misdiagnosed my former client as a growth investor. In order for the expert's charts and recommendations (which had already been shown to be suspect) to have any validity, the "reasonable observer" of the proceedings would have to first believe that my former client had a far more conservative profile than that of growth' investor. Instead of the 10 to 15 percent return that the former client had indicated was his goal on a number of forms he signed and turned in to me, the expert concluded that 5 to 6 percent was a more appropriate investment goal. The fact that prior to coming to see me the client already had a portfolio that generated returns in this range didn't bother the expert.

At this initial stage of his cross-examination, Jim Weller bore in on three key issues:

1. The sloppy and inappropriate methodology the "expert" used in arriving at his risk profile of my former client
2. The extensive documentation that showed the client to be properly assessed as a growth client

3. The expert's astonishing lack of knowledge about the subjects he was testifying about

Jim started out by getting the expert to admit he had openly
and consciously ignored the vast majority of the paperwork that
any registered representative would have had to use to determine risk tolerance. It was not that he had seen them and re-
jected them. Rather, it was pretty obvious that he had pointedly
not wanted to see them.

Q: "Did you review the confidential questionnaire before you
formed your opinion as to the suitability of investments?"
A: "No."
Q: "Did you tell the client that you wanted to see all the docu-
ments he had?"
A: "No, sir."
Q: "Did you see a prospectus receipt before you formed your
opinion as to how Mr. Hine managed this client's accounts?"
A: "No, sir."

I thought that these questions and answers alone should have
invalidated this individual's entire testimony. In another exchange, he admitted not only that he hadn't seen the relevant
documents, but that in one case he didn't even know what one of
them was.

Q: "Did you see this new account application, in which the cat-
egory "long-term growth" is checked?"
A: "No."
Q: "Is this the type of document you use in your business?"
A: "What is it?"
Q: "I just got my answer."

I was really amazed to watch this. The expert admitted that
not only had he consciously performed his analysis without the

basic building-block forms, but that, in this case, he didn't even know what it was. There is nothing more fundamental to the life of a rep than a new account form (NAF), and this expert responded that he didn't know what it was.

I believed that the expert was close to having a meltdown. It seemed to me that it couldn't get much worse for him. In what may have been, to anyone who knew anything about the securities business, the most shocking testimony yet in the trial, the expert just came right out and unapologetically told the panel that even if he had received the forms, he would have ignored all of them. Like a bull in a china shop, he plowed through an astute observation by Ms. Weisman, and proceeded to demonstrate almost unimaginable ignorance of the investment world.

Expert: "I don't care what this questionnaire says—based on what he told me, he did not need 10 to 15 percent. His circumstances—he didn't need—my goal would have been to tell him—even if he did tell me 10 to 15, I would have told him, that isn't suitable for you. You don't need that—why take the risk?"

Panel Member Weisman: "You are rendering this opinion with 20/20 hindsight. You didn't have the information Mr. Hine had. I am trying to sort out where you are getting your opinion from, so I can judge apples to apples."

In her consistent, meticulous, and exceedingly fair manner, Ms. Weisman was trying to get to the truth. I was amazed at what the expert said next.

Expert: "If he said to me, I want 10 to 15 percent, I would have said, 'Go get a letter from your lawyer, go get a letter from your stockbroker, go get a letter from your wife supporting that you are going to take that undue risk—or find somebody else.'"

Can you imagine any registered representative or investment

adviser saying that? He was telling us that he would have told my client "I don't care what you say, I don't care what your goals are, I don't care what you tell me your objectives are—unless you get handwritten notes from your stockbroker, wife, and lawyer, I am not going to handle your account." If this were the standard by which business was conducted, there would be no equities markets—there would be little to no investing at all.

All of this confirmed to me that this "expert" was a joke. A few simple questions from Chairman Besser and Jim Weller had unmasked the expert. But the other side kept their act on. At every break, I asked Jim why the panel didn't stop the hearing, but he explained that wasn't going to happen.

There were two more extremely revealing comments made by the panel members before the Weller cross-examination was over. Jim was going over some more questions about the use of forms, specifically prospectuses. As any rep knows, there is highly specific language in prospectuses that are signed by clients, which make it clear that they have read *and understood* them prior to investing. The "expert" witness had testified that he hadn't read the prospectuses. Referring to this subject, at one point Chairman Besser jumped into the proceedings and succinctly stated:

Chairman Besser: "The witness says he doesn't care—isn't that your testimony?"
Panel Member Weisman: "Thank you, Mr. Chair."

Later in the testimony, Chairman Besser again summed up the expert witness's approach to reviewing documents before making an asset allocation assessment.

Chairman Besser: "He would have ignored the four documents and told him he was not a growth investor."

In retrospect, I believe that these two brief snippets of more than 20 hours of live testimony were very revealing. At the time, they were just another positive indicator for me, though not definitive. By lunchtime, whatever sense of negative momentum I had felt yesterday afternoon had completely vanished.

A Busy Lunch Break—Returning with the Holy Grail

At this point, I was wired and felt a surge of confidence. I just *knew* in my heart that I would be able to get my former broker-dealer's director of research to agree to this. Sure enough, he answered his phone when I called. I told him about the procedure and explained the situation. I told him that it might not be necessary, but if he would be willing to be on standby to testify that the models that had been faxed to me last night were the definitive recommendations for the time periods in question, it would be a huge help.

He agreed to everything I asked. Like a caveman returning with the evening dinner, I came back to Jim and told him what had happened—and that all systems were go. Jim smiled and said, "Great!" I felt fantastic giving him this tool to work with. The team was operating at a very high level.

Hearing the Magic Words: "They're Talking Settlement"

Jim then told me that he had some important news for me. He looked me in the eye and said, "They want to settle." My accuser's attorney had sidled up to Jim on a break and asked, "Do we have anything to talk about?," which he told me meant that they felt they were losing the case and wanted to settle. Though not totally unexpected, I began to think justice was about to be served. My accuser would admit that he had no case. It would be dismissed, and I would perhaps receive something for the trouble he had put me through.

So, I asked Jim, with complete seriousness, "How much are they offering to pay me?" I was dismayed that this wasn't going to happen. In this case, *settlement* meant that they were willing to accept less than the $85,000 (or its new incarnation, $200,000+) to dismiss the case. In other words, I would still be admitting guilt, but they would walk away with less than the unjustified, unsubstantiated fantasy amount they had suggested as their damages.

I asked Jim, "Why would I even consider doing that?" I felt I had proven that I hadn't done anything wrong. The idea that as a result of this I would settle was a nonstarter for me. Jim explained to me, "Tom, a lot of times these cases do settle like this, because it limits the costs, the time, and the aggravation. It gives you some certainty, and you can never tell what might come up later on if we continue to fight it. But it is your decision." For me, it was no decision at all.

A Silent Victory—Though I Would Have Preferred the Noise

Then Jim smoothly rolled out the information that the broker-dealer firm's director of research was willing to be sworn in to the proceedings and testify by phone on this very point—and that we had a way to get hold of him and make this happen today. As in *now*. I could tell that it shocked the other side. I am not absolutely sure that my accuser's attorney knew that this rather exotic technique was permissible. But he certainly didn't expect us to have this level of preparedness. The white belt and his lawyer had struck again. They gave on the point and decided to stipulate that these were suggestions and not requirements.

I had to believe that the other side realized that this would have been especially painful for them to sit through, as, in testifying about the models which I had gotten faxed to me, he would have also made it clear that the expert's models were simply something he had cut and pasted off an Internet site—and *not* the actual recommended models the expert had claimed they were.

Part of me was happy to win the argument and grateful not to have to ask the director of research to go the extra mile and testify for us via telephone. Part of me was secretly disappointed that they hadn't required us to do this because of the potential emotional impact it would have had on the momentum of the case.

I had come to believe from being in that hearing room that in arbitration not everything is weighted in relative importance according to logic and factual information. There is a clear emotional component that is unmistakable. There is negative and positive momentum for each side. And some testimony has a more clearly emotional and devastating impact on the tone of the trial than others.

It would have been high drama to get the director on the phone and go through the solemn swearing-in and questioning. I would really have enjoyed listening to this, but in the end the other side folded their cards on this point. Though it might have been especially satisfying for me to listen to, the fact is his testimony had effectively been refuted. Big points for the Hine-Weller-Herman team.

Starting the Afternoon Session with Even More Indigestion for the Expert

When we got back from lunch, Chairman Besser started the session, as was becoming his pattern, and would remain so throughout the hearing, of starting things off with some good, focused questions. And in doing so, he got out for the record one more real whopper of a mistake by the expert—something to remember him by.

Chairman Besser: "Was Mr. Hine acting as an investment adviser, for which he was paid a fee?"
Expert: "No."

This was a huge admission. Yesterday, they had used my former client's direct testimony to throw up a smokescreen and imply, if not come out and say, that I had discretion from my former client to make trades. The former client had said, at least half a dozen times, some variation of "I left it all up to Mr. Hine" or "I put everything in his hands." The clear impression was that he had, in effect, walked in to my office, plunked down $857,000, said "You manage it," and walked out. To the industry expert panel member, the testimony that the account was "nondiscretionary" meant that I sought the client's approval for trades. Now Chairman Besser asked the question that crystallized this fact and made it plain for all panel members.

If the expert had really exposed his ignorance of our profession in the morning—and he had—he took a flying leap onto a plate of glass with the follow-up question and answer.

Chairman Besser: "Is an investment adviser held to a higher standard than a broker who buys stock?"
Expert: "I believe they have the same standards."

All of a sudden the room got deadly silent. This was information so basic that any registered rep would know it well before his or her first day on the job and the expert witness didn't. As any financial adviser knows, there are two distinct ways in which an adviser can work with a client: as a broker (nondiscretionary account) or as a fiduciary (discretionary account). In some cases, as with the claimant, portions of a portfolio can be conducted under a brokerage arrangement, and other portions as a fiduciary. As a fiduciary, there is a far higher standard of care required of the adviser.

It seemed to me as though everyone other than the expert witness immediately knew what an egg he had just laid. Although Chairman Besser kept a very steady tone throughout the hearing, he was visibly taken aback at this. Jim looked at me with a little twinkle in his eye and gave a half smile. I had to believe his attorney realized what a huge mistake this was, and probably was ready to dive under the table and call for the defibrillator.

But give him credit—the show must go on. After about 10 seconds of silent squirming, he gathered himself and proceeded on as if nothing had happened.

Internet Scheme Exposed

One of the characteristics about the more relaxed rules of arbitration as an adversarial proceeding, as opposed to criminal or civil litigation, is that there is some latitude that is given to each side in presenting their case. Over the course of the expert's direct testimony and cross-examination, it had come out, in bits and pieces, that his models were not what he had represented them to be. They were models, all right, and they were broker-dealer generated, but they were *not* the recommended models for registered representatives to use in helping them make asset allocation decisions.

In addition, in locating the models, the expert hadn't actually spoken with anyone at the broker-dealer's research department. In fact, he hadn't spoken with anyone at their corporate home office at all—not even the receptionist. He had spoken with someone in his affiliated partner company, who directed him to an Internet site. Jim walked him through this, so that the panel could again clearly understand the contrast between his theory and our facts. He had little more than Internet spam. We had the actual official asset allocation models.

As the stress of the cross-examination kept increasing, the expert witness became defensive, then visibly frustrated, and eventually exasperated. As I watched it, I couldn't believe this guy was the best they could come up with.

Before the Weller cross-examination was over, the expert admitted openly that he had made a mistake in claiming that the client had lost any money in the 1035 exchange (the insurance surrender). Chairman Besser, with his penchant for clarity, asked him directly:

Chairman Besser: "So you were mistaken when you testified
that he lost $25,000 by cashing it in?"
Expert: "Yes, sir."

Jim finished up with a few more questions. But the damage
had already been done. The opposing attorney, as he had with
my former client the day before, put together what appeared to
me to be a half-hearted "redirect" set of questions, trying to rehabilitate, to the extent he could, his humiliated expert witness.
And the expert witness got off the stand and later in the day left
the building, never to return at any point in the process.

Duality: The Yin and Yang of Testimony

As I watched the testimony, I could not help marveling how
the legal adversarial world reflected one of the key concepts that
had been a core of my martial arts training: duality. Think of that
classic tai chi circle, with the opposing sides—the yin and the
yang. It symbolizes the idea that the universe works in opposition. Light means that there will be darkness. Heat means that
there will be cold. Good means that there will be evil. All very
philosophical.

On a practical training level, martial arts moves almost always
involve opposing movement. Newton's First Law states that for
every action there exists an equal but opposite reaction. For a
martial artist, each punch forward is made more powerful by
having the retraction (opposing) arm and hand pulled backward.

One of the classic moments in every martial artist's early training is when the instructor stands in a "horse-riding stance" (feet
shoulder-width apart, hips sunk a foot or more below normal
belt level) and demonstrates the difference in power between a
single punch to the solar plexus by itself as opposed to the power
of that same punch in which the opposite arm is pulled backward at the same time and with equal force. Students get to try

this on their own, and the difference is profound. Nearly all martial arts techniques—blocks, punches, evasions—are made more powerful by the proper application of the yin/yang, equal and opposite movement.

As I watched the back-and-forth of the testimony and argument, I could see the yin and the yang in front of me. The claimant got to testify and tell his side of the story. Then we got to cross-examine him and expose the other side. For every fact, there are two opposing ways to evaluate that fact. The courtroom battle was based in part on the ability to prevail in opposition, the yin and yang of legal argument. I began to realize what people mean when they say someone is "thinking like a lawyer." I never set that as a life goal, but here I was, in the arena, and always learning.

At Last, I Take the Stand

One of the unique challenges of formal adversarial courtroom proceedings is that the participant doesn't have control over the timetable. I had expected to be the first person to take the stand, but I wasn't. Although there had been only a day and a half of testimony since we began, it felt like weeks of my life had gone by. I had sat and listened to my accuser and his legal team make their case. I had watched while the arbitration panel seemed to me to be bending over backwards in an effort to give my opponent's group every consideration they could. Finally, it was going to be my turn to tell my side of the story.

As he was in every aspect of this entire process, Jim Weller was exceptionally well prepared. He had scripted a series of questions—all worded with precision, in a nice, clean logical order. The answers to these questions would give the arbitration panel the other side of the story. So far, they had been able to understand our view only indirectly, through the cross-examination process.

Jim started by asking me some very basic questions about my

background and credentials. In a few short minutes I had it on the record that I earned a master of business administration degree from the University of Connecticut with a concentration in finance. I held NASD Series 6, 7, 22, 24, 31, 63, and 65 designations. I held certifications as both a certified financial planner (CFP®) and a certified fund specialist (CFS). I was in my fourteenth year in the financial planning field and had never been disciplined by a regulatory body. With the exception of this complaint, I had nothing on my U-4.

These facts came across with a metronome-like quality. Simple question. Simple, direct answer. Jim felt quite strongly that although their expert witness had essentially imploded, and had been shown to lack credibility, it was important to get these elements of my background on the record. He knew they would form a nice contrast to the background of their expert witness, with his two years in the business, no experience working with clients, and few formal credentials. And, of course, he was the self-described expert, while I was "only" a rep.

In this business, I have prided myself on being very strong in technical analysis, as well as client development and relations. I have a natural analytical bent, and background in computer programming. I truly love studying and interpreting quantitative and statistical information and developing genuinely customized programs for each of my clients that fit their unique needs. The early part of direct testimony laid all of this out. And it was just the start.

Jim then walked me through the facts about my professional history with this particular client. Once again, we presented strong, clear, and compelling information that painted a much different picture than the one that began the trial yesterday morning.

I explained how I had been introduced to this individual. I was introduced to him by an existing client, as is so often the case in my professional life. In this case, the woman who introduced us originally married him approximately two years after I had started working with him. His wife had introduced us. She had been a client of mine for a number of years, had always been pleased with our work together.

But her involvement in this case went far beyond these facts. We brought out the fact that his wife sold real estate professionally, making her another individual in my former client's direct circle who had financial knowledge and access to information and resources if he had had any questions.

Furthermore, we reiterated the fact my former client's wife had attended every single one of the approximately half dozen portfolio review meetings that I had had with him. Those were the meetings at which we reviewed his holdings, went over pie charts, and explained the reasons I had recommended these particular funds to him.

Q: "What was his wife's background?"
A: "She sold real estate. As a client of mine for several years, she knew my style of investing, she knew that I liked to watch the top-ranked mutual funds and rotate into them when appropriate, she knew that I stayed in touch with people in terms of client relationships. Every time I spoke to both of them I felt comfortable, because if there was something her husband missed or didn't pick up she was always there as a backup to ask a question."

During this sequence of question and answer, Ms. Weisman became animated. As Jim and I now understood her intense focus on process and fairness, it was easy to understand why the information about the wife's background, and her attendance at all the meetings, might be of particular interest to her. At one point she jumped in and asked:

Q: "She attended *every one* of these meetings?" (emphasis supplied)
A: "Oh yes, absolutely."

I was unhesitating in my answer. She quickly said, "Thank you." Another little note for her deliberation. I felt that we were making clearer and clearer that the claimant was far from the helpless, financially naïve individual that had been portrayed.

I spoke about some of the other information we would cover in these meetings, including some technical terms such as *price-to-earnings ratios, net assets,* and *turnover rates.* I explained that we would block off from an hour to an hour and a half for these meetings. I made the point that the funds I had recommended to my client, and that were part of his portfolio, were ranked in the top 10 percent of 622 funds.

We had learned our lesson, so my explanations of these topics were precisely as they are with prospective clients—neither talking down to the panel nor assuming any real background. Everything was explained in clear, simple English terminology. At one point, I almost apologized for bringing up some technical terms, but said that some of this explanation was necessary for them to understand how I had worked with this client. As all of this was explained, it shed a totally different light on the image that he and his attorney had tried to paint with his direct testimony.

A Game of Pitch and Catch

It was like playing a nice, comfortable game of pitch and catch. After sitting on the sidelines and working up a slow burn for the last day and a half, it felt great to be in the game.

Q: "When you had these meetings with your client and his wife, did he ever seem confused to you?"
A: "No, he did not."
Q: "Did he ever say to you he didn't understand what you were talking about?"
A: "No, he did not."
Q: "Did he ever say, 'You are talking about P/E ratios, and I don't understand what that is'?"

A: "No, he never did."

Q: "Would he ever ask for additional explanations for things?"

A: "He certainly did, and I encouraged it because I don't expect everyone to know what I know—so I would often break down some of the statistics."

Jim took me through the lunch meeting with the former client and his accountant. Now this meeting, which had been brought up yesterday in cross-examination, took on a fuller and clearer picture—a picture of four people sitting around a table: the client; his accountant; his wife, the long-term investor and real estate professional; and me.

The Investor Scorecard

Jim followed the chronology and got right to the forms that the former client had filled out, which were essential to my ability to accurately develop his risk profile. He went right to the investor scorecard, which he referred to generically as a questionnaire.

Q: "Why do the questionnaire?"

A: "We thought it was very important to sit down early on and throughout the client relationship—to sit down and discuss in detail the client's actual feelings about risk and reward. Because everybody will say—'I am conservative but I want to make money'—a classic joke in financial planning. So we want to make sure if someone says, 'I'm a growth investor,' we would walk through the questionnaire to make sure that we understood and they understood what that meant in terms of risk. In other words, you can't be a growth investor and take no risk."

Q: "Did you form an opinion, an initial opinion, as to what type of investor he was?"

A: " Initially, a growth investor, with this form and throughout our relationship."

Q: "Were there particular questions you looked at?"

A: "Yes. I looked at question 3: 'Which of the following investments would you feel most comfortable in owning?' He
checked 'stocks of new growth companies' as opposed to certificates of deposit or U.S. government securities."

Q: "Were there any other questions which were important to
you?"

A: "Yes, question 4: 'Which of the following investments would
you least like to own?' And he checked the box 'certificates of
deposit.'"

The Killer Graph

Then Jim pointed the panel's attention to the bottom of page
two—a very revealing graph that had obviously been hand
sketched. It showed a vertical line with an arrow at the end of it,
a horizontal line perpendicular to the vertical line also with an
arrow at the end of it, and the "sine wave"—a graphical image
that looked like a roller-coaster—up and down and back up and
back down—through several cycles. Above and to the left of the
sine wave were the words "the market." Below the horizontal
line was written "7–10 years." (See Figure 3.1.)

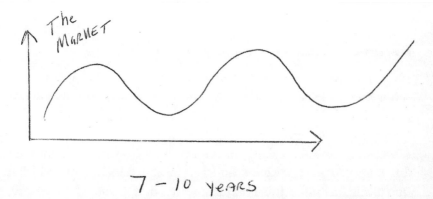

Figure 3.1   Handwritten Graph on Investor Scorecard

It was as clear as could be what this image represented. It showed the client that the market would go up and down over time, and that the proper time frame to consider necessary to reach these financial objectives was 7 to 10 years. And he had pulled out in year four.

Through some simple questions, and my answers, we drove the point home.

Q: "Is that your handwriting?"

A: "Yes, it is."

Q: "Did you draw that image and explain it to your client?"

A: "Yes, I did."

Q: "Why did you do that?"

A: "I draw these lines to show that the market can go up and down—and in fact does go up and down—and the time horizon was important, because when I sit down with an investor, if they are telling me they want to be ahead of inflation, ahead of taxes, 7 to 10 years is the minimum time frame they should look at. It doesn't mean you can't take money out. It doesn't mean you can't move money around. But you should be committed to a program for that time frame. And if you are not comfortable, then we have to reevaluate, and throughout my career I have had people say, 'I had better reevaluate.' We did this because we wanted them to be comfortable with this as a time frame."

Documentation—The Agony and the Ecstasy

As we moved through the story of the client relationship, another key topic was documentation. With regard to paperwork, it turned out that my former client had signed more than a dozen forms, including prospectuses, in which he checked that he was either a "growth" or "aggressive growth" investor. We showed an example early in the relationship in which he had overridden one of the mutual funds I had suggested and replaced it with one he liked better. How could he have done this if he were a docile, unsophisticated investor? The evidence just continued to pile up as I went through my testimony.

During the time period in question, my firm had used two different systems: Microsoft Outlook and a commercial contact management system. In addition, I had contemporaneous notes of meetings, some of which were written in a type of personal shorthand, many of which were on forms that I had worked on with my former client.

There were electronic records of the client's calling in and telling one of our office people in setting up an appointment that he "wanted to get more aggressive" with his investments. In that same electronic note was a phrase about the technology fund he had wanted to purchase. I knew in my heart that these were separate, but related, ideas. He wanted to both talk about the technology fund purchase *and* get more aggressive with his portfolio. But I knew that it could be argued the other way as well—that the technology fund purchase, a relatively small amount as a percentage of his total holdings, would be represented by the other side as the "only" example in which he had wanted to get aggressive.

It was here that I felt a combination of joy and agony, emotional yin and yang. From any realistic perspective, as compared perhaps with the mythical "average representative," my documentation was outstanding. Jim Weller had told me as much. But I still had those holes we had identified, and I knew they would be exploited. Of particular importance was a meeting I had with the client in the fall of 1999, in which he confirmed he wanted to get more aggressive in his overall portfolio, which I did. I definitely took contemporaneous notes of that meeting, but couldn't find them. It just killed me to have nearly perfect, but not perfect, documentation. Strangely, because my records were generally so strong, it seemed to cast a longer shadow on the missing or incomplete documents. Every little thing like this seemed like life and death as far as the trial was concerned.

The Real Asset Allocation Models

We went from record keeping into the broker-dealer firm's actual asset allocation models—the real ones, which I had obtained from the corporate home office, not the "cut and paste off the Internet" ones that had been presented approximately 24 hours earlier. During a sidebar of the attorneys and the panel members, the other side had stipulated that these were, in fact, the "real ones."

Despite this being part of the record, Jim wanted to spend at least a few minutes with me, walking through how I had followed these models. Once again, I used some technical terms, but explained each term concisely but clearly. I showed how the subaccounts of my former client's overall accounts were invested in a manner consistent with the asset allocation models, including products that were categorized as "large-cap growth," "large-cap value," "small-cap growth," "small-cap value," "real estate investment trust (REIT)," and "high-yield bonds." I made clear the high-quality rankings of the investments and the value of diversification as a hedge against market volatility.

When my testimony was done, I felt we had more than answered the challenge of yesterday. Thank God, I had been able to get those models. With them, we presented the panel with dueling portfolios. Looking from a neutral point of view, one could imagine a panel member trying to weigh one against the other. The expert witness was someone who never worked with clients, didn't manage money, had never testified before about asset allocation or suitability. He not only did *not* look at the forms, which normally are the very foundation of a rep's assessment of risk tolerance and asset allocation; he claimed that even had he been presented with this information, he would have ignored all of it and told the client to go get letters from his wife, accountant, and lawyer if he wanted to be a growth investor. He never called his own broker-dealer firm to get information to conduct his expert analysis, but instead had pulled forms off the

Internet. He recommended that this client's funds should have been invested in a stock market index and bond market index—going completely against the principle of diversification. Further, he didn't even know if it would have been possible for my former client to actually purchase the very financial products he had recommended. Finally, he didn't know that there was a difference in standard of care between a fiduciary or "discretionary" relationship and a broker or "nondiscretionary" relationship.

Compare and Contrast

In my own mind, I contrasted all of this with my background, the logic of my testimony, the forms he had filled out, the multiple face-to-face account review meetings, his wife attending these meetings, the documentation of those meetings, the broker-dealer asset allocation models, and the process by which I had invested his funds and managed the relationship. I strongly believed that there was a lot weighing in my favor.

But Jim Weller had repeatedly told me, and I really understood this, that it wasn't over until it was over. He pointed out that although to me it was clear that we had the applicable models and the expert witness did not, it was not necessarily at all clear to the arbitrators. To them, it could have been perceived as just dueling testimony. You could understand it if they evaluated it by thinking "one person says this, and the other says that"—a gray area. And I knew I couldn't afford a lot of gray area if I was going to prevail in the case.

This was more yin and yang, more duality. As the process had gone on, I had partially absorbed how to try and think like a lawyer. It was like having split personalities. My partisan side said that I was in the right, and I had proven it. I was ready to go to war. But the realistic side in me made me realize that all the arbitrators had to do was to think that the claimant deserved some portion of what he was claiming, and it would be a big loss for me.

By the Way, What Damages Are You Claiming?

After testimony was closed, there was a period of discussion between the arbitration panel and the two attorneys, with all of us present. At the request of the panel, there was a preliminary effort by my opponents to calculate their losses from the delay in the technology trade. This led into a discussion of their claim of damages. The initial Statement of Claim filed in September 2002 had used the figure of $85,000. There was a period during the expert testimony where this number seemed to have tripled, to more than $200,000. But I was never clear, and apparently neither was the panel, on what my former client and his attorney were actually claiming for losses.

Ms. Weisman and Chairman Besser were politely persistent in asking my opponent's attorney for this information. It was apparent to me that he was annoying them in his continued refusal to provide a straight answer. Ms. Weisman wanted to know if the original $85,000 stood or if it had increased. What is the claim, and what does it consist of? He dodged the questions by instructing the panel that under applicable law, the panel could award any amount they felt appropriate. Ms. Weisman and Chairman Besser made it clear that they understood this, but that this was not what was being asked. The attorney then made a wandering and oblique reference to the expert witness's (discredited) testimony. "If you buy lock, stock, and barrel into the expert's numbers—and I don't know what the numbers are—190 something thousand dollars—or whatever that number is ... there is nothing in Connecticut law that would limit the panel making an award." I sat in astonishment. He didn't have a particular number in mind, something that was clearly being asked for. He passed up a chance to nail down an actual claim and justification for it. Neither Ms. Weisman nor Chairman Besser seemed to me to be particularly pleased with this little tap dance.

Homework Assignments

Besser, always asking pertinent questions, instructed both attorneys to prepare memoranda within a week. He asked them to include their analysis of "standard of care"—was there a difference in standard of care between a broker and a paid manager—and which applied to Mr. Hine?

Jim and Joan and I had a little summary meeting and then headed off. It had been an amazing two days, but there was more to come. And I didn't even know when the next meeting would be.

The Scheduling Game

Another one of the many little games within a game that claimants and their attorneys use in NASD arbitration is scheduling. They play games with the schedule. As a general principle, time tends to work on the side of the claimant. As long as the issue is being disputed, the notation remains on the rep's record, causing him or her numerous problems. The threat of a big settlement hangs in the air. There is a sense of exhaustion about the whole thing. Why not just cave and settle?

In our case, in scheduling the case, the claimants originally suggested that the entire hearing would only take two days. Jim Weller told me that he was sure it would be at least three days, and probably four days. Based on the claimant's request, the NASD scheduled two consecutive days of hearings. So I left New York on November 4, 2003, not knowing when we would meet next.

Chairman Besser had told both attorneys to have their legal memoranda filed within one week of the end of the second hearing date. I soon found out that the next trial date would be December 8, 2003—just a few weeks away. I went back to my practice full bore, and communicated with Jim Weller about the remaining issues in the direct examination and possible approaches that the other side might take in my cross-examination. By the rules of the proceedings, once the claimant has put on their case, they cannot come back and reintroduce new evidence. I had nearly finished my direct examination, which would obviously be completed sometime on the morning of December 3. The rest of the trial would be about what had already been put on the table.

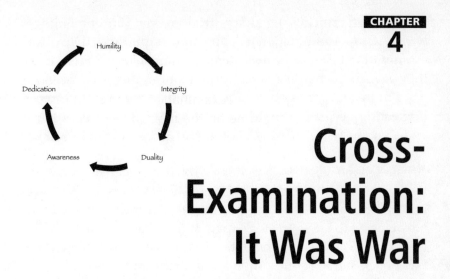

Humility

Dedication

Integrity

Awareness

Duality

Cross-Examination: It Was War

NASD Hearing Day Three— December 8, 2003

Dueling Testimony

Despite what Jim and I both felt were effective cross-examinations of both my former client and his expert witness, and some strong information brought out in my direct examination, we didn't in any way feel overconfident about the outcome. Of particular concern was what the panel made of the expert witness— his charts versus ours. When jury trials boil down to a duel between expert witnesses, it is a murky area. It is easy for a juror, in this case an arbitration panel member, to give some credence to both sides. Mark Twain once said that there are "lies, damned lies, and statistics." His point was that trying to prove something with statistics is suspect.

We also both realized that my own cross-examination was

going to be critical. Legendary trial lawyer Vincent Bugliosi wrote, "Cross-examination takes on more importance than direct examination because juries listen to it more closely. First of all, they realize that unlike direct examination, there has been no dry run in a lawyer's office, and secondly, they find it far more interesting because of its adversary nature" (Vincent Bugliosi and Ken Hurwitz, *Till Death Us Do Part*. New York: W. W. Norton, 1978).

I had done very well playing "pitch and catch" with Jim Weller, the friendly attorney. I had not subjected myself yet to the withering heat of a skilled legal adversary, using every means at his disposal to take my story apart and make me look bad. The weeks between the hearing dates flew by. The next thing I knew I was back in that room, sitting around that conference table.

Dennis Fung and the O. J. Trial Debacle

Many people remember the O. J. Simpson trial and the hours of cross-examination of Los Angeles criminalist Dennis Fung by Barry Scheck, the Simpson DNA expert. Scheck shredded Fung and humiliated him in front of the world. But he didn't stop there. He continued to pound and pound and pound for hours until the end of one day and then another half day. Fung wilted under the pressure, and his inability to counter Scheck's acute questioning and biting sarcasm left a huge hole in the prosecution's case. Beyond the very complex scientific points, the lasting image was of Scheck in total indignation demanding to know this and to know that, and Fung sitting there sullenly hanging his head and giving dull, unresponsive answers—a disaster for the prosecution.

I was determined to be prepared for my cross-examination. I believed the greatest weapon I had was the truth and the facts on my side. But I also had prepared, both with Jim and with the other attorney I had hired. Although I knew cross was going to be tough, I had more preparation than most reps up there for the first time. And I had a competitive spirit. I was not going to let some lawyer trip me up and get a bonus for doing it.

I knew that a skilled attorney could confuse or upset a witness, switch topics back and forth, and the like. And I had seen my former client's attorney in action. He may have come into the meeting late on day one, looking disheveled, but once the lights went on and the hearing went live, he was very focused. And I had been impressed with the fact that even when things seemed to go against his side, he didn't seem to let it bother him. He fought back with every bit of tenacity he had.

The Answer to the Asset Allocation Issue

No matter. I was determined to be a Rock of Gibraltar under the pressure. During the period between the hearing dates, I had come up with a very important observation that I felt would help me enormously. Like a good white belt, I had gone back and taken another look at the numbers and come up with a gem of an observation.

I knew a main line of his attack was to go after me on the question of asset allocation. That really was his whole case. Jim and I felt that, even with the other side arguing their best, we would be able to get the charges about fraud, churning, and the laundry list of most other charges easily dismissed. In our minds, the playing field of major issues was narrowing down to asset allocation. If he could prove I had misdiagnosed his client, or had at any point put him into investments that were unsuitable, he won his case. He was going to ask a series of questions to lead me toward a trap from which I couldn't escape. Little did he know at the time, the trap that had been laid was for him.

To an individual without a financial or analytical background, what I uncovered may seem like an extremely technical point. But any registered representative will be able to understand logic of it in an instant. In determining asset allocation, the simplest way to look at it is what percentage of the portfolio is in equities (the higher-risk vehicle) and what percentage is in fixed income (a low-risk vehicle).

This assessment went back to the original investor scorecard. I could have placed him in one of three categories: income with moderate growth, growth with income, or growth. I had actually, as was my practice with new clients, started him out with a portfolio that was one class more conservative than my rating had been. In his case, this was a moderate growth portfolio. The reason for this is that I am more comfortable starting out a client relationship this way. As we gain comfort with each other, I then revise the allocation based on client feedback.

This was what had happened here. So I was able to testify to this conservative philosophy. He demonstrated his happiness with me by continuing to transfer additional assets under my management and open new accounts. However, the lost notes were a liability. I couldn't absolutely prove that we had discussed upgrading him to growth. However—duality again—I did have all those signed prospectus receipts and new account forms.

The playing field on which this was going to be argued out would likely be the percentage of equities versus fixed income I had him in at any point in time. The expert witness, despite his weak credentials and suspect methodology, had argued pretty strongly that he would have classified my former client into a far more conservative mix of equities and fixed income than I had him in. Throughout most of the relationship, I had him at 80 percent equities and 20 percent fixed income. The "expert" had him as low as 40 percent equities and 60 percent fixed income. Again, using the duality principle and the tendency of arbitrators to give roughly equal weight to both sides of technical testimony, I knew that as arbitrary as these numbers were, it was where the attorney and I would compete.

The bottom line, as far as the hearing was concerned, is that I knew that the client's attorney was going to try and demonstrate that I had exceeded the 80 percent figure for equities and put the client at risk. Conversely, I wanted to demonstrate that I had always kept the client somewhere within the range between 60/40 (equities to fixed income) and 80/20.

The Magical 80 Percent Level

In conducting a detailed retrospective of the account history, there were some times in which my ratio of equities to fixed income did exceed 80 percent, and was as high as 87 percent. It is important to remember that the time in question was in the late 1990s—between 1997 and 2000.

Everyone in the business will recall the stock market boom, driven in part by the enthusiasm for the seemingly (at the time) limitless power of technology to stimulate global business growth. Generation Xers were jumping into the market and posting huge gains, often in Internet-related stocks. Everyone seemed like a financial genius. Even long-term investors, such as my client, could not help but feel the enthusiasm and the growth and want to get in on the gains.

In the fourth quarter of 1999, as the market was really raging and he was feeling a surge of confidence from his six-figure gains, he had made a few moves toward a more aggressive posture. First, on his own initiative, he invested in that technology fund, an aggressive growth fund. Second, he and I had met, and he had wanted to upgrade the aggressiveness of his portfolio, which I did. Once again, the documentation was mixed. I had the signed prospectus receipts, and I also had Microsoft Outlook notes from staff members indicating he had called and wanted to meet me to get more aggressive with his portfolio. But the notes were in a type of internal shorthand and lacked complete sentence structure. I knew what they meant, but I anticipated the attorney arguing the point. And I had no contemporaneous notes from the meeting we had in December 1999. It was killing me inside that I could not locate these, but I had to play the hand I was dealt.

Boom markets present a classic dilemma for a financial adviser. During times of growth, conservative investors feel they are missing out, as they hear stories of financial miracles that their friends and acquaintances are experiencing. Although their portfolio is holding steady and posting some gains, they feel that they are missing out on the windfalls others are achieving. However, once a boom market starts to turn down, those same investors will proclaim that, after all, they were truly conservative and should not have been at risk. This is exactly what was happening in this case.

It's Not Quite That Simple

Another, more subtle, element is that the evaluation of the riskiness of a portfolio by simply measuring the percentages of equities and fixed income is extremely simplistic and not always revealing. Within the classification of equities, there is a wide range of options available at all levels of the risk continuum. The same is true for fixed income, which is by nature generally less risky. However, a given client's portfolio may have fixed income investments that are very conservative or less than that. Standard principles of investing that form the core of many representatives' approach include diversification (to spread risk) and a strong disposition to highly rated mutual funds. So, while the "80/20" idea might hold some attraction to an arbitration panel member, it did not necessarily tell the whole truth about the riskiness of this client's portfolio.

The analysis of the client's portfolio to arrive at this calculation is not as straightforward as it might seem. To do this, it is necessary to go in and look at all of the accounts held for the client, calculate the percentage for each account, and then perform a weighted average of the multiple accounts.

This is not an especially abstract idea, but to arrive at it requires some diligence. In this case, my client had five accounts: three non-qualified variable annuities, one qualified brokerage account (consisting of stock and bond mutual funds) and one non-qualified brokerage account (consisting primarily of utility stocks he had owned before he met me and some exposure to mutual funds). With a sense of mission, I rolled up my sleeves, examined the information I had, and started to crunch the numbers.

A Window of Vulnerability

In this process, I made two important discoveries. The first was that, although for the vast majority of time I had the client in 80 percent equities or less, there were a few times when I went beyond the 80 percent level, with a high-water mark of 87 percent. Ironically, the reason that it reached this height was the significant growth in the value of the equities part of his portfolio, which had a corresponding effect on the relative percentage of equities to fixed income. I felt that any honest evaluation of the overall picture would not lead one to conclude that I had been reckless with his holdings, but this still represented a little window of vulnerability. I knew that with the aggressiveness of the other side's accusations and what appeared to my partisan mind as the sometimes Kafka-esque rules of the proceeding, this was a small opening that they would try to turn into the Grand Canyon.

Then I came to another, far more important, realization. The claimant and his attorney's calculation of "equities to fixed income" (which they consistently referred to by the often used but not technically precise term of *equities to bonds*) contained one minor, but critically important, incorrect assumption. It counted equity mutual funds as "100 percent equities." However, as every registered representative knows, each equity mutual fund contains a mixture of investments with varying degrees of risk. Many of the equity funds hold cash in varying degrees as part of their intentional allocation. This means that, although the mutual fund counts in a raw calculation as "100 percent equity," it is often less risky than that because of the cash position.

Imagine that, when calculating it at some specific point in time, a client's portfolio contained exactly 80 percent stock mutual funds and 20 percent bond mutual funds. But in examining the stock mutual funds, if it is determined that an average of 10 percent of the funds were in cash, this would mean that the portfolio was not 80 percent equities, but rather 90 percent of 80 percent—in this case 72 percent. One could argue that the point is a technical one, but it is also unassailable in its logic. The portfolio in this example was 72 percent invested in equities and 28 percent in cash or bond funds—well within the 80 percent high-water mark in the asset allocation recommendation.

Recalculating Actual Risk

As I laboriously went through the client's five accounts, I could see that this was going to make an important difference. As just part of my professional practice, during this fevered market time, as the market did seem to have some clear downside risk, I was putting my clients into funds that were not only highly rated but also had that conservative component to them. One in particular stood out: A large equity income fund had a 15 percent cash position throughout much of the time in question, and this was a portion of the client's holdings.

When this factor was included in the overall calculation, the client's portfolio was clearly within the asset allocation guidelines. It was a revelation at a late hour that gave me enormous relief, almost a sense of exhilaration. A large part of me was just waiting, hoping, for the attorney to go down the asset allocation road.

Testifying "In the Zone"

Looking back on the whole arbitration case, I almost wish it were videotaped. I have heard the audio, which is very interesting. But it did not quite capture the drama of actually being there. I would have enjoyed watching a videotape of my own direct testimony and cross-examination on this day. I was, as the saying goes, "in the zone"—relaxed, calm, focused, and extremely alert.

It reminded me of my finest moments in karate sparring competition. Through the years of focused preparation, at times one arrives in what appears to be almost a transcendent state, able to perform feats of skill naturally and without forethought.

Baseball players call this "having the game slow down" or "reading the stitches on a fastball." Soccer players at the World Cup level talk about seeing the "instantaneous moment of opportunity," which, properly executed, can become a game-winning goal. In karate sparring, it is as if the entire match is taking place in slow motion. You are able to realize brief instants of vulnerability on your part or an opportunity to attack your opponent and score points. To observers, it seems as if you are performing effortlessly, in a rhythm and flow.

The Awareness Principle

Once again, my martial arts training was blending in with everything else. One of the main motivations for many students to begin practice in martial arts is a desire to measurably improve their ability to defend themselves, and, if necessary, their loved ones. Early in their training, many students will ask an experienced martial artist or an instructor, "When will I start receiving benefit from the training in terms of my ability to defend myself?" The answer is very simple: "Within a few months of beginning training, you will begin to become better able to defend yourself, and this ability will gradually increase as long as you train."

This example illustrates one of the benefits of martial arts training. It involves a gradually increasing awareness of yourself, your surroundings, and your potential adversaries. When one begins the study of martial arts, there is an enormous body of knowledge to cover to simply understand the basics of the art—the basic stances, blocks, evasive maneuvers, counterattacks, self-defense moves, kicks and punches, and forms (or "kata"). Looked at as a whole, it appears to be almost insurmountable.

But, of course, each of these subjects is taught at first in an isolated unit of instruction. Each move is broken down into its component parts and explained. Each move is practiced a component or section at a time. Then, with basic proficiency at that component, the next component is added. Once a move is practiced to an acceptable level of proficiency, then an additional move is added to it. Someday in the future, with enough practice and repetition, all of this becomes a single, fluid exercise—seemingly effortless in its apparently flawless execution. But this is possible only through study of each basic move.

One of the results of all of this training, class after class, tied together as each single strand becomes a part of a rope, is a growing awareness on the part of the student—awareness of his or her actual capabilities, of his or her surroundings, and of the opponent in a sparring situation.

Similarly, I put my mind, body, and spirit into preparing for this case. And by doing so, not just in one intense session but in many preparation sessions over time, I was able to develop that awareness, almost an extrasensory feeling as to the flow of the case, the meaning of testimony, and what to do next. All of my efforts merged together in an insight on asset allocation I felt was extremely important.

We Begin Again with Direct Examination

Something had occurred to me between the first two days of the hearing and this third day, now approximately five weeks later. Although I was obviously fighting for myself and my professional record, I felt when I took the stand, it was as if I was also speaking for, and fighting for, every honest hard-working rep everywhere. I felt that, given the totality of what had happened in this case and the extensive documentation we had backing up everything that was done, we *had* to win this case— for myself and for the profession.

Jim began the direct testimony by giving me an opportunity

to explain to the panel what is involved in making an assessment of risk tolerance and determining asset allocation. I explained that it is a very thorough process, that I continually seek new information and new perspectives to fine-tune my clients' portfolios, and that there is gray area that requires me to make judgments. I explained that asset allocation models vary from company to company—what each broker-dealer defines as "moderate" risk, or "growth" versus "growth and income" is a matter of continual debate. I explained that these recommended models also vary within a company over time; they are not fixed-points on a compass.

Once a model has been determined, there is a tremendous amount of choice and thought that goes into the subaccounts. Although the analysis of a portfolio by "equities" versus "fixed income" is one useful indicator, it is not the only indicator of the risk of the overall portfolio. For example, it would be possible to have a portfolio that was 40 percent equities and 60 percent fixed income that was actually riskier than one that was 60 percent equities and 40 percent fixed income, depending on what went into the subaccounts.

Explaining What Reps Do

Responding to Jim's questions, I did a review of the technical analysis that went into my former client's portfolio in the beginning and throughout our relationship. I explained how I went about thinking through his situation and making recommendations—analyzing funds by price-to-earnings (P/E) ratios and turnover ratios, balancing growth mutual funds with more value-oriented (defensive) funds, offsetting risk and reward, I explained that I didn't buy to make commissions—I thought through everything to build an overall weighted average. My rebalancing was based on changing market conditions and shifts in client risk tolerance.

This type of testimony is very familiar to reps—this is what we do. But Jim and I realized that this might be new information to Chairman Besser and Ms. Weisman, though probably quite familiar to Ms. Dubas, the industry expert.

How I Determined the Client Was a Growth Investor

In response to Jim's questioning, I brought up the fact that when he came to me, this client brought with him a form from an existing account with a major wirehouse in which he was identified as a "growth" investor.

Q: "What are some of the key factors that led you to identify him as a "growth" investor?"

A: "He had identified a 10 to 15 percent annual rate of return as his objective. Generally, I felt that someone in the 10 to 12 percent range was a "growth" investor. Other factors were that he told me he would not need access to the money right away, except a modest amount of income. Growth investors are seeking some growth partly as a way to beat inflation."

We were covering some great territory here. Jim then shifted attention to another of the charges of the Statement of Claim, that of "churning." It was a ridiculous charge, as with the type of investments we had made, it was virtually impossible to "churn." The Statement of Claim had painstakingly listed dozens of trades made over the life of the relationship to buttress the claim of churning. The only problem was that the huge majority of them were rebalancing trades for variable annuities for which no commission was paid. So, Jim hit this head on.

Q: "Is there any incentive to you as a broker to categorize him as a growth investor?"

A: "No. You get paid the same commission in a growth fund or in a variable annuity, which is targeted toward growth and income."

Q: "At any point, did you buy and sell equities to earn commissions?"
A: "Never."

Chairman Besser jumped in and quickly asked:

Q: "Why not?"
A: "Number one, it was inappropriate to do that. Number two, based on the long-term asset allocation goal, you don't need to be buying and selling because the mutual fund manager takes care of that—that's what they are paid for."

As was his style, Besser continued with direct questioning.

Q: "Did you discuss your overall approach with this client—that you invested in mutual funds?
A: "Absolutely."
Q: "So you weren't in the business of recommending individual stock purchases?"
A: "The exact opposite. Not only did I not recommend stocks, when clients came in with stocks, over time I would try to diversify the stocks into mutual funds. We felt it was safer and better for the client to be diversified. If you looked up all the assets under my management, I would estimate that less than 1 or 2 percent of the assets we had overseen were in actual individual stocks."

Covering the Issues One by One

Jim was working off a very well prepared sheet of questions he had broken down into each of the categories we felt we had to address. The next one was the issue of account control. I had been accused in the Statement of Claim of "seizing de facto control" over my former client's account. That wasn't even possible.

Although this was a nondiscretionary account, Jim took a moment to have me explain some key relevant points. I explained that I was not a registered investment adviser or a trustee, that my former client had approved all trades, and that I never wrote a financial plan for him but had acted purely as a broker.

The issue of the client's ability to understand what was going on in his accounts was reinforced by explaining that his wife had attended every meeting I had had with him, her background in investment and real estate, that they had married in 2000, and that she was so happy with my work on his behalf that she had encouraged him to incrementally increase the initial investment of approximately $220,000 up to $857,000. I had earned his trust and respect through performance, which is the way it is supposed to work. I again put on the record that until the sudden end of the relationship, the client, his wife, and their accountant never complained.

There was a particularly effective piece of testimony on some handwritten notes of a conversation I had with the former client, relating to a time in which he had overridden a mutual fund recommendation I had made—one of five funds I had recommended at that time. He accepted four, overrode one, and replaced it with his own preferred fund. How did he have the knowledge and confidence to do that if he were the financially unsophisticated person he claimed to be?

The Technology Fund Purchase

We went through the details on the delayed execution of the technology fund purchase, which was caused by a series of unusual circumstances. His check to purchase the fund was logged by the office on January 14, 2000, which was literally one day after we had switched broker-dealer firms. We had sent out forms to all clients to return to enable us to switch accounts without having a glitch of this type, and had even opened the office on Saturdays to make it extra convenient for clients to come by if they wanted to do this.

The client didn't get his signed form to us until February 15, which we mailed the next day to the new broker-dealer firm. They processed the paperwork, and we placed the trade on March 6. Giving the client every benefit of the doubt, there was a $4,000 "loss" experienced, though in order to have realized this $4,000, the client would have had to have sold the fund at its high point—a rather generous assumption.

Closing Out the Morning Testimony

We finished my direct with two points: the surprise I had when he pulled his accounts and my assessment of the expert's recommendation to put all of a client's equity accounts in the Russell 3000 Index, a single fund.

Q: "What was your reaction when you learned that this client was going to pull his accounts?"

A: "Complete shock. We had always discussed his investments as being a minimum of 7 to 10 years. I had some notes from a discussion just 30 days prior in which he had told me that he was going to be patient with his accounts. He had given me no indication whatsoever of dissatisfaction."

Q: "What do you think about the expert's recommendation of investing the equity portion of this client's portfolio in the Russell 3000 Index—is that an appropriate vehicle?"

A: "No. There are several factors to consider. You don't put all assets in one asset class. At that time you couldn't even invest in that index. It violated the principle of diversification. The Russell 3000 doesn't weight by midcap value—it is just a lump of 3,000 companies. When markets are going down, you are guaranteed to lose money. In a bear market it is the worst thing to own."

With my direct examination finished, we broke for lunch.

Asset Allocation—The Inside Story

In preparing for this moment, I had come to a realization that I had subconsciously known before, but it hadn't really reached the conscious level of my mind with regard to this trial. I realized that it was going to be very important to put the entire asset allocation discussion into some realistic context. As every registered representative knows, this entire discussion about asset allocation and classification is inexact, at best. There are a lot of shades of gray involved. Everyone agrees that the higher percentage of equities in a portfolio as compared with cash or fixed income, the riskier the portfolio is. A portfolio close to 100 percent equities is at the high end of the risk spectrum, and one with almost all fixed income (cash, bonds, or certificates of deposit [CDs]) is at the very low end. But, in between those extremes, what is a fair way to characterize the various stages?

There is an ongoing industry argument as to what represents a truly balanced portfolio—is it 50 percent equities and 50 percent fixed income? Or is it as high as 60 percent equities and 40 percent fixed income? A simple way to think of it is that if your percentage of equities is above 80 percent, it is a relatively aggressive or "risky" portfolio. Between 60 percent and 80 percent is moderately risky, often characterized as "growth and income." Between 40 percent and 60 percent equities is considered "moderately conservative." Below 40 percent is considered tilted toward "capital preservation."

Jim was well aware of what was likely to follow, so he spent some valuable time in direct examination, in which I testified as to the factual basis and logic behind what I had done with this client's assets. He allowed me to get the major points. A key bit of information was that throughout this entire time the client had not once asked to either convert his equities into a less risky vehicle or to change his classification. We had, by my records, 25 phone conversations and nine face-to-face meetings, and not once had the client complained during this period that he was uncomfortable with my decisions or the portfolio mixture.

Had he done so, I would have been absolutely required to immediately address his concerns. Had he instructed me to sell some equities, I would have done so. Had he asked me to reclassify his risk, I would have been required to have him sign the papers to do so, and then I would have had to balance the account, making the transactions necessary to see that he was in his new, less risky, classification. As Jim had instructed me, when he asked me a question, I would not look at him directly, but often pivot and, in effect, give the answer to the arbitration panel. I included them in the answer. When I finished my testimony, I felt we had laid down a very solid case for what I did and an easy-to-follow chain of events and narrative.

Leading Me Down the 80 Percent Road

The opposing attorney took the floor and began to question me, trying to undermine my testimony and to show that I had mishandled his client's assets. As one might expect, given the 20/20 hindsight of being able to look back and see what actually happened in the market during those periods, in his questioning he argued as forcefully as possible that my client was desiring a conservative approach, echoing the wording of his complaint.

As a second component of this argument, Jim and I fully expected that he was going to claim that my decision to increase the aggressiveness of the portfolio in early 2000 was also incorrect. It was clear that the battle lines were drawn at 80 percent. I wanted to demonstrate that I had kept the client's portfolio within an approximate 80 percent equity component, and the attorney wanted to push that number as high as the facts would allow.

The asset allocation models suggested that that the range for his actual classification was between 60 percent and 80 percent equities (strictly speaking, "moderately risky" or "growth and income," not conservative); they were going to use the 60 percent figure as the proper mix, not the 80 percent figure. In his questioning, he kept referring to 80 percent as being "20 percent more risky than the 60 percent figure." I had to keep my cool and just answer the questions. I knew at the end of the day I had the information that would vindicate me.

I could literally feel the opposing attorney's confidence rise as he led me through the argument, piece by piece, after going through the technical information involving the five accounts and the charts indicating the quarterly analyses.

He asked, "Is it fair to say, based on your testimony, that for the quarter ending June 30, 1999, the client's assets were approximately 65 percent in equities and 35 percent in bonds?" "Yes," I answered. I could see where this was heading. He was using the term *bonds* to mean "fixed income," but I wasn't about to correct him. The general point he was making was understood. And I wasn't ready, either, to jump in and correct him with the technical analysis I had done. I wanted to let him walk right into the trap first. It was incredibly exciting to have this little surprise ready to spring.

After meandering through some other side questions, he asked, "So, now, Mr. Hine, looking at this chart, is it fair to say that for the quarter ending December 31, 1999, give or take a little, the client's assets were 70/30, or in other words 10 percent riskier than the 60 percent?" I still wasn't going to do anything to disrupt his momentum. Not yet. "Yes it is." I answered.

With a theatrical flourish and nearly perfect rising of the pitch of his voice, he went for the kill. "Now, Mr. Hine, as we look at the charts for the quarter ending March 30, 2000—if we read these correctly—you had my client in what could be characterized as more aggressive than even the growth portfolio of 80/20, reaching as high as 87 and a half percent equities?

My Shocking Response—The Pivotal Moment in the Trial

I must admit that I was a little theatrical myself. Rather than jumping to answer just as he finished his question, I paused for a moment. I could feel his confidence at its absolute height, and I savored the moment before puncturing it. After that moment, I said, with great clarity and simplicity, "No."

This moment is the reason more than any other that I wish I had a videotape of the proceedings. My recollection, admittedly possibly a tinged recollection, is that the attorney looked like he had just, without any warning, walked straight into a wall. "No?" he asked.

"No," I repeated. I could see the wheels in his mind turning as he tried to figure out what to ask next. It is an article of absolute faith in the legal profession that one doesn't ask in open court a question to which one doesn't know the answer. It is a commandment. Going back to the O. J. trial, people think about Chris Darden asking O. J. to try on the bloody glove. This was my bloody glove moment.

But, according to the rules of the hearing, I actually had to have permission to explain myself. I politely asked him, "Can I explain myself?" He had no option, as the arbitrators were clearly fascinated by this exchange. There was electricity in the room. This was clearly a big moment. He realized he had no choice. He said, "Well, since Mr. Weller is just going to ask you on cross anyway, I might as well hear your explanation."

Inside the Numbers

I calmly and methodically explained the logic of the situation.

"While it may look like the balance might be 87 percent stock and 13 percent bond, if you look at the individual Morningstar reports, which we have here, they show that each manager of each mutual fund maintained their own cash and bond positions, which they could change periodically. And in many cases the cash position was between 8 and 15 percent. So when we say a fund is a stock fund, that doesn't mean 100 percent of that fund is invested in stocks. The manager of that fund may leave money aside in cash, and they decide when they want to buy stocks.

Many of these funds were sitting on up to 15 percent cash, which means that only 85 percent of what you see was in stocks."

It was a pretty technical point, obviously. And I didn't like the sloppiness of referring to fixed income as "bonds," but that was the language being used at the hearing, so on the advice of Jim Weller I used it myself. No matter. It was clear that I had stopped the attorney's momentum dead in its tracks. I could see the blood drain out of his face and the wind go out of the sails of their case. It was subtle but clear. Look at body language, tone of voice, whatever nonverbal cues you want to use. I had the crucial bit of information, and there wasn't a thing they could do about it. I had the floor. The more I explained, the clearer it became to everyone in that room. No matter how you looked at it, at no point was the client's overall portfolio invested more than 80 percent in equities. And, of course, we had already established that these percentages were suggestions, not requirements. It was as clear as it could be. I had met every requirement and kept within every reasonable standard.

When the cross-examination was over, Jim went back over some redirect examination to drive home the key points. When the opposing attorney indicated he had no more questions, I felt we had removed this last major obstacle to a successful outcome.

At some point, one of the arbitrators, apparently amazed but still not completely convinced by what had been said, looked at me and asked, "Did you actually know this at the time?" "Yes, I did," I said.

I went on to explain that this is all part of being a professional in this business. I made it my business not only to be aware of the big picture and the trends in the market, but also to be immersed in the little details. I made the point that anyone who was following the market closely at the time knew that there was in the air a sense that the market might be poised for a downturn. I explained that the fact that these higher-rated funds, the ones I tended to put my clients in, were demonstrating that nervousness by beginning to spread out their own risk within their funds. I made the point that this very tangible piece of information was one of the clear indicators I had to be aware of an upcoming downturn.

The Attorney Fights Back

Give him credit. Right after I felt I had won the argument, he let the moment pass and started hammering me on something else. I had organized quarterly asset allocation charts as part of my preparation for the trial. They did show that the client's portfolio had gotten more aggressive in 2000, triggered, in my mind, by the December 1999 meeting. Of course, we now know that the market started going south, and the charts showed that by the spring of 2001 my client's portfolio, which had swelled from its original $857,000 to more than $1.1 million, went back down to its initial value. When everything was added up, including the $64,000 in income he had taken out, left him with a net portfolio gain of $5,000.

The attorney aggressively challenged why I had made the shift. I pointed to the technology fund as an example of his desire to get more aggressive. Of course, their side had covered this, describing this as his one "flyer," a metaphorical trip to the casino. I also had some notes from staff members. One note said the client was coming in to see me to discuss the purchase of the technology fund and to get more aggressive with his portfolio. But—this killed me—it wasn't written out exactly in a full sentence. So, the attorney argued that the technology fund was the *only* thing he wanted to get aggressive about. Under tough but fair questioning from Chairman Besser, I had to admit that it could have been interpreted either way.

The lack of those notes from the December meeting was particularly glaring. As I had notes from other meetings I had been able to present, the attorney seemed to be able to cast an almost sinister light on the fact that I couldn't produce them. I tried to argue that the overall weight of the evidence, including signed prospectus receipts indicating "growth," was part of a picture. But to my chagrin, a fair-minded person would not walk away from the day feeling I had really closed the sale on this point. The waters were still muddy.

More Questions from Chairman Besser

The day ended with my taking some questions from Chairman Besser, and each attorney giving a five-minute summary of their view of the testimony so far. Besser zeroed in on my classification of my former client as a growth investor. He asked me about the confidential questionnaire, which showed a net score of 93 points. According to the ranges, this meant it could be classified as one of three classifications: "growth," "income with moderate growth," or "growth and income." There was overlap in terms of point score among these three classifications, underscoring that this is an inexact and subjective determination.

Chairman Besser asked how I determined among these choices that this client should have been "growth." I mentioned two critical factors: The first was the persistent listing on numerous forms over a long period of time of his desire for a 10 to 15 percent annual rate of return. The second was the client's representation that he was dedicated to at least a 7- to 10-year time horizon. These two factors, among others, combined along with other indications to put him in the "growth" category.

Chairman Besser asked me to expound a little more about the mix between equities and fixed income. I reiterated that it was a mistake to rely on this simple metric to assess the risk of a portfolio. The allocation within the subaccounts had a potentially huge impact on this as well. He also asked me about what was covered at the meeting with my client, his wife, and the accountant. I explained that I talked about his overall portfolio—what he was in and why. Finally, he asked about the overall performance of this client's portfolio over the 42-month period. I made the point that after having taken out $64,000 in income, the value of his portfolio increased by a net of approximately $5,000—during one of the worst bear markets since the Great Depression.

Each Attorney Summarizes the Case to Date

Chairman Besser asked each attorney to give an overview of the case to date. This gave them each a chance to preview their closing arguments, which would be held on the final day of testimony. My former client's attorney stuck closely to his key themes. He reiterated that this client had historically been a conservative investor, as evidenced by his existing portfolio when he came to see me. He also said that in late 1999 there had been a far more aggressive posture in the portfolio, which in the end cost his client significant money.

As I had come to expect, Jim Weller was extremely well organized and packed a lot of information into his short summary. He highlighted the fact that despite literally dozens of opportunities, the client had never complained. He reviewed the fact that we had met regularly, that the client wanted a 10 to 15 percent return—a dramatic increase from the 5 to 6 percent he was getting—and that he knew he would have to take on more risk to do so. He reminded the panel that the wife was at all the meetings, giving the client a second ear and someone else to whom he could have complained or asked questions.

It Was War

In some ways this day of the trial was my finest hour. I had stood up to cross-examination and done well, though not definitively closed out the case. It amazed me how tenacious the other side was. I came in feeling like my martial arts background made me a warrior who, with the facts I had, could not be beaten. The proceedings showed me that this was not the case.

It was war, and the other side was fighting with everything they had. The two sides of my soul continued in the battle—the optimistic and partisan feeling that I was in the right and had made the case, and the realist trying to look at it from the other point of view and realize that the outcome of the case was still very much in doubt. I could say to myself that they were using bogus arguments and asking me to meet superhuman standards. But the fact was that neither side was a clear winner. I realized that it all might come down to the final day and the closing summary.

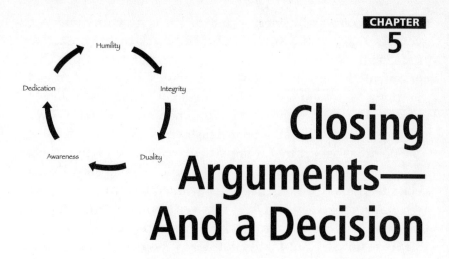

Humility

Dedication

Integrity

Awareness

Duality

CHAPTER

5

Closing Arguments— And a Decision

NASD Hearing Day Four— May 6, 2004

Back into Dormancy

It was a satisfying feeling to have done as well as we did in debunking the theories of the accuser and his attorney and in presenting evidence that substantiated our position. At this point, the case went into another phase of dormancy, in this case for six months. It is one of the real aggravations of the entire process. You go through all this effort and energy to study up, strategize, organize, review and present exhibits, testify, present evidence, and counter charges. Just at the point at which everything is as clear in your mind as it ever will be, the case vanishes for several months, and you go back to your practice.

Having an arbitration case pending means that, in any of a number of ways, as a registered representative you are not al-

105

lowed to conduct business as usual. The complaint remains on your U-4, accessible at NASD BrokerCheck by anyone at any time via the Internet. It could hurt your reputation with a client or potential client, and you wouldn't necessarily know about it. In trying to expand your ability to sell new products or develop new vendor relationships, you are sometimes blocked, as I was, by the scarlet letter of the financial services industry.

The other aspect that was particularly annoying in this case was that when the third day of testimony ended in early December, I felt I had won the case. I just wanted the arbitrators to say what everyone knew—"Okay, this was a bogus charge, case dismissed. Tom, you can go back to your practice with all your rights restored." But that is not how it works. We needed one more day, and it would take place six months later. The feature of the final day would be each attorney's closing argument.

Another Weller Strategy—And I Roll the Dice

As usual, Jim Weller and I continued to stay in close touch, e-mailing each other back and forth and trading thoughts on what we wanted to do in order to wrap up the case in the strongest possible way. He came up with another strategy that had some risk in it, but a lot of potential reward. He explained both sides to me.

Jim suggested what we might want to do is to subpoena my former client's records and find out what his investment pattern had been after he had stopped working with me. Jim explained that this was a move that could work for us or possibly against us.

If it turned out that the client had changed his pattern to a more conservative investment philosophy, it could bolster his claim to the arbitrators that he was, at heart, a more conservative investor than my assessment had indicated. It could well be that his negative experience with the bear market had caused this conservatism, but there it would be for the arbitrators to look at and for his attorney to argue in closing arguments.

However, if it turned out that in working with another broker his portfolio had approximately the same level of risk in it as when he was with me, it would really undercut their argument. It would enable us to argue that I had properly assessed his risk profile and the investments I had recommended for him were suitable. A big-time yin and yang example.

Because this decision was coming so close to the end of the case, it had a heightened sense of importance. Once we had decided to issue the subpoena, there was no turning back. If it turned out to be potentially damaging to our case, the other side would have the information. The toothpaste would be out of the tube. Jim did his usual great job of clearly laying out for me the pluses and minuses of each choice.

I like to think that many of my decisions are based on logic. I tried to assess the pluses and minuses and weigh them. But, ultimately, this was a true "gut" decision. I knew this man. I had worked with him. The individual he and his attorney were portraying was simply not an accurate picture of who he was. He was a very astute individual who knew what he was doing and liked to direct the decisions of his life. I had him properly assessed in the first place. I just believed that he went to another broker and continued to invest in the same way he had with me. I told Jim to go ahead, roll the legal dice, and issue the subpoena.

When he received the information, Jim immediately called me. He wanted to fax it over to me and have me interpret it. When I read the sheets, I felt like a kid on Christmas morning. My former client's portfolio with his new broker was, overall, at least as high in risk profile as the one I had him in. Home run. I tried to control my enthusiasm as I went over with Jim the various investments and the risk associated with them. All of a sudden, I was really looking forward to the final day of the hearing.

Dedication and the Martial Arts—Kaizen

The final martial arts principle that came into play at this point was that of dedication, also known as *Kaizen*. Martial arts dedication is the driving spirit to train. A martial artist is in constant pursuit of a state of perfection that will never be obtained, a perfect synchrony of mind, body, and spirit. It is the spirit that causes good students to follow their instructor's suggestion to do a single form 100 times, until they nearly drop from exhaustion. It is the kernel of dissatisfaction that burns in the heart of the martial artist who examines every workout, every belt test from a critical eye, asking himself or herself, "How can I do this better?"

That spirit, of course, is not confined to martial arts. It is the spirit of the inventor, the humanitarian, the athlete, those who strive for excellence in every endeavor. In his own way and in his own craft, Jim Weller exemplified this black-belt principle perfectly. Despite the fact that I was only one of many of his clients with cases going on, he was never satisfied with the state of the case. Like me, he continued to "tear it down and build it back up" again and again. This last strategic effort was just one good example of this principle in action.

The Stockholm Syndrome

By the time I got to the hearing room, it had a feeling of familiarity. So much had transpired in here—and at such a high level of emotion and concentration. I had a strange experience that Jim and Joan had warned me about. It is a variation of the "Stockholm syndrome," in which people held hostage tend, over time, to form a type of bond with their captors. A similar thing happens in arbitrations. You are in close quarters with your adversary, someone you know. Your legal representative and his are doing battle. It is very intense.

But, from time to time, there are little humorous asides. Someone mixes up someone's name, someone says something self-deprecating, and instinctively everyone, including the arbitrators, laughs. Humanness breaks out and takes over. These little events sprinkle into the proceedings at unexpected times.

The result is an almost subconscious letting down of the guard, a subtle sense of familiarity that develops with the people who have been in that room with you. I could feel this force. Coming back in, it was like old home week—a school reunion. I did not want to let up, even for a moment. I didn't know what little thing in the end might sway the outcome. I forced myself to put on my "game face" and concentrate even harder.

Truth is, unless their side or the arbitrators called me to testify, which we didn't expect, I was just a spectator on this day. My part was pretty much done. The case was in the hands of James Weller, Esq.

Risky Business

I was delighted to have Jim's cross-examination of my former client as an important part of the morning's hearing. I strongly felt that both he and his attorney knew exactly what was coming. They had received a notice of our subpoena and had been able to also receive copies of the information we obtained as a result. I knew they were going to try and spin this to the best of their ability, but it wasn't something that was easy to spin.

The facts were pretty clear. My client, after transferring his accounts from my former firm to another broker, had continued to invest as a growth investor. In fact, some of the investments could be considered "aggressive growth." The absolute smoking gun was a letter he had written to his new broker indicating that this set of investments "best suited his investment objectives." Incredible. After all the caterwauling about how I had put him in "unsuitable" investments, he had gone right out and gotten into some more risky business.

I was happy that I had made the decision to find this out. I had evaluated the situation, gone with my instinct, taken a risk, and, as a result, given Jim Weller one more tool to help me make my case. I had learned to temper my enthusiasm, as I had come to really understand the yin and yang, the dualism, of this stuff.

What seems like a big victory can collapse into a puddle. So I wasn't taking any victory laps. As always, watching Jim in action was highly dramatic——I knew more or less what he was going to do, but watching the execution of the plan was a thrill and a pleasure.

It was clear to me that my former client had been coached that under no circumstances should he admit what had happened. But he had to answer the questions and looked foolish avoiding them. He squiggled and squirmed and Jim kept firing away.

Q: "You would agree, would you not, that after we have reviewed all the aspects of your portfolio with your new broker, it was very similar in risk to the one you had with Tom Hine?"

A: "The investments were different."

Q: "I understand that. What I am asking you is that, after we have gone over the portfolio you had with Tom and the one you had with your new firm, you would agree that these portfolios are very similar in their degree of risk?"

A: "I am not really qualified to make that determination. That is why I have someone to advise me."

Q: "Let me try this again. After your experience with Tom, in which you said that the portfolio was too risky, wouldn't it be natural for you to be extra cautious about risk when working with your next broker?"

A: "I trusted his advice. I liked what he had to say. I don't consider myself an expert in these matters. What he told me made sense."

It was an interesting back and forth. My former client had been coached that he couldn't yield on this point. But Jim, with the skillful phrasing of his questions, was making it clear to the arbitrators, I hoped, that my former client had continued to invest more or less as I had projected him—in what we referred to as a "growth" investor.

No Perry Mason Moments

I was a little disappointed in the lack of fireworks, but happy to see the way Jim had laid out the facts and taken my former client through a sequence of questions. I had learned throughout the hearing that the "Perry Mason moment" was not going to come. The moment where the witness breaks down, confesses, the innocent man is let off, and everyone goes home happy, just wasn't likely to happen in this case. I am not sure it happens very often in any case.

After some questions back and forth from the arbitrators to both attorneys on various points that had come up in testimony, it was time for closing arguments. In my mind, I had imagined that each of the attorneys would take the stage and proceed to make a multihour, brilliant, carefully crafted speech—full of drama, anecdotes, humor, questions, and dramatic pauses. I pictured them walking up and down, pacing, gesturing with their hands, imploring the arbitrators to find for their client. This was not what happened.

I was a little shocked when Chairman Besser instructed the attorneys to make their closing remarks and "try to keep them to half an hour." I couldn't imagine how either side could review and summarize their case in such a short time. I found out that my Hollywood notions were way off. This was real life. And what we had was two good but also fatigued attorneys who were trying to do their best to pull everything together and give a cogent review. And rather than have the uninterrupted attention of everyone for their close, it would be interrupted frequently by questions from the panel.

A Familiar Refrain

Their side went first. I was a bit surprised to see how low key and meandering my former client's attorney was. He didn't seem to have a great deal of energy, nor did he appear to be particularly well organized. But he had crystallized the case down to a couple of clear points and questions. It had gotten down to a familiar refrain. He was back hammering away at the issue of suitability.

He went over the shift of late 1999 and early 2000 and asked, "Where is the documentation for such a shift?" Well, the documentation had been there for the most part, but the loss of those December 1999 meeting notes stuck out like a sore thumb. I vowed never in the rest of my career would I allow myself to be exposed to this because of a lack of documentation.

Once again, I had to give him credit. He hung on to his case like a bulldog. It seemed like he had been able to totally block out of his mind the very damaging, to my mind, testimony of his client earlier in the hearing. And he just focused in like a laser beam on his key points. He clearly had conviction, and he was closing as strongly as he could.

Assessing the Expert

When the attorney was trying to review the case made by the expert witness, Arbitrator Weisman jumped in and asked about his credentials: "How should we assess them?" The attorney replied, "He has excellent credentials." This rang hollow, I felt, to everyone in the room. At least I hoped so. Acutely aware of every little minor shift in momentum, I felt this might be a good sign, but I realized I wouldn't know until the decision was final.

In what passed for a final burst of momentum, the attorney asked the panel to consider the effect these investment decisions had had on his client's life. "It all gets down to whether or not the initial assessment and the shift in March of 2000 was the right diagnosis. If not, a $100,000 mistake was made."

I was struck by two points. First, he seemed to have finally given up entirely on the line of thinking that the original diagnosis of my former client as a "growth investor" was correct. He seemed to be hanging his entire case on the portfolio shift in early 2000. I was also amazed that here we were at the end of the case, and their side still had not settled on what the damages were. They had gone from $85,000 in the Statement of Claim to more than $200,000 when the expert witness testified, to "190 something thousand" in the day three summation, and now to $100,000. But no justification, no breakdown. Rather, a general plea to throw some money at my former client to compensate for his losses in a down market. I didn't know if this would work. I hoped it wouldn't. But Joan and Jim had both warned me about the tendency of some arbitrators to want to balance things out. If they applied the "50 percent theory" to any of the wandering numbers for claimed damages ($85,000, $220,000, and the latest entry, $100,000), I had lost. I was burning inside listening to this.

Then, he was done. He had fired his last shot. Then he did the strangest thing. He wandered over to the window and started staring out of it, seemingly oblivious to what was going on in the room. It seemed to me to be incredibly disrespectful to everyone in the room. But the arbitrators didn't say a word about it. Joan and I looked at each other with a question in our eyes. What was he thinking? We'll never know.

Weller Closes the Case

In the back of my mind, I had been thinking about the closing argument during the entire trial. I knew it was the crowning moment. Vincent Bugliosi wrote: "It is not uncommon for me to prepare most of my argument before the first witness at a trial has ever been called. As soon as I learn the strengths and weaknesses of my case, I begin almost immediately to argue these strengths and what I am going to say in response to the anticipated defense attacks on the weaknesses" (Vincent Bugliosi and Ken Hurwitz, *Till Death Us Do Part*. New York: W. W. Norton, 1978). I knew that Jim had been crafting this part of the trial since we started working together. My anticipation was high.

When Jim Weller went to make his final summation, he had an aura of tremendous calmness but determination around him. It reminded me of watching great martial artists as they prepare to spar in a tournament. There is that last moment, the deep breath, the look out onto the competitive arena, and then they plunge in. Jim told me later that he had, from our first encounter, believed in me and in my case. He felt an obligation in this closing argument to transfer that belief and clarity to the panel of arbitrators. I listened to him with near reverence as he began to address each issue.

"This doesn't even come close to a 'violation of high standards.' NASD Rule 2310 provides an appropriate benchmark. Rule 2310 states what a broker is supposed to do. A discrete broker such as Mr. Hine is supposed to look at a customer's financial status, he is to consider his tax status, consider his investment objectives, together with other such information considered to be reasonable to be making recommendations to a customer. Tom has clearly met this standard in every way."

It was a great way to start. I loved the confident, declarative, aggressive tone. Jim wasn't meekly saying that I had crept just beyond the standard, but far exceeded it. He then went back to a theme he had developed at other points in the trial. He reviewed all the evidence of my diligence in meeting the proper standard of care. Although all of this had been testified to at various points, it was very powerful to hear it presented in sequence.

Uncontested Facts

"It is significant that a number of the facts in the relationship are uncontested. There is no question that Mr. Hine sat down with the client at the beginning of the relationship. The client testified to that as well. … There is no question that they met and they spoke on a regular basis. The client testified that Mr. Hine showed him pie charts showing how his assets were allocated. The client testified that he was shown the Morningstar reports. The meetings, the communication between the parties are very well documented. … The fact of the matter is that there was regular contact made between Mr. Hine and the client. They spoke on the phone; those calls are documented. They met from time to time; again, those are documented. Mr. Hine, I would submit, met the NASD standard—trying to find out what was in his client's mind without climbing into his head. He asked about his financial status. He found out where he was in life. He found out about the fact that the client had some commercial property that generated some income. He found out what his goals were, what his objectives were."

"He had him fill out a questionnaire. He wanted a 10 to 15 percent return. This was different from what he had been earning, which was a 5 to 6 percent return. Based on all of that, Mr. Hine decided that this client was a growth investor. I don't think there has been any dispute that if this characterization were correct, the funds that were chosen were appropriate."

"Our exhibit 96 summarizes the documents that the client filled out. He signed these documents. Included in these documents, if he had any issues, if he had any concerns about what was being suggested to him, if he didn't understand something was growth or G&I, if he didn't understand if something was conservative or more aggressive, his obligation was to make further inquiries."

"You Would Stand the Securities Industry on Its Head"

Jim then went straight at the expert's testimony and theorizing, upon which the entire premise of the case was built.

"The expert testified, and I do believe there is a real issue about his qualifications to testify about unsuitability. He has no background or experience to testify as an expert on suitability issues—never offered testimony on suitability. It is on his testimony that the entire case by the claimant on suitability is built. On cross, he said he never looked at any of these receipts where the growth box was checked off, and I asked him if it would matter and he said it wouldn't matter—so these 17 documents would have had no relevance to him. I would submit that to completely disregard these 17 documents where he checked off "growth" would stand the securities industry on its head."

With that phrase, "would stand the securities industry on its head," Jim Weller captured the essence of our case. This was a phrase that I am sure he crafted in his many hours of Bugliosi-like preparation. It was perfect. He was telling the arbitrators that this one case had significance beyond its effect on the parties involved. If this client—who had lost no money; who had had numerous portfolio reviews; who had signed off on 17 documents; who had had constant communication from me, which was well documented; who had put himself of his own volition into a high-risk tech fund—could recover money from losses in a bear market, then you might as well open up the ATM machine for every investor everywhere. No broker or investment adviser could survive in such an environment, and the securities industry would become a piggy bank for anyone with a hard luck story. The concept of risk/reward would cease to exist. That, really, was what was at stake in this case.

Jim's thoroughness, preparation, and determination really shone through here. All of our preparation; all the details; all the observations; all the notes exchanged; all the work that he, Joan, and I had done came together in a quietly glorious, symphonic moment.

It was a contrast to my client's attorney, who, though he had had a few moments of clarity, had nothing like the force of narrative that Jim Weller had. Jim stuck to the basics, unafraid to repeat what had been said before. He had what seemed to me to be unstoppable momentum. It didn't seem like anyone in the room was looking at their watch to see how long he was speaking. He was quietly but clearly commanding the stage.

"The client is an intelligent man; he was a successful business man. It strikes me, members of the panel, the relevant question is: was he capable of understanding this material—was he capable of asking questions if he didn't understand. There is a plethora of cases to the effect that if you sign a document, you have to read it. If you don't understand it, you have to ask questions. The only exception to that is—"

Chairman Besser, always totally in the moment, blurted out, "Fraud!" Jim smoothly continued, "And there has been no testimony at all that Mr. Hine said anything that misled the client on what he was signing."

Then Besser jumped back in and made what I felt was a huge statement at this time. " It's even stronger than that—if you sign it, you are bound by its contents whether you read it or not."

My pulse skipped when he said that. I wanted to jump up and say, "Hallelujah!!!" If he said what I thought he said, and meant it, the conclusion was obvious. My former client's "Rain Man" defense was null and void.

Jim continued. "He had abundant resources—his wife sold real estate, and she was at every meeting. So he has a resource there. At one meeting, Mr. Hine sat with the client's accountant. The client never availed himself of that opportunity. If he had questions, why didn't he ask them? He didn't."

"Mr. Hine looked at a lot of things in making his recommendations. The role of a broker, not a discretionary broker, is to look at all that information and get to know the client to the extent that he can and make recommendations, and that is what he did—he analyzed the funds, he analyzed the Morningstar ratings, and he made suitable investments. When the client closed his account and went to the next broker, he bought the same type of funds, so if that was a problem for him, why did he do the same thing again?"

Jim later explained to me that this entire line of argument was known legally as "ratification." The client, by his participation in all of these various activities—portfolio reviews, prospectus reviews, telephone calls, opportunities to ask questions—by his actions (signing the documents, attending the meetings) and by his inactions (never objecting, never complaining) is ratifying the process. A good trail of documentation, as we had, is the proper defense to a claim of unsuitability.

No Damages, No Harm, No Foul

Our opponents had been singularly reticent to directly tackle the issue of damages. Jim Weller was not at all reticent. He went right to that subject next.

"The issue of damages—how was he damaged? Well, what would have happened if the account had gone up at the end rather than down—would we be here today? The comment by my opposing counsel said 'probably not'—and I suggest that that is a striking point. I mentioned this in my initial memorandum of law: 'The law does not permit an investor to stay and see how things would work out after discovering the past alleged impropriety which brought him to the decision to stay or get out—and recover damages."

"I Ask for a Dismissal of All the Remaining Claims"

"The whole issue of ratification—the client never complained. He had meetings at the office with Mr. Hine. He could have spoken with other people at the office if he was concerned about speaking to Mr. Hine. He never said anything for three and a half years. You can't say it was unsuitable and sit back and do nothing and see how it works out and if it works out, fine, then you are not going to complain, but that is exactly what happened here. There were no letters sent. There were no complaints made. None whatsoever.

"At the end of the day it was uncontested that this client had no out-of-pocket losses, which is a standard means of evaluating a claim. Again, and finally, it strikes me that at the end of the day this case is clearly about ratification. The client never complained to anybody. He sat by. He's an intelligent man; he had no issues about whether particular funds were appropriate, whether they were consistent with his objectives. All he ever had to do was ask—and he never did that.

"I would ask for a dismissal of all the remaining claims

against Mr. Hine, and I would ask that his record, which is presently clean, be maintained in such a fashion."

When Jim said those final words, I felt another flush of emotion. It took me back to the beginning of the case. I had done nothing wrong. Jim was saying as much. And he wanted a dismissal of all remaining claims. What a performance—in my mind, Bugliosi-like.

The major events of the day had transpired, but we had not finished. Chairman Besser and Arbitrator Weisman had a long series of questions about the technology trade. Clearly, this was still an issue on their minds. Arbitrator Weisman, a pro right up to the end, asked my accuser and me to state clearly and for the record that we felt we had received a full and fair treatment—a great way to end.

When you are done with an athletic contest, you are exhausted but at least have the clarity of an outcome as some compensation. In this case, I didn't have that. Jim and Joan and I spent our usual period of debriefing. We all agreed that it had gone as well as it possibly could. We also all agreed that we didn't know how it was going to turn out.

It was a long drive home, with a lot to think about. The words of both the opposing attorney and Jim rang in my mind. The opposing attorney had really been tenacious. He used his lawyering skill to make the best case possible for his client. He painted the claimant as a sympathetic figure who had trusted me, and I had led him down a path that had damaged him.

I know I was rooting for my own side, but I kept turning it over in my mind. I thought Jim really nailed it. His phrase, "stand the securities industry on its head," had to be sticking in the minds of the arbitrators. If they were going to award a client with no net portfolio loss damages on the basis of a couple of ambiguous documents and missing notes from a client meeting, then what chance did any rep have of ever prevailing in NASD arbitration? I wore myself out thinking about it back and forth. I felt like a Court TV talking head, reviewing my own trial in my mind.

For better or worse, the case was in the hands of the very capable arbitration panel. Although I had a sense that this professional nightmare was nearly over, it was no time to celebrate. I went back to my practice and back to work.

We Focus on the One Remaining Vulnerability

This process led Jim and me to what was, we now believed, the only true vulnerability I had. The reason I didn't recognize it earlier in my preparation was it didn't seem like that big a deal. The original complaint, which had been filed in September 2002, was filled with inaccuracies, gross mischaracterizations, and wild charges. It included a laundry list of charges, most of which were clearly unsupportable.

However, there was one item that had come up in the trial which I now realized was a genuine mistake, an issue in which my accuser had a legitimate cause for complaint. Despite the fact that it was a fairly technical point and had facts that could be construed in either his favor or mine, I felt that to be truly secure in the outcome, Jim and I needed to be able to dispose of this matter.

It Fell Between the Cracks

The client had brought in a check to be deposited into his account, which it was. He wanted to purchase a technology fund in early 2000, a time of significant volatility in the market, especially in the technology sector. Our firm accepted the check and deposited it into the appropriate account. However, we were unable to execute the trade right away. We had switched broker-dealers in January 2000. The account into which the check had been deposited was from the former broker-dealer. To be able to execute the trade, we needed the client's signed transfer forms indicating his consent to switch his accounts to our new broker-dealer.

At the time of this changeover, my office had sent out forms to clients to sign. The client had not returned the signed form, and so the money sat in his account with the former broker-dealer. The letters that had been sent to clients indicated the urgency of signing and returning the forms and informed the clients that our offices would be open for several Saturdays to make it convenient for people who wanted to come in person to sign. By any reasonable standard, we had more than fulfilled our obligations to the clients. However, this issue had fallen between the cracks.

The market went up in the first quarter of 2000, and the fund he had wanted us to purchase had increased in value. Later in the year, it came back to earth, as did so many of the technology funds during that period. The client claimed that he had experienced a loss based on the increase in value between the time at which the fund would have been purchased had the forms been properly signed and its peak value.

The Power of 20/20 Hindsight

While I understood that my firm had some culpability in the matter, it also seemed to me to be a case where reason and common sense might be taken into account. What evidence is there that the client would have had the wisdom to be able to call me up at the exact height of that particular fund and sell? Why should he be given the opportunity to retroactively claim a loss that allowed him to use the power of 20/20 hindsight?

There was another element to the charge that cut against the essence of the entire case the accuser and his attorney had built. In their entire presentation, they had postured that my client was a hardworking and professionally successful but relatively financially unsophisticated individual.

Their entire plea was that his risk profile was conservative, and that I had invested his money as if he had a more aggressive profile. Their complaint alleged that had I followed his desire for a conservative approach, he would not have "lost" the asset value he was complaining that he had. Of course, he hadn't lost any net money at all, so the loss really was a loss based on a projection. In any event, throughout the trial, the accuser was presented as wanting to play it safe and I had thrown him into riskier investments.

In this specific instance, they were claiming that he lost money because of a delay in putting him into a fund that was transparently aggressive—risky. The client had actually called me up with an article he had read about the fund, telling me he wanted to buy it. This particular type of transaction is sometimes referred to as "unsolicited," meaning that the client himself or herself had decided to invest.

We Decide to Make an Offer to Take This Issue Off the Table

After reviewing all the facts and the arguments, pro and con, Jim and I concluded that we should consider approaching my accuser's attorney with an offer to settle this specific issue and remove it from the trial process. This practice is one aspect of the NASD arbitration process that is fair and helpful to both sides. The parties can agree to resolve any aspect of the complaint at any point in the trial up to the rendering of the final verdict by the arbitration panel.

In this case, this specific issue was the only vulnerability we felt we had. Although in a perfectly neutral world, my own sense of fairness made me wonder what responsibility, if any, a client is supposed to have, I also realized that an arbitrator could look at this as a mistake on my firm's part and a legitimate complaint on my accuser's part.

At this point, strategy became very important. My original goal had been complete vindication from the process—a total clean bill of health from the trial. If that were not possible, as it now appeared it might not be, there was an extremely important second goal. If an NASD arbitration panel grants an award of $10,000 or more, this result is permanently on the registered representative's U-4 record.

In this case, the accuser had claimed initial losses of $85,000, and had increased that hypothetical figure to $220,000 during the trial. However, Jim and I thought he had lost badly in the hearing. In our view, the only small piece of his case that had any validity was this specific issue. The question we had was how receptive he would be to a side agreement to remove this from the case.

Our feeling was that if the other side felt that the hearing had gone in their favor, they would turn this type of offer down, feeling that the arbitration panel would include this amount of "loss" in their final ruling. No matter how we calculated it, Jim and I couldn't see how a panel could possibly justify awarding $10,000 or more for this one complaint. But, since we honestly felt it was our only vulnerability, why risk it?

In making this suggestion, we were signaling our confidence. We were asking the accuser and his attorney, "Do you want to get this relatively small amount of cash right now? Or do you want to risk getting nothing at all in the end?"

We Make an Agreement—Clearing the Way for Final Resolution of the Case

Jim approached the attorney. After a series of negotiations, we made an agreement. It required me to make a payment of a higher amount than Jim and I thought was warranted under the circumstances. But in exchange, they agreed to eliminate the issue. In the ideal world of what is fair, I wasn't delighted to make this agreement. After the case was over, the opposing attorney said that he felt his client was being aggressive in the amount he asked for, and for which we settled. But in the overall goal of being able to go back to my practice with a clean bill of health on my U-4, it felt like a good decision.

I Receive the Final Answer—Vindication

Six weeks later, I received the answer. It came in the form of a fax to my office. I received a call from Jim Weller's office telling me that they had received the final conclusions of the arbitration panel. Although I had been aware that I would get this call at some point, all of a sudden my adrenaline was pumping and my emotions racing. This was it.

The result was exactly what I had hoped for, yet it was still a thrill to hear and even more of a thrill to read in black and white. On the fourth page of this very formal, legalistic document were the key words under the section entitled "Award."

> After considering the pleadings, the testimony and the evidence presented at the hearing, and the post-hearing submissions, the Panel has decided in full and final resolution of the issues submitted for determination as follows:
> 1. Claimant's claims are denied in their entirety.
> 2. Any and all relief not specifically addressed herein is denied.

It couldn't be any clearer than that. I read back over the document and caught some of the key phrases. I particularly enjoyed the section that stated: "All awards are **final** and are not subject to review or appeal by the arbitration panel or by NASD Dispute Resolution, Inc." It was clear that this decision was final. Jim had explained to me that the possibility of further appeal in the courts was almost nonexistent, requiring the other side to prove that one of the arbitrators had hidden a major conflict of interest or something equally egregious.

When I had an opportunity to reflect, I took some time to look back and try and learn from what happened. How and why did I win? What actions could I now take that would safeguard me to the maximum extent possible from a future claim of a client? How could I use the lessons I had learned to strengthen my procedures and improve my client communication and documentation?

I believe that there were a number of reasons I was able to prevail:

- I had the basic facts on my side. While no one likes to experience a loss of value in investments, in order to be compensated for those losses, you should be required to prove that the registered representative did not appropriately do his or her job. And I had provided this client with my standard level of care, which is quite high. We had met many times and he had constant access to my staff, and not once did he ever complain about the advice he had been given, right up until I received a copy of his Statement of Claim. That had to count for something. He had ratified my advice.

- The documentation. Starting with the original questionnaire, going through numerous signed prospectus receipts, new account forms, records of phone calls, records of meetings, and that particularly damning letter to his subsequent adviser stating that the aggressive funds he was going into "better met his investment objectives."

- The legal representation. I realize that Jim and Joan do this as their profession. Still, their work was very impressive to me. I got the chance to see another legal team in action against us, and I felt that we consistently had an edge—in preparation, organization, and the ability to respond to challenge.

- The arbitration panel. I have heard nightmare stories from acquaintances of mine of arbitrators who seemed clueless during hearings, even one case of an arbitrator falling asleep during a case that involved a multimillion-dollar claim. As it turned out, I had a panel of exceptionally capable, committed professionals. Chairman Besser was tough on our side at times, but he was equally tough on our opponents. Arbitrator Weisman was very focused on the process and ensuring that each side had an extremely fair hearing. Arbitrator Dubas said very little during the proceedings. But I am sure she provided valuable industry expertise and perspective on the technical and analytical issues as the panel deliberated.

- I really believe that the core principles of humility, integrity, duality, awareness, and determination, which had been so strongly reinforced over years of martial arts training, pulled me through the most stressful challenge of my professional career. I did not learn these principles from my instructors—I

learned them from my parents. But the principles were reinforced over years of training in a very powerful and, I believe,
permanent way. The principles became my touchstones. I
firmly believe that the years of training my mind, body, and
spirit in Shotokan karate deepened my sense of right and
wrong, of what to do under pressure, and a determination to
see the case through to the conclusion.

In retrospect, the whole NASD arbitration system seemed
pretty brutal to me. I couldn't get out of my mind that my
claimant and his attorney had willingly charged me with a number of things they had to know were fallacious. They had me
hung out to dry for 21 months, with my reputation sullied by the
fact that the claim had been filed.

But in the end, in this case, I felt justice had been done. The
cost had been high. I had put in every bit of spirit and energy I
could, so I would have no doubts when it was all over. The costs
of potentially losing were, to me, simply astronomical. So I had
to count my blessings. I had survived. I had heard of other reps
who also felt they had done nothing wrong, who didn't have the
same outcome that I did.

I also came to conclude that I was, at some level, fortunate that
it had all turned out this way. Without getting those asset allocation models, with a different panel, with arbitrators who were
sympathetic to my former client and felt he needed redress, I
could easily see how it could have gone differently.

Strengthening the Business

When I finally had the sense of finality, I experienced an enormous feeling of relief and gratitude. I told my staff. They were
well aware of the situation, but we had made an agreement not
to discuss it, as we had no control over the outcome. We wanted
to dedicate ourselves to improving the business and serving our
clients. I could feel everyone's spirits lifted by the news. But it

was short lived, and, true to our sense of purpose, we returned to our work.

In true "Kaizen" spirit, I made some changes to improve the business. I was in the process of instituting a comprehensive system of client communications and activities, and I accelerated this. I standardized using a service called Copytalk to dictate myself a memo after every face-to-face client meeting or important phone call. That memo was then e-mailed to me. At my instruction, my staff cleaned up the memo and put it into a proposed letter. I reviewed the letter and sent it in the mail. I had learned in the arbitration process that arbitrators place more credibility in a witness who claims not to have received an e-mail than one who claims not to have received good old U.S. Postal Service snail mail. This just became another level of the business for me. I know my clients feel well served and well communicated with.

I instituted other changes as well. I receive an annual compliance audit from my broker-dealer firm. I decided to add another layer and pay for an outside firm to conduct their own audit. I like the feeling of security it gives me. As careful as we are, something could get missed. Having two annual audits doesn't make the system completely goof-proof, but as close as humanly possible.

I thanked Jim Weller and Joan Herman for the outstanding work they had done, for Jim's brilliant advocacy, and for Joan's valuable words of advice. Jim told me that I had been a dream client and that the verdict was the correct one. My staff and I could now return to the business at hand with renewed vigor.

FIVE BLACK-BELT PRINCIPLES TO PROTECT AND GROW YOUR FINANCIAL SERVICES PRACTICE

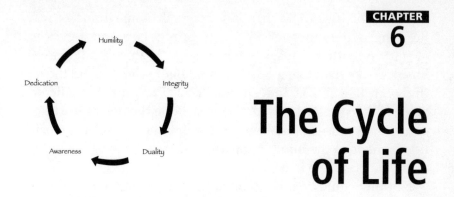

The Cycle of Life

"Our life is frittered away by detail—simplify, simplify."

—Thoreau

There have been books written about how to protect a financial services practice. There have been many books written about how to build and grow a financial services practice. The purpose of Part Two is to explain how to do both at the same time—to protect and to grow.

One of the most disheartening things that happen to many reps at some point relatively early in their careers is that they go to a seminar or conference at which a "top-producing rep" is featured. It might be a million-dollar producer or even a three million–dollar producer. It is someone who represents a level of success that only a small percentage of people who start this business will ever reach.

A little starry-eyed, the rep looks forward to meeting this hero figure in the flesh. And then it happens. In some innocent way, the name of the superstar rep will be brought up, and some kind of snide or cutting remark will be made. "Yeah, right. I'd have a business like that, too, if I didn't mind being slimy." And the rep finds out that this is, indeed, the "buzz" about that particular star. He does well because he dances along the line of unethical behavior. A sense of innocence is lost. But, far worse, an association is made in the mind of the aspiring rep: "To be great in this business, you have to be unethical."

Nothing could be more damaging than to imprint that belief and carry it around with you during your career. If you genuinely believe that, you have built an almost insurmountable roadblock in your career path. If it really is true that to get to the top you have to take advantage of people, then you, an honest "good guy" rep, wouldn't want to ever get there, would you?

Human nature is such that in any profession, there will be members who will elevate the profession and others who discredit it. The vast majority of people who enter any vocation, whether it is medicine, firefighting, teaching, or investments, have good intentions and fundamental integrity. But it is just as certain that a small number will lack that basic integrity. Some of them will get away with their behavior for years, even forever. Others will engage in behavior so egregious that at some point they will be marched off in handcuffs in a perp walk and get on television.

Tom Hine tells the story about the first time he heard a disparaging comment about a top producer:

> I was raised by Catholic parents. My father was a Korean War–era veteran. We were brought up to believe in the American dream—work hard, be honest, and you can succeed to the limit of your ability and effort. I remember distinctly the first time I heard the "that top producer is slimy" comment. I was very young in the business. All I was thinking about at that point was survival. I wasn't thinking "million-dollar producer." I just wanted to be able to stay in the

game. The first time I heard that type of comment it felt like a punch in the stomach. It offended me. It upset my sense of the way things should be. And it made me vow that whatever results I might have in this business, no one would be able to accurately say that about me. I wanted my fundamentals to be so strong, my commitment to integrity so complete, that if I ever did succeed, I could become the counter to this example.

Now it is more than 10 years later. With the help of some fine people who are on my staff, we have built Capital Wealth Management, LLC from inception in 2001 to more than $1.5 million dollars in annual revenue in 2006. We are driven by a desire to really make a difference in our clients' lives, to give them a level of care and service they could not get anywhere else, and also to build a company that we are proud of—one that succeeds because it does the right thing. A company that others can look at and say: "It is possible."

As Tom went through his NASD hearing, he found himself relying on five fundamental principles. They were introduced in the trial in sequence for a reason:

- *Humility*—a starting point principle, a place to begin. Humility requires us to approach every person, every challenge, every situation with head metaphorically bowed respectfully and with that most wonderful of assets, a genuinely open mind. With humility as a starting point, we can then proceed to:
- *Integrity*—the logical second principle in sequence. For any idea, plan, or goal to be worthwhile, it must be rooted in the truth. Shakespeare wrote: "This above all things, to thine own self be true." For any endeavor to have a truly happy ending, integrity must be built into its core. Having built the strongest possible foundation with the principles of humility and integrity, we proceed to:

- *Duality*—a principle of perspective. Duality is a reminder to check ourselves before leaping ahead on impulse—to try and first see and understand the other side. Imagine a glass with water filled to the halfway point. The optimist states that it is half full. The pessimist says that it is half empty. Duality makes us realize that it is both. With head bowed, eyes clear, and an alert, flexible mind, we proceed to:
- *Awareness*—the principle that tells us to observe, to use the powers we have been given to see the world as it is, not merely the way we might wish it to be. This principle reminds us that it is more important to understand than to be understood. It warns us that however good or bad our present circumstance might be, there is always something around the corner. Now armed with these four principles, we reach the final peak:
- *Dedication*—the spirit of *Kaizen*, the Japanese term for continuous improvement. This principle reminds us that there is an infinite horizon. It impels us to seek a state of perfection that we know we will never reach. Now having reached this highest principle, the proper way to be sure we keep growing every day of our lives is, obviously, to return to the first principle, humility, and start all over again.

The principles define a system for personal development and change that is easy to follow, and that, if followed, will bear fruit. Expressed in an image, they look like Figure 6.1.

This is the cycle that was used at the beginning of the first five chapters. It describes a simple system of universally understood concepts that fit together into a formula, an integrated conceptual road map for success. Call this the Cycle of Learning. Looked at vertically, the principles are:

- Humility
- Integrity
- Duality

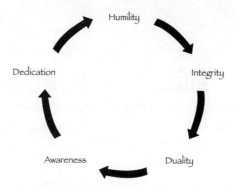

Figure 6.1   The Cycle of Learning

- Awareness
- Dedication

HI DAD!

The authors take a moment to salute their dads. Both are now deceased, but lived rich and robust lives. Both were war-era veterans who loved America, loved their wives, and loved their children. Both exemplified through their lives the lessons they had learned and passed them on to their children. Hi, Dad.

The idea of a sequence of principles being used by people in a cyclical manner to improve their life quality or inner character has been around for centuries.

In his autobiography, Benjamin Franklin described his system of 13 virtues. His plan for lifetime self-improvement revolved around the idea of working on each virtue for one week, then on to the next, through four cycles each calendar year. When he would complete the thirteenth virtue, he would return again to the first, ideally strengthened by his work over the past 13 weeks, now seeking a higher level of living. Franklin modestly stated toward the end of his life that if he had the opportunity to live again, it would be his fondest wish to correct in another life the mistakes he had made in the first. He was an individual of humility and enormous accomplishment in many fields of endeavor.

In 1935, a failed stockbroker from New York City met a troubled physician in Akron, Ohio. Both had been afflicted with a hopeless drinking problem for most of their adult lives. Touched by what they later described as the healing energy of a Higher Power, together they began a society that came to be known as Alcoholics Anonymous. Three years later, the 12 Steps were first published.

The first step requires an act of complete humility with the proclamation of the individual's powerlessness. These 12 steps described a program of recovery, which today is practiced by more than 2 million formerly suffering alcoholics worldwide. The steps have been applied to helping people recover from other addictions. When the individual completes the twelfth step, he or she is encouraged to begin again at the first step, with another proclamation of helplessness. Successful practitioners of the 12 steps believe that continued practice of the steps, in a cyclical manner, is a formula for continued abstinence and personal growth.

In 1989, Stephen Covey published *The Seven Habits of Highly Effective People* (New York: Simon & Schuster). Covey's core philosophy of principle-centered leadership helped to lead the movement that is in full gear today toward improved business ethics as a foundation for success—by individuals or organizations. The habits are described in a cyclical fashion, each building on the foundation of the previous habit. When the cycle is completed, individuals are encouraged to start at the beginning again, in a loop of continuous self-examination and self-improvement.

Having defined this somewhat interesting but rather abstract system of sequential, cyclical principles, is it possible to bring it to another level of practicality for the entrepreneur–financial adviser? Is there a way to enhance this system so that we have an image we can work with that captures, in a single unified graphic, all of the key information we need in order to protect and grow our financial services practice?

The answer is "Yes." Add a yin and yang image inside the cycle, and make each half represent, in equal portion, the two challenges of building a successful financial services practice, one that is built to grow in a healthy way forever (see Figure 6.2).

Outside the circle are the five principles in sequence. These principles remind us to always start at the beginning, with humility, then to add integrity, and go through each principle to the final one—dedication. And now, having achieved that highest principle, we begin the journey again, this time boosted by the journey we took before. As we continue to embed these principles and make them a part of all that we do as professionals, the bar is automatically raised. We barely have to even make an effort to do so.

Protect and Grow are shown in both English and Japanese, out of respect for the generations of Japanese heroes of martial arts and Eastern philosophy. Protect and Grow are the yin and yang of building a financial services practice. They seem to oppose one another, yet they simultaneously complement each other. Neither can dominate the other. If Grow became impossibly

Figure 6.2   The Cycle of Life

strong, then Protect would get weaker, and eventually the system would fail. If Protect became impossibly strong, it could choke off the creativity and oxygen that is Grow. Both need each other.

Master Sang H. Kim is an internationally respected instructor of multiple martial arts, author, and producer of successful videos. In describing the relationship of yin and yang, he says, "Harmony becomes unbalanced when the stronger of two forces prevails over the weaker. The status of balance and unbalance fluctuates constantly throughout life" (*WTF Taeguk Poomse*, Turtle Press, 2002).

All business growth and management can be visualized as a dynamic, fluid competition and collaboration between Protect and Grow. The goal is a type of dynamic equilibrium, which leads inevitably to health and a type of prosperity that is far beyond that which can be measured in dollars—the knowledge that you are a useful individual in this world, performing work that genuinely contributes to the well-being of your fellow human beings. This is why you got into this business, isn't it? When in your professional life you are being used for a useful purpose, when you are engaged in work that has meaning and value—when what you do on a daily basis helps other people live fuller lives, you have reached a major milestone in life, one that many people never reach.

Cognitive psychologists tell us that when you are finished reading this book, you will forget a good portion of what you have read in a relatively short period of time. But as you read the rest of this book, really imprint the cycle, which we shall call the Cycle of Life. It contains, in a single image, an entire training program on how to protect and grow a financial services practice. When you reach a professional dilemma, whether it is in sales, marketing, operations, service, staffing, financial management, or compliance, the five principles with the Protect and Grow in the yin and yang can give you an immediate guideline on what to do next. If you simplify your life and your practice, and invest time and energy inculcating these principles, success, however you choose to define it, is inevitable.

As is so often true when working with universal principles, and especially with Eastern philosophy, it helps to take the long view. As chief executive officer of your financial services practice, what is your vision for your business? If you had a narrow vision, or merely a short-term profit goal, you could twist the Cycle out of shape, put your foot on the accelerator of "grow," and, at least for a while, nearly forget about "protect." You could cut those corners. You could use your knowledge and power to maximize your short-term gain at the expense of the long-term benefit of your clients.

And it just might work for a while—maybe a year or a couple of years. But if you take the longer perspective, you can see that there is no way that it would work. If you intended to build a business in such a way that you could be in the business 20 years from now, working with some of the same clients, or their offspring, you would then be forced to live by solid principles. You would want to use the Cycle of Life and build your business on eternally sound universal principles.

What is wonderful about the Cycle of Life, however, is that it is far more useful than giving us an image to remember by which to manage a practice. If you look carefully, you can see many other applications. After all, isn't Protect and Grow the very reason our clients come to see us in the first place? How many times have you had a client or potential client tell you that their investment philosophy was "conservative with growth"? The ultimate contradiction—the yin and the yang. The truth is that they do want both, and your job becomes to help them meet their objectives in a world in which there are no guarantees. The Cycle of Life can be adapted to parenting, studying, or almost any endeavor. But we will start out by describing how to use it to protect and grow your financial services practice.

To Protect and Grow

"The perfecting of one's self is the fundamental base of all progress and all moral development."

—*Confucius*

The Cycle of Life gives us a simple image, a path to follow, and a game plan. But it does more than that.

Part Two is not meant to be a detailed step-by-step operations manual on the nuts and bolts of building a million-dollar practice. Some fine books have been written on the subject. Of these, the one that has had the most influence on Tom's career is *Tested in the Trenches* by Ron Carson and Steve Sanduski (Chicago: Dearborn Trade Publishing, 2005). This book describes, in precise detail, a nine-step plan for building and sustaining a million-dollar financial services practice.

Ron Carson has been referred to as the "Tiger Woods of Independent Representatives." As of the writing of this book, for 14 years in a row, he has been the number one producing registered representative for Linsco/Private Ledgers, the nation's largest independent broker-dealer firm. Ron is president of Carson Wealth Management Group, a comprehensive wealth-planning firm with more than $1 billion in invested assets.

For many registered representatives, it is a dream to build a practice that produces $1 million in annual revenues. Carson Wealth Management Group has annual revenues in excess of $7 million. Ron and Steve are principals of PEAK Productions, a financial adviser coaching, software, and consulting company. Through this program, Ron and Steve have taught and mentored many advisers around the country into building their own practices, many of which have reached or exceeded $1 million.

Tom Hine has been a student in PEAK Productions continuously since 2002. He has adapted many of the ideas described in *Tested in the Trenches* and detailed in the PEAK Productions coaching program to building Capital Wealth Management, LLC, from its inception in 2001 to its current status in 2006 as a business that produces $1.5 million in annual revenue.

Significantly, the philosophies described in *Tested in the Trenches* and explained in greater detail in the PEAK Productions coaching program do not focus exclusively on building a practice devoted to achieving business metrics. The system is holistic in nature, and helps its students build lives that are diverse and fulfilling, allowing each individual to define success for him- or herself.

It begins by encouraging each person to achieve personal and professional clarity through a "blueprinting process," which includes clarifying personal values, finding a meaningful life purpose, developing a compelling vision of the future, and developing a personal and professional mission statement. The result of this is a set of "SMAC-Certified" (Specific, Measurable, Achievable, Compatible), which become the core of the rep's strategic and operational plan for personal and professional growth.

Other steps in the system involve recruiting and building

a strong, service-driven staff, building a brand, focusing marketing efforts on top clients and prospects, and delivering outstanding client events. Beyond Ron's personal record of accomplishment, and the clarity of this game plan for development, perhaps the most widely copied concept that other reps have adapted to their own practices is "Systematize Everything." To continue to grow a wealth advisory business, Ron describes the need to systematize virtually every aspect of the business's operation.

Adapt, Don't Adopt

The challenge of change and growth is part of every rep's daily business life. As the saying goes, "If you do what you always did, you will get what you always got." In order to build a practice, to strengthen client service, to improve one's professional knowledge, to recruit staff, to acquire new clients and assets under management, change is required. New tools and ideas must be developed.

Reps are fortunate in that much of the conceptual groundbreaking work has been done in this area, and it is easily accessible through books, seminars, and coaching programs. The raw material by which to build a practice is easily available. Ron Carson and others who have described their own unique approach to building a million-dollar practice provide a cornucopia of ideas from which to choose. In this book, Tom provides some of his own unique ideas to add to this wealth of available knowledge.

Any practice will reflect the uniqueness of the individual who builds it. Therefore, in looking through any success methodology, whether it is Ron Carson, Tom Hine, or any of the other individuals in this field, it is wise to follow the precept "Adapt, Don't Adopt." The truth is that if you are reading this book, you probably have your own client base and you want to protect and to grow it.

As a starting point, realize all the things you have already done to get to wherever you are in the profession. How many people have come and gone while you have stayed and built? You obviously are doing many things right, and in making changes, you want to not only keep these core strengths but continue to build on them. As you look to use a system by which to improve your business, pick out an idea or maybe two. Ask yourself, "How does this relate to me and to my practice? Where and how can I apply it? What adaptations do I need to make in order to implement it?" As you implement, you continue to tweak and tinker. That is the nature of entrepreneurship. If over a period of a year, you have successfully implemented two or three major ideas into your practice that have helped protect and grow it, you have had a great success.

There Is No Magic Bullet

There is no single idea or series of ideas, no matter how powerful, well articulated, or brilliantly implemented, that provide a 100 percent guarantee of success. No matter how well you market yourself and your services, there will be clients who will not come to work with you and you will never know why. No matter what level of service you provide to your clients, some will leave, and some will leave and come back. No matter how fastidious you are about following procedure, communicating with your clients, training your staff, and following up, mistakes will be made every year you are in the business. This is not a revelation. It is a statement of reality.

As a parent, you know that no matter how much your love your children and do everything you can to teach them and to protect them, they ultimately are on their own. As a business owner, no matter how careful you are in selecting, training, and managing people underneath you, they will not be perfect. As a wealth adviser, no matter how well you know your client, study the markets, and learn about new products, your advice, at best, helps your clients to manage risk but does not eliminate it.

So if you are looking in this book for the single "aha" moment, the magic bullet, that will insulate you forever from any risk of a future customer complaint, or even the possibility of having an award against you, you will not find it. If you are looking for the perfect step-by-step formula to follow to grow a business, you will not find it.

NASD Arbitration Solution

So, if perfection is not obtainable, then what is? What *is* the "NASD Arbitration Solution"? It is *you*. As the legendary comic strip character Pogo said, "We have met the enemy and he is us." In the yin and yang of that idea, we are our own worst enemy and our own greatest resource.

The NASD Arbitration Solution is you, as a registered representative, deciding, hopefully partially on the basis of what you have read in this book, to have a new level of energy and commitment to your profession. Now that you have the seen the details of the arbitration process, what changes do you need to make in your practice in order to protect it? What holes are there in your system through which could slip the client who will someday become a claimant? What reasonable steps can you take to plug those holes?

Many of the answers are already known to you. As Chris Gryzen, vice president of compliance at BancWest Investments and specialty faculty member at Creighton University, said, "Many of the complaints are completely avoidable. It's not a matter of a registered representative not knowing what to do. Rather, it is a case of them not doing what they already know." So, what are you currently not doing that you already know? Pick a spot and begin working on it. Then build from there.

The NASD Arbitration Solution is you, the rep, committed to a future in which you have a clear personal and professional vision, and you are building a practice that has a level of service that would make it inconceivable for anyone to ever think of filing a complaint. That vision and practice are backed by a system of overwhelming documentation, in which your electronic and paper audit trail is so clear, your records so well organized, that you not only can serve your clients to the highest possible level, but in the event there is controversy, you will have the means to defend yourself, which will make it nearly impossible to penetrate the walls of your practice.

Ultimately, in the long term, both in life and in building a financial services practice, simplicity is the answer. Be principle centered. When in doubt, do what you know is right. Sometimes that might mean turning down the chance for short-term gain, in exchange for the knowledge that you are building a business and a life, on the strongest foundation—that of values which are universal and easy to understand. The Cycle of Life is a tool with which to do that. The next step is up to you.

Humility

The White-Belt Attitude

"It is better to be interested than to be interesting."

—Lee Brower, Strategic Coach

I t seems almost self-defeating to write about humility. Humility has an evanescent quality. It seems as if the moment you proclaim it, you lose it. You can hear the snickering in the background. "Sure, he is a humble guy. Just ask him."

And yet when we recognize true humility in others, we revere it. Mother Teresa and Pope John Paul II were among the most influential people in the world for decades. Billions of people from every continent were in awe of their humanity and humility. Through lives of service, they exemplified the highest of human ideals.

Doris Kearns Goodwin's book *A Team of Rivals* (New York: Simon & Schuster, 1980) detailed President Abraham Lincoln's amazing ability to hold the nation together during the Civil War.

Lincoln's cabinet was filled with men of high intellect and ego, rivals with one another, many of whom believed themselves to be of superior intellect and ability to Lincoln. The book describes example after example in which Lincoln's personal graciousness, humility, and ability to forgive treachery won him the admiration of his adversaries and kept the nation held together through its darkest hours.

On July 4, 1939, Lou Gehrig of the New York Yankees stepped to the microphone in a packed Yankee Stadium to deliver what was his farewell address to the sports world. Gehrig, a graduate of Columbia University and a man of relatively few words but heroic sports feats, was in severe pain, suffering from amyotrophic lateral sclerosis, a terminal illness, now known as "Lou Gehrig's disease." Despite his pain, he proclaimed himself the "luckiest man alive." Gehrig's speech, a moment of complete humility, is considered one of the great moments in sports history.

Humility is one of the most powerful human traits. It indicates a soul that has been tempered with wisdom, a spirit made larger through gratitude, and—one of the most powerful of all tools in the universe—a mind that is open and seeking the truth. Humility is a wonderful starting point for martial artists or investment advisers.

Humility is not a technique. It is an attitude. It is not a sales tool. It is a state of mind and spirit. In 1936, Dale Carnegie wrote *How to Win Friends and Influence People* (New York: Simon & Schuster, 1936). The book sold 16 million copies worldwide and can still be found in most large bookstores. The core of the book was a series of suggestions so unexceptional as to be almost astonishing. The book included such chapters as "Six Ways to Make People Like You" and "Twelve Ways to Win People to Your Way of Thinking."

Carnegie emphasized, however, that he was not recommending tools for manipulating others into doing what you want them to do. He was suggesting a new way of life. As you grow your practice, develop your professionalism, and continue to mature as an adult, the development of genuine humility will be a natural outcome of this process.

Stephen Covey brought a new perspective to humility. It was one of his seven habits of highly effective people: "seek first to understand, then to be understood"(*Seven Habits of Highly Effective People*, New York: Simon & Schuster, 1989). He referred to it as the Principle of Empathetic Communication.

Humility is not only a desirable personal quality; it is also one of the most practical business tools imaginable.

"I Could Be Wrong"

In conversation, and as a basic attitude, always leave open the possibility that you are wrong, even if you believe you are not. The reality is that you may be. And good human relations practices tell us that if you admit up front that "I may be wrong," it is hard to offend someone or get into an argument with them.

Clients often come to a rep with a challenge to the rep's advice. Clients themselves are often high-energy, success-motivated individuals who are recognized in their own profession and used to being right about things. They talk with their friends and acquaintances and hear about someone who, reportedly, is doing better with their investments than they are. They come to you with a bit of an attitude about it. Their tone of voice just reeks of "I'm right and you're wrong."

It is very tempting at this point to pull out your "expert" hat and put it squarely on top of your head, then to launch off into some technical financial analysis that shows you can run rings around their theory. You may win an argument and lose a client.

So, you say, "Well, that is a very interesting idea. It has some pluses behind it. And, of course, I could be wrong about this. But let me give you my take on what I think is actually happening."

It is not necessary to accept the invitation to every argument to which you are invited. With some simple conversational grace, self-restraint, and the right attitude, you can defuse these situations quite easily.

You can use "I could be wrong, but . . ." as a mantra. It shows that you have your ego in check, that you are not wearing blinders. It shows that you have an open mind. Even on subjects where you are "sure" you are right (have you ever been "sure" of something that you later found to be incorrect?), "I could be wrong" protects you in the one case in a thousand that you hadn't counted on.

"Never Say Never"

This is also a philosophy, a reality, and a bit of practical conversational advice. We are in the business of trying to make the future less uncertain. We are trying to give our clients a clearer glimpse into the future. With our experience, the hours of study of markets, academic preparation, and research tools at our disposal, it stands to reason that over a long period of time we will be able to help clients improve their chances to achieve their financial objectives—to both protect and grow.

Yet, none of us can see the future. In the early 1990s, did any of us truly know that the Internet was about to burst on the scene and change global business forever? In the late 1990s, did any of us know that the attacks of September 11, 2001, would cripple the global airline industry? Do any of us truly know what the world of 2010 or 2015 will be like? We can look at our projections and charts of the past, and the best we can do is give a best guess.

So, Never Say Never is another good, simple rule to follow. How many times have you spoken with a rep who, in relaying an incident in his or her career, said, "I never thought that X would happen, but it did."

Instead of "never," you can simply substitute "The odds of that happening are remote" or "Based on everything I know, I would be extremely surprised to see that come about." You protect yourself and demonstrate good manners and an open mind at the same time.

"Let Me Clarify"

Clients often express the desire for contradictory outcomes. They are "conservative with growth" investors. When the market goes up, they feel as though their portfolio is not aggressive enough. When the market goes down, they feel it is too aggressive.

Clients will discuss the asset allocation that you have for their portfolio. They will express a desire for change—getting either more aggressive or safer. If you listen carefully, there is no real clear decision that their words reflect. They may mention in a meeting or a call that they, in general, want to move in one direction or the other. They may leave a meeting in which there is some ambiguity as to what they actually want you to do. It may be moving some assets, selling some assets, or some other strategy.

The answer to this, the humility principle in action, is the "let me clarify" discussion in which you walk through with them what they have told you and asked if they want you to take a specific action. It may be that they do, and having had a chance to reflect on your previous discussion with them, they actually do want to go ahead and make a change. It may be that they were just "thinking out loud" and in the end don't really want to change.

By calling them and stating that you want to "clarify," you are allowing them to restate, rethink, or finalize an action. Whatever it is, you want to be the balancing wheel, covering the "other side of the story" (duality principle). Once you have done that and they have signed off, what is left is to execute the action and document the discussion with a follow-up letter or e-mail.

"I wanted to call back and clarify what we talked about yesterday. Given the volatility of the market and some recent developments in the world, you mentioned that you might want to convert some of your assets to cash. Is that something you are firm in wanting me to do, or was that just a topic for discussion?"

If they say, "No, I would like to have you sell X amount of assets," you say, "That's fine. I just want to walk you through the other side of this. You are right in that there are signs the market seems a little shaky in the short term. But overall it has been on a gradual upward trend. Three months from now or six months from now, if it bounces back and continues on the upside, you may look back at this and find yourself upset that you missed out on some opportunity. Are you comfortable with that?"

Having talked this through, you execute the decision and document your discussion, including your own "other side of the story" input, in a follow-up e-mail or letter. You have shown respect to the client, you have given them responsible advice. You have fulfilled their wishes. And you have protected yourself with your advice and the documentation if later on they regret this decision.

Admit Mistakes

Hopefully, this will be a relatively small number of occasions, but there are occasions in which you should admit a mistake and take action to correct, however momentarily painful. A top producer told us of an example in which he had made a trade in a client's discretionary account. Although he believed this was in keeping with a discussion they had had, when he informed the client a few days later, the client was upset that he had sold this particular asset. The client claimed that had the rep called ahead of time, the client would have never approved selling that particular asset. What was worse was that had he not sold the asset, it would have gained in value by $12,000 during the short period in question.

It was a dilemma. This, after all, was a discretionary account. To an extent, this was an example of a client's asking to employ the power of "20/20 hindsight." However, after thinking it over, the rep called the client back, apologized for the mistake, worked with the trade desk, reacquired the asset, and took the $12,000 hit. It was a valuable client, an important gesture, and a sobering lesson.

The Power of the White-Belt Attitude

In the description of Tom Hine's NASD hearing, there is a description of the "white-belt attitude," also sometimes known as the "beginner's mind." The essence of the white-belt attitude is that, whatever level a martial artist may have achieved, he or she approaches each class, each challenge, each moment with enthusiasm, an open mind, curiosity, and a drive to improve.

During Tom's trial, the white-belt attitude helped him to look at the NASD arbitration process with a hunger to understand it. He became a student of his attorney, Jim Weller, asking dozens of questions about process and strategy. On his own initiative, he came up with some ideas and information, coming from a fresh perspective, which helped him succeed in the case.

A rep told a story of someone in professional sports who exemplified the white belt attitude. This person was in grade school when his father took him to a doubleheader between the New York Mets and the Cincinnati Reds in 1964. The leadoff hitter for the Reds drew a walk to open the game. He dropped the bat and raced to first base, as if he were trying to beat out an infield hit.

"Who is that and why did he do that, Dad?" the young man asked. The father replied, "That is a guy by the name of Pete Rose. He was the National League Rookie of the Year last year. His nickname is Charlie Hustle. And he plays the game the way a lot of the great players played it back when I was growing up." For all of the controversy of his later years, Pete Rose loved playing the game of baseball. He never lost his enthusiasm for the sheer joy of a man playing a boy's game—a white-belt attitude.

The white-belt attitude is a fantastic asset in building any career, but especially a financial services practice. It will help you want to learn more about every aspect of the business and seek the advice of others who have achieved what you want. It will help you become genuinely interested in the stories and problems of your clients, asking questions, understanding their thinking, alive and marveling in the uniqueness of each individual.

Humility and Gratitude

The simplest and most effective way to develop humility, which is the driving force of the white-belt attitude, is through gratitude. It has been said that if you truly desire wealth, seek an attitude of gratitude. There are people in this world who are worth billions but do not have genuine gratitude and are therefore unhappy. They have the Midas touch, but make those around them miserable.

Then there are those who have very little in terms of material possessions, but great spiritual wealth due to an attitude of gratitude. When you feel yourself getting off track, when you find yourself getting annoyed and stressed, when you feel overwhelmed by the pace of life or its challenges, stop and count your blessings.

Whatever circumstance you may find yourself in, there are dozens and hundreds of things to be grateful for. Do you have decent health? What would a person who is sick and dying give for one day with the health you have? If you didn't have good health, what price would you pay to have it?

Do you have children? Are you grateful for them and the gift of daily challenge and imperative to grow? It is an irony of life that parenting gives us an opportunity to grow up, something that supposedly took place when we were younger. Parenting is about becoming a better person, a more tolerant person, a more unselfish person, a person whose actions are more value driven. Are you grateful for your children and their love for you?

Are you grateful for your clients? These people could have any one of hundreds of people helping them steer through the perilous shores of the finances of adulthood. They have chosen you. Are you grateful for the opportunity to serve them? Have you told any of them this recently?

It is said that to develop self-esteem, one must do esteemable acts. Humility can be sought and acquired through action. Take some time to give of yourself to others who have no way to repay the favor. It might be volunteering at a homeless shelter. It might be work on behalf of a cause in which you believe. Some volunteer work and doing things for people without anyone's knowing about it are sure ways to develop gratitude and, with it, humility.

One of the most powerful expressions of humility is the prayer of St. Francis of Assisi. He lived a life of simplicity and service to his God and to others. His prayer is written here not as a religious statement, but as an example of true and deep humility.

The Prayer of St. Francis

Lord, make me an instrument of thy peace.
Where there is hatred, let me sow love.
Where there is injury, pardon.
Where there is doubt, faith.
Where there is despair, home.
Where there is darkness, light.
Where there is sadness, joy.

O, Divine master, grant that I may not
So much seek to be consoled, as to console.
To be understood, as to understand.
To be loved, as to love.

For it is in giving that we receive.
It is in forgiving, that we are forgiven.
It is in dying to self that we are born to eternal life.

Integrity

Look in the Mirror

"This above all things, to thine own self be true."

— *William Shakespeare*

Integrity is such a revered trait that it is woven into our civic mythology. Children in school are taught the famous story about George Washington and the cherry tree. The lesson is that in the end virtue is rewarded.

Warren Buffett, legendary investor, lectures at colleges and universities. A recording was made of one of his standard lectures about "qualities of character." He was speaking before the master of business administration students at the University of North Carolina at Chapel Hill. Buffett asked the room of approximately 100 graduate business students to do a thought experiment.

He asked them to imagine that they had the opportunity to invest in the business future of one of their classmates. It was a long-term investment, and they would be paid based on the financial performance of the person they selected. Inherited wealth wouldn't count. It had to be based purely on merit and business performance. Under the rules of the thought experiment, students were not allowed to vote for themselves.

"So," Buffett asked the spellbound students, "who would you vote for?" He didn't follow through with ballots and an actual vote count. It was just a thought experiment. But Buffett explained to the students that he had performed the full experiment many times with other groups. And always got the same result. There would be a very small percentage of the students who received the vast majority of the votes. Two or perhaps three students, depending on the size and other characteristics of the class, would emerge as the top vote getters.

"Why is this?" Buffett asked the students. He explained that the top vote getters were rarely the top students, though often they were near the top. They were not necessarily the students with the best score on the graduate business board exam. But they were always individuals of outstanding character. Students who showed up at every class well prepared. Students who were impeccable in integrity, as evidenced by the interactions with their classmates. Students who, in short, had qualities of character.

Buffet concluded his experiment by telling the students that the wonderful opportunity of being alive is that we all know what those qualities are. And we all have access, 24 hours a day and seven days a week, to try and live up to those qualities.

If you meet individuals who have reached the very top of our profession, you will find, almost without exception, individuals of sterling integrity. Perfect? No. Able to walk on water? No. But individuals whose word is absolutely dependable.

In the description of his trial, Tom spoke of martial artists "practicing in front of a mirror." The mirror reveals all flaws of form, as well as reflects exercises that are performed well. Self-examination is one of the most difficult human steps to take, but one of the most necessary in order to improve.

As you build your financial services practice, be willing to "look at yourself in the mirror." Don't gloss over your personal strengths or those of your practice. Without them, you would have no practice. But it is far more fruitful, from a development standpoint, to put in clear relief your own weaknesses and those of your practice. These will tend to run along parallel paths.

If you are a great technical analyst but dislike the activities of marketing, you run the risk of having a small number of extremely well-educated and well-serviced clients. If you are a natural networker, an extrovert, someone who loves to meet new people, you run the risk of attracting people to you, but not having the systems in place to be sure the details of their service are fulfilled. In the end, you may find that you build up people's hopes, then disappoint them with your service level.

The way to growth, for both of these extremes, is to follow the game plan in the Cycle of Life. Protect *and* Grow. Continue to strengthen those elements at which you already excel. But have the humility to examine your weaknesses and the desire to correct them. It is said that "reputation is what people think of you; character is what you really are." Devote yourself to a career, in fact, a lifetime of balanced growth. Let your good and always improving character define your reputation. Follow one of the precepts of Shotokan karate. Seek perfection of character, and let your reputation take care of itself.

Practice in Slow Motion

When martial artists are learning techniques, such as for a specific kick or punch, instructors often teach them in super slow motion, exaggerating each aspect of the technique. Students are then asked to repeat the technique first in super slow motion several times, then in slow motion several times, then at normal speed several times, and through gradations until they reach top speed. By building slowly in the slow motion foundation, maximum efficiency is attained. Performing techniques extremely slowly requires additional muscle control. It is actually more difficult, and more beneficial, to perform a technique in super slow motion than at regular speed.

For the beginner, it is very tempting to want to rush through this and go to fast speed immediately. This not only has the momentary satisfaction of feeling the speed and power of the action, but it also has the added element of hiding any mistakes that are made in technique. Ultimately, however, the solidness of your foundation will determine the height you can reach. If you have rushed through the technique and chosen the shortcut, you will eventually lack the full power that the technique can yield.

Financial advisers have similar temptations. In the enthusiasm of the sales process, it sometimes is tempting to skip a step, such as taking the time to explain with great clarity the downside risks and disclosure of expenses involved in making a specific recommendation. Similarly, although the immediate reaction may be a rush of adrenaline and a feeling of accomplishment, it is at the long-term price of risking being undermined by the termites you have allowed into your foundation.

Account Minimums

Most registered representatives want to grow their business. A simple enough statement. Then why do so many get to a certain level of production and can go no further? In some cases it is a fallacy that they have embraced, such as, "I would have to be slimy to be a top producer and I don't want to be known as slimy; therefore, I am going to retain my virtue by not growing my business." It looks ridiculous to read, but this is an actual conversation many reps have had with themselves.

In order to grow a financial services practice, one of the simplest ideas that works is account minimums. Tom Hine has been in the Quest for Excellence™ Coaching Program continuously since 2002. He credits this program with a lot of ideas he has implemented and that have improved Capital Wealth Management, LLC. But none anywhere nearly as important as account minimums.

In theory, a good account minimum to take on a client with investable assets would be the amount of gross annual revenue that one's practice produces. So, if your practice produces gross annual revenues of $250,000, then $250,000 becomes your minimum. In practice, adjustments and modifications are almost always part of the implementation process.

Ron Carson, having tested all of these ideas in the trenches, helps reps anticipate the difficulties they will face when first setting an account minimum. He warns that it will seem impossible at first and that it may ruin your business. You won't be able to find any new clients at all, so the thinking goes, and it will hurt the business.

Ron emphasizes that this changeover is made gradually. For any potential clients who are in various stages of becoming clients, the minimum does not apply. It does apply to all new potential clients after the point at which it is being implemented.

Tom's first effort to implement account minimums occurred in 2003. He had reached $1 million in annual revenue. He set his minimum account at $500,000. Tom verifies that Ron's advice held for him. "I could feel that sense of panic. I remember telling my staff, and they were for it in theory, but I could tell there was some skepticism about whether I was actually going to do it. It helped that I had put myself on the line about it. I just forced myself to do what Ron had taught me. I learned that the process requires that you grow in your thinking. You learn that, with the right approach, it often requires no additional time to bring in a client with $500,000 or more in assets than it does for one with $100,000. But the great thing is that one of the larger clients is equal to five of the smaller ones. What happens is a whole series of changes take place. Because of your new goals, you have to hire new staff or improve your existing staff. You create more service capacity in your system. And, Ron says, you are going to compromise. A little, not a lot. But you will always compromise some. In my first year, I had set $500,000 as my minimum, and I recall bringing in a client with $425,000. But that was still larger than most accounts I had previously gone after. All of this activity also has an impact on the staff. It increases their own pride in the business and makes everybody raise the level of their game accordingly—a fantastic process.

In year two, I kept pushing myself and raised my minimum to $750,000. Well, that worked, and I compromised again, but the compromising was at the $700,000 level. A year earlier, $700,000 was a fantastic size client. Then, in 2005, I made the big leap to a $1 million account minimum. So once again I compromised, now at the $900,000 level. My new standard is to bring in a client who has the capacity to bring in $1 million in investable assets. What is great is that this is a process of personal and professional growth, and a major factor in how we were able to bring the business in five years up to $1.5 million in annual gross revenue.

As you look at your own practice, ask yourself: "What type of practice do I want to have?" There is nothing in the world wrong with keeping your practice at whatever level you wish. But be honest with yourself. If you truly desire growth, then you need to be willing to look at yourself and your practice in the mirror and do some things that are currently uncomfortable.

Taking the Tough Phone Calls

Another personal integrity challenge in building a financial services practice is being willing to immediately take a "tough phone call." This does not mean that, if you have a system for taking phone calls that specifies times when you do this, but you get a client who insists on talking to you now, you have to break out of rhythm and take it immediately. It does mean that at the soonest possible time in your normal schedule you will call that person back. None of us like to deliver bad news or be blamed for bad news. But this is the profession we have chosen, and it is part of what we get paid for. Taking the tough calls will strengthen your own professionalism and also build the strength of respect and rapport you have with your staff.

"To Be Fair"

One of the greatest signs that you are practicing your profession the right way is when clients say to you, "I know you would never mislead me. You have always been fair in everything you have said." This is a sign that you have not only done the little things like following up on details. It is deeper than that. It means that throughout your relationship you have been fastidious about covering both the upside and the downside of investment products. This is keeping with the NASD principle "Know Your Client."

It is easy to sell the upside and then gloss over the downside. It is not lying, exactly. It is more laziness. It is far better, in both the short and long term, however, to cover both sides of any investment decision. You become the source of information and the balancing wheel for your clients.

After you cover the good points, the reason a client might want to invest in a particular product, you say, "Now, to be fair, it is not all good. Here is something you need to consider." A simple, but powerful, idea. An integrity check.

Walking Away from a Sale

It should be a rare occurrence, but one of the most character-building experiences in this business is to have the knowledge and conviction about when to walk away from a sale.

A top-producing rep told this story. "Early in my career, I had a wealthy client with an eight-figure net worth. He had approximately $250,000 invested with me at the time. He was happy with our work together and asked me to get aggressive with an additional $300,000. He wanted me to invest it in the Asian markets, as he had some knowledge of the Pacific Rim economies and he felt they were poised for growth. He even told me that if he lost the entire $300,000, it would be okay.

It was very tempting. But after thinking about it, I just knew in my heart it was not the right thing to do. I didn't have the knowledge or confidence about that market. And I didn't want to try and have him pay for my training. Knowing that I was risking losing his business entirely, I politely thanked him for the opportunity, but turned it down. Inside I was thinking, "Not on my watch." Now, more than 10 years later, he is still a client, with more than $5 million invested with me. And he has given me two fantastic referrals."

"The Hard Way"

Harlan Sanders became famous in the 1960s and 1970s as the Kentucky Colonel, the inventor of Kentucky Fried Chicken. What is interesting about Colonel Sanders is that he started the business while he was in his 60s, with little formal education and almost no assets. However, he was armed with a good product, a dream, and a life philosophy that he had developed. It is called "the hard way":

> It is comparatively easy to prosper by trickery, the violation of confidence, oppression of the weak … sharp practices … cutting corners … all of those methods that we are so prone to palliate and condone as "business shrewdness."
>
> It is difficult to prosper by the keeping of promises, the deliverance of value in goods, in services, and in deeds . . . and in the meeting of so-called "shrewdness" with sound merit and good ethics.
>
> The easy way is efficacious and speedy, the hard way arduous and long. But as the clock ticks, the easy way becomes harder and the hard way becomes easier.
>
> And as the calendar records the years, it becomes increasingly evident that the easy way rests hazardously upon shifting sands, whereas the hard way builds solidly a foundation of confidence that cannot be swept away.

—Harlan Sanders, 1937

Duality

Yin and Yang

*"Do I contradict myself? Very well, then, I contradict
myself. I am large. I contain multitudes."*

—*Walt Whitman*

The concept of duality—of the simple, but profound image of
yin and yang—is one of the most universally recognized elements of Eastern philosophy. Yin and yang represents the idea
that throughout the universe there are opposing forces and principles, which ultimately seem to need each other and to complete
each other: male/female, cold/hot, light/dark, health/sickness,
happy/sad, fire/ice, wealth/poverty, good/evil, negative/posi-
tive, material/spiritual, protect/grow, red state/blue state,
Venus/Mars, sales/compliance.

In the universe, opposing forces struggle against one another,
and at the same time need each other. It is a relationship of both
opposition and symbiosis. Neither force prevails, for if it did it
would kill off the other force, and then die off itself. The result of

these struggles of opposition is the dynamic energy that helps to drive the universe.

Imagine happy or sad without the other. It is inconceivable. As difficult as sadness can be, it also provides the perspective with which to feel the uniqueness and value of genuine joy.

Try this thought experiment. Imagine it were possible for one day to mandate that there be no human sadness. For one day, people would feel no disappointment, no bereavement, no loneliness, no heartache, no negative emotion. There is no concept of sadness in the human mind or heart. It has been taken away. At first, it might sound great. But think about it. This would drain life of emotion. Sadness is part of the richness of being human.

A Day without Humor

Now try a related thought experiment. For one day, there is no humor. There is no concept of humor. There is no sense of humor. Nothing is funny. That day, if you could somehow imagine still knowing about humor but it did not exist for a day, might seem the longest day of your life. Humor is a wonderful thing. We have access to our sense of humor 24 hours a day, 365 days a year (366 on leap years!). Yet often, in the stress of answering e-mails and hitting deadlines, we don't smell the coffee or the flowers, and we miss the joy of living.

The essential lesson of duality is that there is another side to everything, and that solutions often are found only after one genuinely understands the opposing sides of an issue. Every argument has a counterargument. Every point has a counterpoint. The University of Virginia Law School has a tremendous moot court competition each year. Some of the winners have gone on to great distinction in the legal field. There is an elimination tournament, and the finals are highly publicized. They are presided over by a major figure in the legal world. Supreme Court justices have presided over some of these events, which have been televised locally. Sometimes the same cases are tried in the semifinals and finals. There have been occasions where the winner successfully argued on one side to win the semifinals and the other side to win the finals. Think about that. If you understand duality, it makes perfect sense.

Opening Your Mind

What can come out of your awareness of duality is a more flexible, open, and responsive mind. Exposing yourself to viewpoints contrary to your own is one of the best ways to develop your own sense of duality and grow as a person. How often have you had a civil argument with someone who had very different political views from your own? It is much easier to spend time talking politics with people who we know agree with us. It turns into a back-patting session. Yet how much, really, is gained from that kind of activity?

If you are a sports fan with favorite teams, when was the last time you had an extended civil discussion with someone who is as enthusiastic a fan for your rival? If you are committed to a religion, one of the most interesting things you could do is to have an extended, civil discussion with someone who is equally passionate about a religion whose tenets are different than yours. One of the greatest human qualities is empathy, the ability to understand someone. Stephen Covey's Principle of Empathetic Communication is "seek first to understand, then to be understood." Covey is not only providing a wonderful tool for business success, but a challenge to grow as an individual. If you do indeed seek first to understand, and second to be understood, life will go much more smoothly, and you will continue to grow as a human being.

Duality and Clients

Working with clients is filled with duality. The classic definition of the investment "philosophy" that most people would use to describe themselves is "conservative with growth." We all have clients who:

- Want to grow their assets but not accept risk.
- Want to earn more money but don't want to write down goals and a plan for success.
- Want to take out income but maintain principal.

One of the keys to working with clients is to understand their duality, not be frustrated by it, and to realize that one of your roles is that of educator and counselor. You may have a client who has a net worth many times that of your own. Yet in the realm of investments, he or she is coming to you for your advice and assistance. That individual may be very emotional about his or her assets and need the counsel of a qualified third party. There are times when it is like the relationship of parent to child. You explain the rules of risk and reward, explaining the positive aspects of products as well as their disadvantages.

Here are some brief examples in which your ability to present the other side of the issue will help your client understand that although the desire to have it both ways is understandable, it is not realistic:

- When clients complain about your fees, you can simply say, "I understand your concern. But I had to make a decision in building the business. It was low fees and poor service or competitive fees and great service."
- When clients in a relatively conservative portfolio complain about poor performance, remind them that they always have the choice to become more aggressive, though at increased risk.
- When clients focus on the Dow Jones Industrial Average, but also want true diversification, remind them that the Dow, while heavily publicized, is a measurement of an extremely narrow group of companies.
- When clients dislike life insurance but own annuities, remind them that annuities contain death benefits.

Imagine recording every client meeting or phone call you have had in a week's time. In your mind, play them back and listen to them. Your discussions should be filled with duality—examples you give that make clear both sides of the issues you are discussing.

Dancing in the Gray Zone

One of the core responsibilities that every rep has to his clients is to accurately assess their risk profile, develop a portfolio of suitable investments, and then work with them through the inevitable ups and downs. Given a long enough time horizon, the same client can at times believe that he or she is placed in investments that are either not aggressive enough or too aggressive.

When the equities markets are rising, clients who have a more conservative portfolio hear about the gains others are making, and, at some level, blame the rep for not having them in an aggressive enough mix. When the markets are in a period of fall, clients who enjoyed the swelling of value from a boom market will turn on the rep and blame him or her for not being conservative enough. This is part of the business. There is no absolute scientific method to perfectly diagnose any individual, or on how to advise them when either their personal circumstances or market conditions change. The future is always an unknown. This sometimes emotional process of give and take with clients can be thought of as "dancing in the gray zone."

Warning Signs that a Change May Be Indicated

It is understood that every client situation is unique, and that NASD Rule 2310, "Know Your Client," must be a foundation for any work with clients. "Know Your Client" does not pertain only to the beginning of the relationship. It is an ongoing process. Over the course of a relationship, due to changes in a client's life circumstances or market conditions, it may be appropriate to consider revising an individual's risk profile and rebalancing his or her portfolio accordingly.

Here are some possible indicators that this might be considered:

- Sporadic phone calls, either to the rep or to his or her staff, that are not related to quarterly performance reports or normal meetings. These calls may indicate nervousness about the market or indicate a change in personal circumstance. A single call is not necessarily cause for concluding that a change is appropriate. A series of calls may be. If you hear the phrase "I can't sleep at night" or "I am up all night worrying about this market," that is usually a red flag to review where you are. Sometimes the expression may be used as a colloquialism when the client is not that concerned.
- A change in health or family situation. Clients react to change differently, based on their own values and view of the world. However, when there is news of a significant personal or family change, it needs to be factored into the rep's ongoing view of that client's risk assessment.
- Without warning, the client's spouse may start calling in offering new information about the client's health or well-being.
- Relatives start expressing a great interest in the client's assets.
- The client confides to staff members or advisory board members complaints about the service that he or she is reluctant to directly address to the rep.

"Let's Talk Through and Clarify Your Position"

When a client decides that he wants to make a major change in his portfolio, the rep needs to carefully consider the entire set of circumstances. The decision may be inconsistent with the client's long-term objectives and be driven by short-term emotion. It is possible that implementing the decision will be something that the client will come to regret.

It is imperative in these circumstances that the registered representative utilize the duality principle and help the client think the decision through. Here is a short example of a client who wants to sell in a down market: "I understand what you are saying, and your thinking. But I want to walk you through how this may turn out, so if you do go ahead, you have done so after having completely thought this through. It could be that three to six months from now this downward trend will have continued, and you will be happy that you did this. But it is also possible that the market may rally, and in three to six months, this decision will have cost you some significant value. It is my belief that you are properly situated for the long term of 7 to 10 years, which is what we have always discussed. It is your money, but whatever you do, I want to make sure I have advised you of the other side, so that if it does not turn out as you thought, you don't blame me for not having talked you out of it."

These discussions are among the most delicate that a financial services professional will have with clients. This is just an example. What is important is that you are presenting a balanced point of view and giving the client a perspective based on all your work together, and not just based on the feelings of the moment.

This discussion then becomes documented in a rep's notes and should become the subject of a follow-up e-mail or letter. Tom sends letters documenting client review meetings through the U.S. Postal Service for several reasons. First, he believes that it has a greater impact than an e-mail. People get e-mails all the time, which get deleted or forgotten. It is much rarer to get a personalized piece of mail. So, it has greater impact. In addition, he believes that in the event that there is a dispute as to whether a client received communication, greater weight is given to traditional mail than to e-mail—there are no spam filters for traditional mail.

When a Major Change Takes Place

When it is decided that there should be a major change in a client's portfolio, it is best to have a face-to-face meeting, if at all possible. This gives the client an additional opportunity to understand the level of seriousness involved, and also gives the rep the opportunity to make sure that the client understands the full implications. This gives another opportunity to review just what is being done, from both the upside and downside. Whatever decision is made is again reinforced through a follow-up letter.

Duality in Building a Practice

Building a practice is filled with what sometimes seem unsolvable dilemmas. These include:

- How do I grow by getting new clients while serving existing clients?
- How do I set high account minimums but cope with my fear of chasing business away?
- How do I hire, train, and manage people while also doing my core job?
- How do I acquire knowledge and get more credentials without hurting production?
- How do I bring a highly qualified rep into my business and protect myself from having him or her steal my clients?
- How do I take on the expense of investing in people, equipment, and facilities without the guarantee of future income?

These dilemmas have certain elements in common. One is that they contain duality and require your ability to understand both sides of the issue. Second is that they are problems others have had and have solved.

Entrepreneurs tend to be self-reliant, self-motivated people. By their nature, they are willing to take a risk and believe that they can live by the product of their talents. Along with that can come a sense of isolation, a feeling that they can't reach out to people and trust them. Ultimately, this can express itself as a sense of "terminal uniqueness"—that the particular combination of circumstances one faces is somehow unique in human history. Nothing could be further from the truth.

One of the best starting points to solve any problem is to believe that there is a solution. If you don't believe that, you will not be able to use your creativity and other resources to successfully solve it. Next is to realize that in most cases, others have faced and solved the very problem you are facing. So the next thing to do is to find out or figure out what someone else did with the problem you are facing.

Then you go into "entrepreneurial problem-solving mode." One of the most desirable qualities a person can have is that of being "solution focused" rather than "problem focused." Some people become experts at describing or defining the problem itself. They seem to take joy in expounding at great length and in living color about all the elements of the problem, and the dire consequences that will occur if it is not solved. While well meaning, they can contribute to a problem's becoming an unsolvable crisis. By obsessing about the problem itself, they (consciously or unconsciously) steer a group to do the equivalent of the driver who sees a large pothole up ahead and fixates on it. In one part of the mind is a desire to avoid it. But by staring at it, they lock in and drive right into it.

Duality teaches us that for every problem, there must be a solution. Become solution focused. Once you have defined the relevant parameters and elements of a problem, put your mind and creative energy toward solving it and bringing in other people who will help solve it.

Wanting It Both Ways

Reps can fall into their own little dilemmas, which become for them unsolvable problems. They may wish to:

- Earn more but don't want to have a written business plan or goals.
- Achieve more but don't want to invest in a coaching program.
- Grow more but not change what they are doing.
- Protect the clients they have but not go out and get new ones.
- Market for new business but not put in place systems to continuously improve their procedures and service.
- Be taken seriously by people as a top producer, or be seen as an individual on the way to big things, but have their main business e-mail address ending in yahoo.com, aol.com, msn.com, or peoplepc.com.

All of these issues are problems with a solution. All of them are problems that have been solved by others, some of whom have written books describing how to solve them. In order to continue to grow, both as a person and in business, it is helpful to understand duality and to commit to continued knowledge and maturity. With that will come growth of the business and an increasing sense of self-fulfillment.

One of the most famous written pieces on the subject of duality can be found in Ecclesiastes. One need not have any religious views to benefit from its wisdom:

For everything there is a season, and a time for every purpose under heaven:

A time to be born, and a time to die; a time to plant, and a time to pluck up that which is planted;

A time to kill, and a time to heal; a time to break down, and a time to build up;

A time to weep, and a time to laugh; a time to mourn, and a time to dance;

A time to cast away stones, and a time to gather stones together; a time to embrace, and a time to refrain from embracing;

A time to seek, and a time to lose; a time to keep, and a time to cast away;

A time to tear, and a time to sew; a time to keep silence, and a time to speak;

A time to love, and a time to hate; a time for war, and a time for peace.

Awareness

The Third Eye

"When the student is ready, the master appears."

—*Buddhist Proverb*

Four Olympic Gold Medals

Al Oerter is a permanent part of Olympic history and inarguably one of the greatest clutch performers in the history of modern athletics. He was the first person ever to win the same event in four consecutive Olympic Games. As a 20-year-old student who was attending Kansas University, he won the discus throw at the 1956 Melbourne Olympics on his first throw, a personal best and Olympic record. Four years later in Rome, he won again, setting another record, exceeding his previous throw by 10 feet.

Despite a severe rib cage injury, he won again in 1964 at the Tokyo Olympics. In Mexico City, in 1968, he confounded the experts by winning another gold medal and setting another

Olympic record. In three of his Olympics he set personal records. He was never favored by the sportswriters of his time to win in any of his four Olympic Games.

In describing why he was able to do this, Al explained, "I really think there were two reasons. The first was attitude. I never went to any Olympics with the goal of winning a gold medal or setting a record. My entire vision, and my complete focus in all of my training, was to get to the Olympics and, in that most important of all athletic competitions, do my absolute best. As a result of this attitude, I didn't feel the pressure to win. I had the attitude that it was the greatest thing in the world to be able to go out and compete. And I have told people many times, 'I feel bad for you if you don't understand how great it is to be out there competing with the best in the world.' I believe that athletes who don't understand this, not just in their minds, but also in their hearts, are missing something really important. I feel sorry for them."

Al also described what he thought of as the "technical" secret to his success. "I had this ability during a competition, when the stress is the highest, of somehow being able to see what I was doing, and make little minor corrections in technique. This was well before the days of videotape and digital cameras. So I had to do it on my own. The discus is an event in which any little quirk or tweak will throw you off. Guys would get into the ring, have a bad throw, and just be unable to correct what they were doing wrong. I almost thought of it as an out-of-body experience. It was almost as if I was hovering a few feet above and to the side watching myself throw" (John Brubaker interview, 1984).

There is perhaps no better description imaginable of the "Third Eye" concept. Individuals who work very hard to develop themselves, physically or artistically or in any endeavor, are able to draw on new and deeper levels of reserves. They find in the depths of their soul, through training, self-discipline, and effort new plateaus of energy, insight, and stamina.

How Do You Appear to Your Clients?

It is almost a parody. Turn on one of the many television programs that feature investment-oriented "talking heads." Some will be sane and intelligent. Others will appear loudmouthed and over the top. Some of these shows degenerate into towel-snapping behavior, where one self-proclaimed guru is trying to talk over another. How do you appear to your clients? Some sanity and humility will help make sure you do not remind them of the more extreme caricatures of these talking heads.

The Client-Centric Business

In the 1980s, management consulting guru Tom Peters astonished the business world with his book *In Search of Excellence* (New York: Warner Books, 1982). He examined companies that he considered to be at the top of their diverse, respective fields. One of the key common denominators of these innovators and market leaders was the ability to see their own businesses through the eyes of their customers. This is the business equivalent of the Third Eye.

Study virtually any successful business and you will find that the people leading the business have an acute and ongoing understanding of those they serve. ESPN is a classic in the media world. Watch the commercials in which ESPN promotes itself. They are uniquely tuned to a primarily, but not exclusively, male audience who are fanatical sports fans. Try this: Record one of their commercials and show it to someone who does not fit this description. They won't have the slightest idea what the commercial is about. But those who are in the "club" love them. ESPN has a genius at understanding its audience.

You will find that those people who have built large and successful practices similarly are uniquely attuned to their clients. This goes far beyond the requirements of NASD Rule 2310, which tells us to "Know Your Client." People who build highly successful financial services practices not only know the clients on an individual basis, but also are very aware of and often connected to the groups they belong to and circles in which they travel. Social circles have a type of often unwritten "code" in terms of how members recognize each other and even the language they use. The more you can become absorbed in knowing your clients and their circles, the stronger a relationship you can build with them.

If you want to transform your business, one of the surest ways to do it is to turn it into a client-centric business. Most of us feel we are already doing that, but there are often many levels beyond what we are currently doing. One of the most unpleasant things to do is to try and put yourself in the shoes of your clients and see the "movie" that they see when they interact with your business. It is a strange quirk of human nature that we can easily spot the flaws in others but have blind spots toward our own. Have you ever known someone who, it seemed, every time you met, had spilled something on his shirt? Yet, he may as well have been totally blind to this little quirk and thus unable to correct it. Businesses are the same way. Unless you are willing to expose yourself to the short-term pain of really looking at what you don't do well, you are nearly doomed to keep making the same mistakes.

In taking this type of inventory, you want to see your business not only at its best, but also at its worst. Use whatever issues you may have in service or operations to try and literally see and feel how the customer feels. Then put into place systems and policies that can prevent such problems in the future. This is an organic and never-ending process.

For years, financial services practices were marketed on the basis of access to unique or especially valuable products. In the twenty-first century, with so many products that are so readily available and contain any feature imaginable, this does not represent for a registered representative a truly unique selling proposition. So, differentiation and distinction can come from a different source, emphasizing the uniqueness of process instead of products.

The Three-Meeting Rule

Tom Hine has adapted some of the tools from his years of experience and also from various coaching programs to create an extremely client-focused system at Capital Wealth Management, LLC. No individual can become a client without having three meetings. This single feature is itself somewhat unique. Often, financial advisers are known for coming in too early in a process and trying to "close a sale" and get the prospect to begin turning over assets. Tom's system, when properly implemented, eliminates a prospect's sense of being "rushed." And, of course, the meetings themselves take place over time, on a schedule that the prospect establishes. This is explained in a flowchart, entitled "The Meeting Process at Capital Wealth Management, LLC" (see Figure 11.1).

Fact-Finding Meeting

The process begins with a "fact find" form, which is filled out by a prospective client and returned to the firm. This 17-page form includes basic information about the client's background, circumstances, and objectives. This is followed up by a "balanced wealth introduction meeting," in which Tom or one of his advisers uses a large board to walk the client through the Balanced Wealth Process™.

This meeting covers a wide range of personal and professional topics. The system is completely flexible, and is shaped to meet the unique background and needs of the prospective client. Tom or one of his advisers takes notes on each of those areas, and also lets the prospective client know more about Capital Wealth Management, LLC, and the way in which they conduct business. The "Meeting Process at Capital Wealth Management, LLC" is explained in detail. Through this process, Tom or one of his advis-

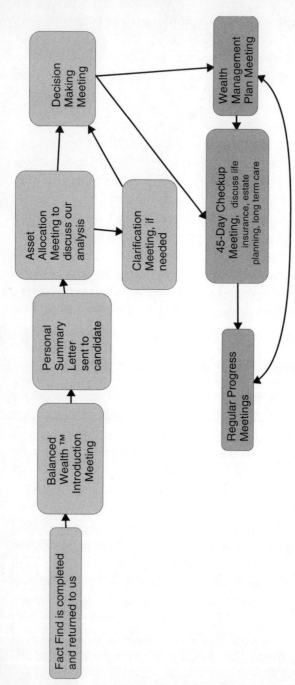

Figure 11.1   Becoming a Client at Capital Wealth Management, LLC
Source: Capital Wealth Management, LLC.

ers gets to know the client, and the client gets to know the adviser, without the pressure of worrying about making a commitment in terms of investing.

The notes from that meeting are then inputted by the staff through software into a Balanced Wealth Profile™, which is reviewed, finalized, and then sent to the prospective client, along with a letter that summarizes the main points of the meeting. Tom uses Copytalk to dictate those memos right after the meeting. Tom first got this idea from Ron Carson in the PEAK Productions coaching program, and has used this service since 2002. The return memos are then refined, turned into a letter, reviewed, finalized, and sent as part of the package to the individual. Assuming that there is continued interest in taking the next step, Tom and his staff put together a proposed investment plan, and schedule a meeting, if it has not already been done.

Asset Allocation Meeting

At this meeting, which is scheduled based on the client's timetable, the proposed investment plan is presented and discussed. Based on feedback from that meeting or other subsequent communication, the plan can be modified. If necessary, a clarification meeting is held. Based on the client's interest, the next meeting is a decision-making meeting.

Decision-Making Meeting

This is the meeting at which a prospect becomes a client. It is described as a decision making because there are two important decisions made. The first is by the client who has decided to commit a certain level of investable assets for the firm to manage. The second is the series of commitments that the firm makes to the client in terms of the process going forward, including multiple methods of communication and the opportunity for the client to, at any stage, ask questions and receive assistance.

It is clear that this meeting is really the first formal step in becoming a client at Capital Wealth Management, LLC. There is a scheduled 45-day follow-up meeting to discuss life insurance, estate planning, and long-term care. There are additional wealth management plan meetings, regular progress meetings, and wealth management network meetings. The entire system is designed to provide maximum support to the client as well as a strong feeling of control and predictability.

A Robust System of Support and Activities

Beyond this formal structure that applies to each client, Tom has a robust system of activities and events that provide further opportunities for clients to interact with the business and to get feedback. He says, "In doing the right thing for clients, you can't go too far today. We constantly try to update clients in several different formats, and we add new ideas every year." Here is a sample of activities at Capital Wealth Management, LLC, many of which are being used at other financial services practices:

- Client phone appointments when needed.
- Client office appointments when needed.
- Ad hoc calls that come in.
- Two client seminars each year. The fall seminar is a client educational event that features a speaker or a theme (such as "long-term care"). Topics are chosen from client feedback (such as the client advisory board), which is solicited as part of the preparation. The spring seminar is a client appreciation event.
- Client conference calls.
- Client web site. This allows clients to access their account values. It also includes a financial calculator, links to other financial web sites, and a calendar of events.
- Client e-zine. This is a biweekly electronic magazine, produced by a staff member. A master schedule is prepared 12 months in advance of topics. Articles of interest are identified, and permission is secured to electronically reprint them.

- Biweekly market commentary, which is included with the client e-zine (thanks to Ron Carson of PEAK Productions for this idea).
- Client advisory board. This is comprised of four to five couples who serve on a volunteer basis. Couples are rotated out after a term of 24 months. All clients are encouraged to communicate concerns to the board. The board meets twice annually and advises the company on service issues, and provides recommendations on how to better serve the clients. They are recognized at client events and with an annual dinner. Board members are considered by some clients to be easier to approach, giving the company feedback it might not otherwise receive.
- Periodic client surveys.
- Birthday and anniversary cards.
- Periodic mailings of deadlines and announcements.

The Yin and Yang of Rule 2310

"Know Your Client" is a fundamental of this business. But it goes beyond being able to recite how many children a client has, what clubs they belong to, or the names of their pets. At a deeper level, it involves understanding them, and yourself, so well that you are aware of concerns they might have about changes in their lives or their assets, as well as how they will react when you do something. Tom tells this story:

> Whenever there is a bit of a market freefall, I am used to getting calls from nervous clients. In fact, I am pretty good at knowing just who they will come from and when. So one day I decided to get proactive. We were in a bit of a market fall-off, so I went ahead and called some of my clients—before they called me. I received different reactions. Many of the clients later thanked me for going the extra mile and thinking about them. But, notably, a few of them told me, "You know, I wasn't nervous at all until you called. Then I

started getting nervous. I figured you wouldn't call unless there was really something to worry about!"

Awareness of the Industry

If all you ever do is focus on clients, you will know them quite well but may run the risk of not providing them with the best advice possible. So, another aspect of awareness is being a true "lifetime learner" with regard to financial services, products, and trends. We live in an age in which there are many venues for the continued development of this knowledge. As you develop this knowledge, it builds upon itself and becomes part of the repository of experience, which is a large part of what your clients pay you for.

Going Against the Grain

Sometimes awareness will help you make a decision that is counter to conventional wisdom. Tom tells this story:

> During the recent bear market, many advisers stuck to their guns and kept clients invested for the long haul, as they had been told to do. But I diverted here, and when it came to proactive management, I rebalanced many of my clients into bond funds and bear funds in 2001–2003. Sometimes you have to break with tradition and do what your gut instinct tells you is right, even though you face a lot of opposition at the time. I did rebalance clients back into the market in late 2002 and early 2003, and I may never do this again in my lifetime, but at the time I am glad I did what I did to protect client accounts.

All clients have their own unique circumstances and personalities. If we know them as well as we should, we will be able to make the occasional intuitive decision that is the right one. Tom says:

I had a client who was going through some financial challenges and needed more income, yet did not want to risk the principal of the investment account. This particular client had panicked and gone to cash earlier in the year. When it came time for me to present a variable annuity with a guaranteed minimum withdrawal rider (GMWB)—a clearly good sale at the right time—my gut instinct told me that this client would love this product when things worked. But if things did not work out, and another down market occurred, they would not be happy with the lack of liquidity and other restrictions. So the money was left in cash in a brokerage account temporarily, rather than tie some of it up in a variable annuity, even though the annuity was otherwise the appropriate decision.

The Challenge

Developing a dynamic, client-centric business that provides outstanding service and expert analysis is the challenge that all of us who have financial services practices face. By continuing to grow in knowing your clients, in your knowledge of investments, in your analytical ability, and in your self-knowledge, you are on the road to better service and more dedicated clients. Increasing awareness is a daily challenge and opportunity.

Every phase of evolution commences by being in a state of unstable force and proceeds through organization to equilibrium. Equilibrium having been achieved, no further development is possible without once again setting out on a journey of a thousand miles, which begins with the next single step which lies at your feet.

—William James

Dedication

Kaizen

"When you aim high, you hit high."

—*Henry H. Hine*

The four previous principles in the Cycle of Life involved what is in your soul (humility, integrity), your mind (duality), and your five senses (awareness). Kaizen is about what is in your heart. It includes vision, passion, courage, and a relentless desire to excel, to take the next step toward an impossible goal that you know you will never reach. It is the driving force that, over the course of a lifetime, makes the difference between merely marking time and having a lasting impact.

Kaizen in Japanese means "change for the better" or "improvement." In the second half of the twentieth century, the term *Kaizen* came to be associated with efforts to improve industrial and workplace productivity. After World War II, many of the leaders of Japan put their minds to mastering the possibilities of

189

improving industrial production. Out of this came the ground-breaking work of such individuals as W. Edwards Deming, considered by many to be the father of the quality management movement, and Frederick Taylor, whose name became synonymous with manufacturing efficiency.

In twenty-first-century business, *Kaizen* refers to discrete events, often within manufacturing environments, in which a selected multidisciplinary team is given the task, under an aggressive deadline, of working together to reinvent processes that will yield ambitious, measurable standards of productivity. Together, they examine every process and procedure involved in a production task. They tear it apart and put it back together again. After the Kaizen "event," the new processes are, hopefully, implemented across the organization.

Continuous improvement is the core philosophy that drives many quality management programs. The concept is that it is possible, and should be required, to have a continuously improving level of measurable performance, in virtually all areas of an organization. What began as a manufacturing initiative has become adapted to organizations of all kinds. The key is to establish metrics, analyze and improve processes, eliminate waste, and drive productivity improvements.

In the martial arts world, Kaizen is a spirit—the spirit of a true warrior, who does not train in order to defeat others in battle, but rather to improve himself or herself toward a state of perfection that is unobtainable. It is the force that drives a martial artist to train to exhaustion, and then train some more. It is the power that enables people to dream a seemingly impossible dream, and then have the fortitude to make it come about. It is a combination of imagination and persistence—a vision of what is possible, backed by a relentless drive to fulfill the vision.

Kaizen is found in inventors, entrepreneurs, and athletes. Michael Jordan became famous for his feats of basketball wizardry and his indomitable spirit to win. But part of his legend is that he didn't even make his eighth-grade basketball team. How many times have you heard people talk about the "crushing defeat" they experienced in life that became a defining moment. Kaizen is a type of spiritual energy that believes that no setback is final. It is embodied in Winston Churchill's thought that "Victory is never final, defeat is never fatal—in the end it is courage that counts."

Motivational guru Anthony Robbins says that high achievers who become the benefactors of mankind often possess what he calls a degree of "unreasonableness"—a stubbornness that refuses to accept defeat. He talks of the "unreasonableness" of the Wright brothers in their belief in the possibility of flight, which today is the aviation industry.

Thomas Edison is remembered for his inventive genius. However, without Kaizen, an indomitable spirit of persistence, his raw intellectual capability might never have borne the fruit of so many inventions that are now part of daily living. Edison carefully catalogued his experiments.

Motivational speaker Zig Ziglar tells the story about a newspaper reporter who came to interview Edison as he was approaching his ten thousandth unsuccessful experiment to invent an incandescent light bulb. The reporter asked Edison, "How does it feel to have failed 10,000 times to invent an electric light bulb? Edison is reported to have said, "You are a young man, with a lot to learn. I have not failed 10,000 times. I have successfully found 10,000 ways which do not work." Ziglar tells that history records Edison "failed" 4,000 more times before finding the one way that works. A thoroughly "unreasonable" person, and we all are the beneficiaries of his unreasonableness.

As the world prepared to celebrate the new millennium, all sorts of lists were made about the twentieth century: greatest athletes, greatest actors and actresses, greatest businesspeople, and so on. On virtually all of the lists in the field of popular music, at or near the top was John Lennon's song "Imagine," despite the fact that there dozens of other songs that achieved far greater commercial success. "Imagine" represented to people a hopefulness—a sense of possibility, of what could be in the future.

What are you "unreasonable" about? What would you like your life and professional work to stand for? Part of the Ron Carson system of goal setting involves the "epitaph" question. Carson encourages people to sit down and write their own epitaph—the one they would like. What do you want your life to stand for? What would you like to leave behind?

The greatest tragedy, on a personal level, is for a person to go to his grave with "his best music still in him." We are fortunate to be alive at a time and place when it is more possible than it ever has been to take an idea, a vision, a hope, and turn it into reality. In the twenty-first century, ideas have more power than at any time in human history. Look at the story of Google—an idea, a vision, a rather simple one, which has become a regular part of many of our daily lives and even our vocabulary. The founders of Google.com have turned a noun into a verb.

One of the most effective ways by which you can tap into the power of your own idealism in creating an outstanding financial services practice and a life of fulfillment is through the self-development made possible through coaching programs.

As this book is being completed in May 2007, Tom Hine is simultaneously in three coaching programs. He believes that the investment he makes in his coaching programs is perhaps the biggest bargain in the business today. Tom has said on many occasions that perhaps 50 percent of the new ideas he has gotten that have helped him build Capital Wealth Management, LLC, from inception to $1.5 million in annual revenue come either from the programs themselves or from people he has met while in the programs. The opportunity to spend time with other high-energy, goal-oriented achievers is in itself a major plus. As is often said at these programs, "More is caught than taught." Everyone in the profession has the opportunity, if they choose, to be part of a good coaching program.

Quest for Excellence™: PEAK Productions

Quest for Excellence™, the coaching program offered by PEAK Productions (www.joinpeak.com), was developed by Ron Carson and his partner Steve Sanduski. It teaches the methods used by Ron Carson to build a $7 million a year business. Ron has been the number one producer for Linsco/Private Ledger, the largest independent broker-dealer firm in the country, for more than 16 consecutive years. As Tom says:

> When I first started the program, what hit me hardest was the power of Ron Carson's example. Ron truly has developed ideas and, as he likes to say, "tested them in the trenches." Our business is so competitive, and it amazed me that someone who developed these great ideas and systems then turned around is willing to share it with people all over the country, people who arguably are Ron's competitors. Ron is really open—he tells what he did right and what he did wrong. For someone who has such phenomenal production, I have found him to be genuinely humble and approachable. What I have found is that nothing makes Ron or Steve happier than to hear of someone adapting the ideas they learned in this program, and achieving new levels of success and fulfillment.

The two areas that Tom first learned in the Quest for Excellence™ program, and then successfully implemented to build Capital Wealth Management, LLC, are systematization and account minimums. The coaching program describes in detail the systems for marketing, operations, and client service. Tom credits this and the insight he gained on how to successfully overcome his own fears and natural resistance to implementing account minimums as major contributors to his career.

Strategic Coach

In August 2004, after having been in PEAK Productions for two years, Tom enrolled in Strategic Coach. Whereas PEAK Productions is very grounded in the day-to-day nuts and bolts of the business, Strategic Coach gives the "30,000-foot view." Strategic Coach is composed primarily, but not exclusively, of individuals in the financial services industry. Approximately 60 percent of its participants are in the financial services industry. However, it includes entrepreneurs and other individuals with high-end professional practices.

Participants in Strategic Coach are grouped by earning power, which means that individuals are spending their meeting time sharing challenges and solutions with other individuals at their level. Through increased performance, individuals can move to the next level.

One of the greatest benefits of participating in a coaching program is to spend time with others who have achieved as much and, in many cases, more than you have. Tom tells the story of his first Strategic Coach meeting:

> I flew into Chicago and got in ahead of time. I was very psyched to meet the other people. I was in with the group who had a gross income of $1 million or more. I was at a table of eight. We were casually dressed, and it was very relaxed. People started introducing themselves to each other, asking each other, "Did you fly in?" I said that I had. Then, as the conversation went around the table, I realized that five of the eight people had flown their own planes to the meeting. I felt like I was the guy in Section 8 housing. At another meeting, I remember speaking with someone who built a business and was worth $15 million. I asked him how he chose his financial adviser. It is amazing how approachable these people are.

One of the great benefits of Strategic Coach is that participants have access to the intellectual incubators in the industry and get a glimpse into the emerging issues, trends, and the leaders who will help drive the industry into the future.

Tom says, "Strategic Coach has phenomenal tools. I come away from every meeting with my mind buzzing with new ideas. In fact, the challenge has been to resist the temptation to come back from a meeting and just start changing everything based on what I just heard. We are encouraged to make change slowly, like a golfer with his swing."

Tom first got the idea to try and write a book at a Strategic Coach meeting. He says, "The famous author David Bach was a member of Strategic Coach. I briefly met him once. I started hearing what he did and said, 'Why can't I try and figure out how to write a book?'" Tom believes that without being in Strategic Coach, this book would never have been attempted. Tom remains in this program on an ongoing basis.

Ultimately, Kaizen is not just a concept. It is a driving force—a life force. It suggests to us that reward is impossible without risk, and that the courage to put forth best effort is, in itself, a type of reward. These ideas were captured in Theodore Roosevelt's remarkable speech, which has often been excerpted under the heading "The Man in the Arena." Roosevelt gave this speech at a time when one gender predominated. Clearly, his ideas belong to all of humankind:

> It is not the critic who counts; not those who point out how the strong have stumbled, or where the doer of deeds could have done them better. The credit belongs to the man who is actually in the arena, whose face is marred by dust and sweat and blood. Who strives valiantly. Who errs and comes short again and again, because there is no effort without error and shortcoming. But who actually strives to do the deeds. Who knows the great enthusiasms, the great devotions. Who spends himself in a worthy cause. Who at the best knows in the end the triumph of high achievement. And

who at the worst, if he fails, at least fails while daring greatly. So that his place shall never be with those cold and timid souls who neither know victory nor defeat.

**—Theodore Roosevelt, "Citizenship in a Republic,"
speech at the Sorbonne, Paris, April 23, 1910**

HOW TO PREVAIL IN AN NASD ARBITRATION HEARING

What's the Cost?

N ASD arbitration is extremely costly to the rep, even one who achieves the best possible outcome. There are 10 categories to consider.

Time

Time is a major category, under which there are six subcategories:

1. ***Time to research the case and prepare a summary for the attorney(s).*** This is not as easy at is sounds. It involves a thorough review of extensive electronic and paper documentation: all disclosure forms, notes of meetings, correspondence

with the client, and any interaction between the client and staff. Because it is essential that the rep form the strongest possible foundation and become an expert in his or her own case, this is not an activity that should be delegated to others.

2. *Time spent with the attorney(s) preparing the case.* In order to fully prepare for hearings, a rep will want to have several face-to-face meetings with the attorney. This will also involve time to prepare for those meetings, including travel time.

3. *"Extra credit" research projects.* A rep who is committed to a total effort will often conduct additional research, which may be to gain additional information about the complainant or to consult additional outside professionals for their expertise.

4. *Added staff time.* It is a sound practice not to have arbitration preparation cut into normal client acquisition and service time. Many reps will have their staff work overtime to prepare for the arbitration. This may involve organizing charts and graphs, which can be invaluable in a hearing.

5. *Trial time.* Arbitrations can take several days of testimony time. If the hearing goes to three days or beyond, rarely will those three days be consecutively. Often, they are spread out over many months. Each hearing date requires preparation time, as well as time for analysis and additional research on issues that have come up in testimony. Days leading up to hearing dates ("ramp-up time") are often heavily dominated by preparation. On days subsequent to a hearing date ("ramp-down time"), many reps report staying in "full trial mode," responding to issues that have come up and tracking information down for the attorney.

6. *Additional client time.* Being in arbitration can change the way a rep views his or her normal business activities. Many report a heightened awareness of "what could go wrong" in working with clients, and being gun shy about making recommendations, which would be part of a normal business process. One said, "I started picking apart what my prospec-

tive clients were saying, and asking myself, 'Is this someone who might sue me?'"

Money

As with time, there are costs that are both obvious and subtle. There are seven subcategories of financial cost of arbitration:

1. *Errors-and-omissions insurance deductible.* This is the amount the rep has to pay to the errors-and-omissions carrier at the start of the case. Deductibles used to be as low as $500. As of March 2007 they are as high as $40,000. Given current trends, it would not be surprising to see the deductible going to $50,000. Notably, this deductible is *not* refunded in the event that no arbitration award is given from a full hearing. It simply underwrites the cost of the legal defense.

2. *Staff overtime.* This pays for evening and weekend work that is part of the case preparation, especially organizing charts.

3. *Travel costs.* These can involve traveling to see the attorney as well as the hearings themselves. This can include overnight stays, meaning that there are hotel, parking, and dining expenses.

4. *NASD filing fees.* No matter what the outcome of the case, the rep has significant filing fees, which can total $4,000 or more.

5. *Additional professional services.* Some reps hire a backup attorney and/or additional expert professionals, which are out-of-pocket expenses.

6. *Side settlement.* At any point in the process, there is the possibility of the two sides in an arbitration settling any part of the contested claim and, in effect, "taking it off the board." This means the panel will not consider it as part of their deliberations after the hearings have been completed. Taking advantage of this, to improve the chance of no award or a small award, can cost several thousand dollars.

7. *Opportunity cost.* This is an assessment of what type of income one would have been able to generate without the arbitration process. This can include the loss of new clients who might have been acquired with the time, self-confidence damage, and a curbing of some of the normal business practices (such as selling a certain type of product) out of fear.

Emotional Stress

Many reps report that by far the most damaging aspect of the process personally is the emotional stress, strain, and resulting loss of confidence. This can include a sense of being wronged, angst over what might have done to prevent the claim from being filed, anger at the system itself, a feeling of shock at the inflammatory and accusatory language of the Statement of Claim, anxiety about the possibility that an award will exceed the carrier's limits, and worry about how the process will affect the rep's personal and professional future. Some report receiving medication to help cope with the stress and sleeplessness.

Client and Prospect Relationships

With the amount of press coverage of investor lawsuits, highlighted by big-dollar payouts, clients and prospects are more prone than ever to ask a rep about his or her record. Often, they may not know the terminology, but they might ask, "Have you ever been censured?" Others are more sophisticated. U-4 issues hang like a shadow, threatening to damage the rep in a number of ways, including relationships with existing clients. One topproducing rep tells of a prospect with multiple millions of dollars of investable assets who asked if the rep would be willing, during an exploratory meeting, to go onto the web and show his NASD record. He did so, and the fact that it was completely clean allowed the discussion to move forward.

Heightened Supervision

This is one of the more subtle costs. During an arbitration, or after completing one in which there is any award or a settlement of $10,000 or more, reps are subject to increased scrutiny on their trades, on new account forms, and on all product lines. They are at a higher risk of an audit from their broker-dealer firm. Some outside licenses and certifications (such as CFP) may require that you submit reports of the progress of your NASD arbitration and its conclusion. This extra pressure can undermine the confidence of the rep, as well as the morale of his or her staff.

Restricted Broker-Dealer Movement

When a rep leaves a broker-dealer, a notation is made on his or her U-5 form. If the separation was voluntary, there should be no negative consequences on your career. However, if it was "for cause," it will make it difficult, if not impossible, to secure a relationship with another broker-dealer. With an ongoing arbitration on your record, it is safe to assume that most broker-dealers will want a full description of the charges involved and your defense for them. A broker-dealer firm may be reluctant to start a relationship with a rep who has an arbitration ongoing, no matter what the facts of the case.

New Product Appointments Slowed Down

Most product applications for reps involve questionnaires that include a broadly worded question along the lines of "Are you, or have you ever been, under any investigative proceeding?" If your case is ongoing, you must answer "Yes" to be truthful. This can substantially slow up new product appointments or approvals.

One rep reported an incident that took place while he was in the middle of an arbitration proceeding, which he eventually won (no award). He had a client who desired a $5 million life insurance policy. Due to some of the specifics of the client's background, the rep determined that the best outcome would be obtained by working through a third-party adviser. Because of his pending arbitration case, his appointment for this product was held up, and the client pulled the case. This rep has never done business with this third-party adviser since. He felt that the "guilty until proven innocent" philosophy was totally unjustified.

Outside Business Dealings

Arbitrations fall under the broad definition of "legal proceedings" for the purposes of a wide range of business activities. These might include renting office space, applying for commercial credit, forming new relationships with centers of influence (such as CPAs or attorneys), or selling or buying a practice.

Prospecting, Sales, and Recruiting Staff Members

It is an axiom of sales that the most difficult objection to answer is the one that doesn't come up. Reps spend significant time over a period of months, if not years, and fail to land certain potential clients. In some cases, it may be that a prospect checked your NASD record under "NASD Broker Check" and didn't tell you about it. If you are currently involved in an arbitration, that fact will be available. If you have had an award or a settlement in excess of $10,000, that information will also be available.

As many reps mature in the profession, they begin to implement account minimums and raise those minimums over time. It is reasonable to assume that as you approach clients with larger portfolios, they will take more care in investigating your background prior to deciding to work with you. One rep reports that right after his successful arbitration hearing (no award), he met a client with a $5 million portfolio of investable assets. The first question he was asked was "Do you have a clean record?" The answer was "Yes," and the discussions have continued for more than a year.

This same principle can apply to recruiting top staff talent. Reps report having had some of their top prospective hires utilize NASD BrokerCheck as part of their own due diligence before making a decision to accept an employment offer from a firm. One rep reports having brought in a new associate, who told him, "I was impressed that you were a $1 million producer with a completely clean U-4." As with prospects, U-4 issues can create a taint with staff that cannot be erased, and the damage from which can never be fully known.

Groupthink—Viral Contagion

Attorneys for complainants in investor suits use a type of "reverse affinity marketing," encouraging complainants to recruit other complainants to file. As many reps use referrals as a major lead source, this can backfire with one unhappy client. This can create a herd mentality, which can spread like wildfire throughout a rep's client base. The damage caused by one unhappy client can increase exponentially in the hands of an aggressive attorney. There are reports of some plaintiff attorneys taking out local advertisements that specifically say, "If you worked with (Broker X), you may have a case to recover your market losses."

Calculating Damages

In Tom's case, which was detailed in Part One, the legal fees paid by the insurance carrier came to approximately $50,000. Tom bore additional direct out-of-pocket costs of more than $30,000. This included filing fees, other NASD fees assessed after the decision, added attorney fees, staff overtime, and travel costs. In addition, Tom estimated that a reasonable application of an hourly evaluation of the worth of his time, cost him another $50,000 in lost income. So, without any additional calculation for emotional stress and subtle costs, a relatively simple case that was completed with no award to the claimant had a total economic cost of $130,000.

Case Studies

Part One told the story of Tom Hine's arbitration case, from beginning to end. Here are interviews from four other registered representatives who went through arbitrations. Each story, told in the actual words of these reps, contains its own unique lessons.

Case 1

"With my career on the line in a multimillion-dollar investor suit, one of the arbitrators fell asleep at the hearing."

—A Top-Producing Midwestern Rep

I have been in the business for more than 20 years, and it has been fantastic to me. My staff and I have built a lot of wonderful long-term relationships with our clients. Our company often has a feel to it of an extended family. We genuinely love working with our clients and helping them to achieve their goals in an uncertain and ever-changing world.

I had one experience with arbitration and to this day it still has an almost surreal quality to it. I received a call in January 2000, right at the height of the bull market. This prospect had significant stock options in a booming tech company, which was the rage of the Midwest at that time.

We met in March on an exploratory basis—a fact-finding mission. At the time, that stock was trading at $128 a share. Counting the stock options, he had investable assets in excess of $20 million. At the time he called me, his portfolio had reached the point where it was just sufficient to provide him with the income he believed he needed to have. But he had gotten greedy.

Right off the bat he told me, "Don't even talk to me about selling any of it—this stock is going to $200 a share." He had high-growth-market fever. I told him that he ought to consider a hedge strategy, or at least be open to looking at it. At this point, he still was a prospect—these were preliminary discussions.

As happens with many prospective clients, it was hard to get him to commit to coming in and sitting down with us. He kept doing the "potential client dance." I had put together a proposed financial plan for him, but I couldn't get him and his wife to come in to the office and discuss it. The stock started to plummet. It went down to $73 a share. I wrote him a letter, which stated, "I strongly recommend you diversify," and I suggested a number of possible ways to do this. We had a number of phone calls during this period in which I continued to recommend he consider selling the stock. All calls were well documented.

By the time he decided to bring his assets under my firm's management, the stock was down to $28 a share. I worked with him to make the best of the situation, which obviously had deteriorated in the tech bubble burst. It was, by that time, a familiar story. He was one of probably millions of unhappy investors who had seen a big decline in their portfolio value.

Two years later, out of the blue, I was attending a major sporting event and I got served with a complaint by an attorney for this client, asking for damages in the amount of $14 million. Incredibly, they wanted the differential between the stock at its highest price and its lowest. He wasn't even a client for the majority of the time the stock value went down. It was absurd but frightening. If they were awarded the full amount, it would have exceeded the errors-and-omissions (E&O) carrier's per-claim limit by $5 million, an amount for which I would have been personally liable. It was clear—they were shooting for the moon and planning to take no prisoners along the way.

The E&O carrier told me that they felt the client had no legitimate claim, but that in cases with this level of exposure it was often a common practice to negotiate some settlement "to get it to go away." Just the magnitude of the claim gave it a credibility that the facts didn't support. Imagine the discovery on a $14 million lawsuit. We got estimates of $700,000 for legal fees. With this much money at stake, expert witnesses come out of the closet.

It was a nightmare. I started to think about what was about to unfold. I figured they would fish through every client I had. I could imagine an attorney out there making presentations to all of my clients, sniffing for anything they could use in a trial.

Well, the case went ahead. My former client played the "unsophisticated investor" role, something I now know is very common in these cases. One of his outrageous prehearing claims that came out in discovery was that he had never received multiple e-mails, which I had sent him. I knew he was lying about this.

Our preparation was very thorough. Our research had uncovered that my accuser was a beneficiary of a trust that he hadn't disclosed, increasing his actual net worth by well over eight figures. As part of our discovery, we subpoenaed his computer files and obtained a completed copy of his hard drive. We paid a forensic technology specialist. He was able to recover those e-mails, which had been received, but had been erased from the drive. This guy was really playing hardball. This was criminal activity as far as I was concerned.

The hearing went on for more than a year, and it was incredibly stressful. There were all kinds of delays, lawyer games. I hated it. When we presented our smoking gun, I felt that at least one of the arbitrators was receptive, but the head arbitrator wasn't showing his hand at all. With my career on the line, the third panel member, a public arbitrator, fell asleep during the hearings.

When the hearings ended, my attorney and I felt we had won hands down. A few months later we got the panel's decision. They awarded my accuser $50,000, a number that had no rhyme, reason, or justification whatsoever. It was almost as if they were rewarding him for filing a claim of that size—a terrible message to send to reps and other investors.

Before this all happened, my record keeping was excellent. Now it is beyond excellent. I took some additional steps with the purpose of making sure nothing like this ever happens to me again.

Case 2

"If a client was ever going to sue me, I was afraid this would be the one."

—A Top-Producing New England Rep

I have heard that even the most ethical and careful rep stands a decent chance of having at least one client sue them at some point in their career. It is a type of occupational hazard. In my sixteenth year in the business, I went through an NASD arbitration. I fervently hope it is the last such experience of my career.

I have always had a little unease about clients who start working with me when the equities markets are roaring. It has a feeling of a problem waiting to happen. I had a client come to see me for the first time in early 1999. He was in his early 50s and contemplating an early retirement from his employer of 30 years. The company had offered him a buyout with one year's severance, and the rates for medical benefits would be locked in for his lifetime. In many ways, it was an easy decision for him to accept their package, find other employment for several years, and bridge into retirement.

At the time, he had approximately $750,000 in assets, comprised of $200,000 in certificates of deposit (CDs), which he didn't want me to touch, and $550,000 in a lump-sum distribution, which he wanted me to invest. He came into my office with reams of information about stocks. He had been an investor for years on his own, but wanted an adviser to help him as he made this career shift.

After going through my due diligence, and understanding his goals and risk tolerance, I constructed a portfolio for the $550,000, which met with his approval, comprised of approximately 70 percent stocks and 30 percent fixed income. The equities markets started to drop. I told him it was okay to change course, but he assured me he was fine, committed to long-term investment. The freefall continued. Then 9/11 hit, and it got even worse. It was a very scary time for a lot of people—falling markets, anthrax, governance scandals, and global uncertainty.

In the spring of 2002, he called me and said, "I have to get out." He was down a couple of hundred thousand dollars at this point. I could feel his angst, but I tried to convince him to hang on. We went through this for three days in a row. I said, "History tells us that the markets will come back. But if you are sure this is what you want to do, then go ahead." He sold out and within a few months we were no longer working together.

Three months later, I received a demand letter from him, asking for restoration of his lost assets. It was written with such a level of sophistication that I was sure an attorney had drafted it. He calculated his losses two different ways and gave me two options—a choice between $250,000 in damages or $500,000. I notified the broker-dealer and was told that they would handle the case on their own until further notice.

I can't say I was shocked. I knew it was a big mistake for him to sell out at the bottom, but it was his decision. When I told my wife about it, I said, "If a client was ever going to sue me, I was afraid this would be the one."

The case went quiet for more than 18 months. In March 2004, I received his Statement of Claim. He had filed with the NASD for arbitration. There was an additional element, caused by the broker-dealer firm's delay in having notified the errors-and-omissions carrier of the dispute. They had let a deadline pass, which meant under the terms of the policy, they were not required to provide coverage. It was agonizing, in that it would have been a simple matter for me to make that phone call as soon as I received the demand letter.

This meant that I had to fund my own legal defense, with the possibility that I might be able to recover the expenses after the case was resolved. In addition, it was uncertain whether or not I was legally exposed for the settlement or award, if there was one. This dramatically increased my anxiety level on what was already a highly stressful situation.

I got very practical and started working with my attorney to prepare my case. The whole specter of the thing was really daunting. I felt I had to fully fund a very vigorous legal defense, because if I didn't and lost I would forever regret it. But these are real dollars you are spending, tens of thousands of dollars plus the NASD fees.

As the case proceeded, I was amazed at how tilted the system is to the complainant. The other side kept missing deadlines, with no negative consequences. It seemed to me like a scheme to try and pressure me into a settlement. I held firm. I had impeccable documentation of the entire relationship and I believed strongly that I had provably exceeded the standard of care required.

At the hearing, my former client tried to paint himself as very simplistic in financial matters, despite his years of experience as an investor. One of the most important parts of my defense was the fact that he had the $200,000 in CDs, which in the overall scheme of things offset the risk element of the equities. Including the CDs, he in actuality had a 60/40 portfolio, not 70/30. I made the point as strongly as I could in the hearing, but the other side challenged it. I had no idea what the arbitrator thought.

One of the really bizarre elements of the case was the behavior of the opposing attorney, who was a professional acquaintance. Prior to the start of the hearing, he went out of his way to be overtly friendly to me, asking about my family, wishing me well in the hearing. I couldn't believe it. This was the same guy who had written a scathing indictment of my professional behavior and was going full speed ahead on a lawsuit for half a million dollars!

Before the hearing, he treated me as if we were long-lost college roommates meeting at a reunion. Once the hearing started, it was like someone had flipped a switch and he became a fevered, passionate, indignant, hard-edged legal advocate. I wondered at what type of personality would permit this type of Jekyll and Hyde behavior. It seemed amazingly manipulative to me.

We had competing expert witnesses. I had prepared an analysis of what would have happened had he followed my advice and held on to the investments, and it turned out that within three years, he would have recovered virtually all of the value of his portfolio. When the hearing was over, I was emotionally and intellectually drained, with no idea of how it would turn out.

I waited and waited for the decision. It was like a ticking time bomb in the back of my mind at all times. The news finally came without warning—a call from my office to call the attorney. I knew it had to be the news I was waiting for. Ironically, my wife was in the car with me when I found that that no award was given. I had won completely. I felt a flood of emotions—relief, joy, and reprieve. At that moment, the full force of it hit me and I broke down and wept. I consider myself to be a pretty strong individual, but I had not realized the level of pressure I had been internalizing for so many months.

Since the experience, I have made some adjustments. I had a situation with a client that was making me uncomfortable. He would call my office and complain to me or my staff about his portfolio performance. But when he would come in and meet me face to face he acted very friendly and buddy-buddy. I nipped it in the bud and gracefully exited from the situation.

The other extremely important lesson I learned is the importance of getting good information and acting on it. At the time I notified the broker-dealer, I felt I had done everything necessary to protect my interests. Now I know that I should have gone the extra step and immediately called the errors-and-omissions carrier, to get on the record that there was a potential dispute.

Strangely, I believe the experience strengthened me as a professional. It strengthened every area of my practice. I have recovered my full confidence, though it is always layered with caution and thoroughness—a great combination.

Case 3

"My fate was in the hands of people who didn't know what they were doing."

—A Southern California Rep

After graduating from an Ivy League college, I spent the first 15 years of my career in corporate America as a systems engineer. When people hear that, they immediately suspect that I am at heart an analyst, a number cruncher. It couldn't be further from the truth. I got into this business because I love working with people, and it gave me an opportunity to help guide people through life's difficult transitions.

I had been in the business for about 12 years when, in the mid-1990s, I was taken to arbitration. My client was a retired nuclear engineer who had a portfolio that was split 50-50 between limited partnerships and mutual funds. He had asked me to provide him with inflation protection, and I was successful in doing that. He was highly diversified. The funds did well. The partnerships did not.

I had to finance my own legal defense. The case dragged on

and on. I ended up paying my lawyer $110,000. We paid $15,000 for an outside expert and still lost the case. I kept borrowing and borrowing and borrowing. It was a major business interruption and an emotional disruption.

You get so depressed. You have a three-day meeting where you listen to out-and-out lies and you are made to seem like a criminal. How are you supposed to go out and put on a good face to your clients? The time drain is huge. The emotional drain is even bigger.

The arbitration hearings were a nightmare. I had a three-person panel. Two of them were from outside the industry and they had no idea about some of the most basic aspects of the investment business. The one industry expert was no expert either. So my fate was in the hands of people who didn't know what they were doing.

You are always told in this business to document, document, document. This was one case where it didn't matter. My attorney told me that he had never seen anyone who had documented as well as I had.

When it was all over, I had a judgment against me for $45,000. I have no idea how they came up with that number. Of course, they don't tell you the reasoning—they just send you the bill. At the time, I had been in the industry for 12 years. My wife took it even harder than I did.

When it was over, I didn't tell anybody about the arbitration. Here it is now a decade later and I have rarely told anyone about it. It was so humiliating—an ugly stigma. Like your daughter had a drug problem.

Case 4

"Everybody has to get paid—how I was pressured into an unjustified $17,000 settlement."

—A Female Rep from a Mid-Atlantic State

I had been in the business for more than 15 years without a

single complaint against me. Then one day I was shocked to receive notification that I was being taken to NASD arbitration by a former client, who had lost no money in her investments, but wanted a settlement of $140,000, an amount with no factual basis or justification.

I didn't even realize it was possible for someone to do this and be accepted as credible. I always thought that people who filed for arbitration were people who lost money, usually a lot of money. I also naively assumed that that most of these cases that were filed were ones in which the rep had clearly done something wrong. Neither of those applied here.

I did all the things I was supposed to do—called my home office, got assigned to an attorney, organized all the information for the attorney. I was expecting that the attorney was my advocate—someone to represent my side. I didn't realize how the system actually worked.

I was frightened and a little ashamed about the whole thing, so I didn't call and reach out to other reps who had gone through this to the degree that I should. I couldn't believe what my lawyer told me—that if I took this to a hearing, I would probably lose. Incredibly, *not* because I did anything wrong, but because my client was a widow in her 80s. The lawyer explained that arbitrators tend to have sympathy for someone like this.

As the thing moved forward, I felt as though I had no control over the process and no say in what happened. The lawyer mentality was driving the process to an unfair conclusion. My lawyer kept telling me that I had to settle—the carrier didn't want to go to a hearing. I was told to cut a deal and move on, go back to my career. It was as if all the parties had gotten together in a room without me and agreed—this is what we are going to do.

I started to cave, feeling like I had little choice. So I started arguing about the amount, which was purely made up anyway. The crowning statement of the whole process was when my attorney told me that I needed to agree to a certain amount. He said to me, and I quote, "Everybody has to get paid." The whole process was predetermined and, frankly, my role, my thoughts were completely inconsequential. I was nobody.

I felt completely helpless. The proceedings were more about the legal game than the facts of this specific complaint. However, and get this, they had all talked and agreed to this sum long before they asked me if this offer was okay with me. They were simply going to intimidate and coerce me into complying whether I wanted to or not. They said that if I wanted to go to arbitration, they would not represent me. I would be on my own. I said that was fine, it was worth it to me. Then they said that my broker-dealer firm and the E&O carrier would not support me. Eventually, I gave in and agreed to a $17,000 settlement, something I deeply regret and resent to this day.

One of the great ironies is that toward the end as I saw what was happening, I got over my fear of talking to other reps about it and I had put out a couple of phone calls to people who had been in arbitration, to get some advice. Within a few hours of my agreeing to settle, I got a call back from one of them, encouraging me to fight it. Too late. I'll never forget that.

The whole process was a nightmare. It cost me financially and took away an enormous amount of time and mental energy. It changed my view of my clients, and caused me to be more suspicious of them and their motives, something I really dislike. It has permanently damaged my professional record and decreased the economic value of my practice as an asset. But the worst thing was the damage it did to my dignity, my professional reputation. And the thing I can't get out of my mind is that I didn't do anything wrong.

The Lawyer's Perspective

How to Prepare and Try an NASD Arbitration Case

JAMES W. WELLER, ESQ.

For many registered representatives, NASD arbitration is the first time in which they had been engaged in an adversarial legal proceeding. The purpose of this chapter is to provide an overview of the NASD arbitration process, with an emphasis on what a registered representative can do to assist the attorney to achieve the best possible outcome.

Arbitration vs. Civil Litigation

NASD arbitration may be thought of as a "quasi-legal process." It is similar to civil litigation in that attorneys almost always represent the parties in the dispute, there is a presentation of documentary evidence, each side may issue subpoenas, there is sworn testimony (direct, cross-examination, redirect), and each side gets to make an opening and closing statement.

However, there are some very significant differences. The NASD designed the rules under which arbitrations are conducted to simplify the process and reduce the costs, as compared with litigating in the court system. Depositions are not taken as part of the discovery process. Most documents are easily accessible, without major expense. Many of the documents in cases are stipulated to as authentic by both sides with little or no challenge and entered into evidence. There is typically a minimum of motions involved.

NASD arbitrations are presided over by an arbitrator or an arbitration panel rather than a judge. Standards for what would be acceptable as evidence are far more lax than in civil litigation, giving both sides of the dispute some significant leeway. Hearsay evidence, which is theoretically forbidden from civil litigation (unless permitted by an exception), is often allowed.

NASD arbitrators have the opportunity to directly question witnesses, clarifying testimony and crystallizing key issues in the dispute. Arbitration outcomes are considered final, with almost no opportunity for appeal. Unlike judicial decisions, arbitration outcomes are not required to and often do not include the reasoning of the arbitrators, only the amount of the award, if an award is given. As of this writing in 2007, there is significant discussion within the industry about changes in the process that would result in requesting or requiring arbitrators to provide reasoning with their decisions.

The Claimant

The claimant is the investor who has filed the claim. Prior to the hearing, the registered representative is the key to helping the attorney understand the background, nature, and disposition of the claimant. Is he or she highly educated or not as educated? Is he or she an experienced or inexperienced investor? What is his or her professional background? What is the factual basis for the claim? Did the rep have any clue that a claim might be filed against him or her by this particular client, or was it a complete surprise? Are there issues in the claimant's personal or professional background that might help the attorney better understand them?

Throughout the process, the registered representative should do everything possible to help the attorney understand the claimant. Details that might seem minor to a rep can be crucial to an attorney in forming a clear picture of the claimant, his or her motivation, and how he or she might react to the pressures of an NASD hearing.

The Claimant's Legal Representation

As recently as 20 years ago, the NASD arbitration process was far less formal and legalistic than it is today, resembling today's NASD mediation process. Disputes were often settled by bringing in both parties to a single arbitrator, having each side explain their view, and going over the relevant documents. An arbitrator would evaluate the conflicting claims, review the evidence and the testimony, and, within a few weeks of a hearing, make a decision, which could include an award. Arbitrations often took place within a single day, in many cases requiring only half a day of testimony and examination.

Today, the entire process is far more intense and legalistic. Though it is not required that they do so, claimants almost always utilize the services of an attorney. The claimant's attorney generally receives part or all of his or her compensation in the form of a percentage of any settlement or award. The claimant and his or her legal representation seek the highest possible amount in damages that can be justified, through whatever logic. In addition, there is a natural motivation for the complainant's attorney to try and settle prior to a hearing.

In many NASD arbitration cases, the complainant's attorney (and his or her particular style) represents an unknown. He or she may be very skilled and experienced in NASD arbitrations

or have little experience. He or she may communicate frequently with the representative's attorney, or infrequently. He or
she may be aggressive and confrontational in settlement discussions and in the hearing or more soft-spoken.

Because of the increasingly large financial stakes involved,
there has been a rise in law firms that specialize, sometimes exclusively, in NASD arbitration. These firms take a very aggressive and well-organized approach to each case. There are
forums for the sharing of information regarding trends and successful or unsuccessful strategies among plaintiff attorneys.
Reps involved in an NASD arbitration and their attorneys
should assume that the claimant is being represented by an extremely skilled and well-prepared legal team.

The Registered Representative—The "Respondent"

In NASD arbitration, the registered representative named is
considered the "respondent." This is the equivalent of the "defendant" in a civil or criminal judicial case. The registered representative will play a central role in determining the outcome
of his or her case. Some registered representatives regard the
NASD arbitration process as an annoyance and a distraction
and, consciously or unconsciously, "outsource" its handling to
the attorney and the broker-dealer. This is a major mistake.

The registered representative can have enormous input at
every stage throughout the arbitration process. By providing all
relevant documentation, by being completely truthful with the
attorney, by being engaged in and committed to the process, by
making sound decisions at every stage, a registered representative can significantly influence the final outcome. The quality
of the legal work performed on his or her behalf can be no better than the quality of information, follow-up, and cooperation
of the client. A registered representative who is well prepared
on the facts of the case and responsive to the attorney's requests
for information and clarification and presents himself or herself

well under direct and cross-examination can have a hugely positive effect on the outcome of the case.

The Registered Representative's Attorney

Some NASD arbitration cases are handled primarily by an attorney working directly with the registered representative. Other cases will involve a more robust defense effort, including a paralegal, other attorneys who are sought for advice, and an expert witness(es). When the effort involves multiple individuals, the lead attorney takes on the additional role of coordinator of the legal team. To achieve the best result possible, all members of the team must perform their roles to the best of their ability and work together in a cohesive and coordinated fashion.

It is unusual, but not unheard of, for a registered representative to have a degree of input into the selection of an attorney. If so, you can utilize a number of research tools. The information that would be of interest is the attorney's experience in NASD arbitration—specifically, how many total cases have been handled, how many cases were taken through a complete hearing, and the results of those cases. There is no substitute for experience, and an attorney who has had a significant number of cases (at least six or more) go through to conclusion has a strong basis from which to represent you. If you have the ability to suggest legal counsel, and there is no one in your area with NASD arbitration experience, look for an experienced litigator.

The attorney has multiple responsibilities. The primary responsibility is to the client—to provide the best defense possible, within the constraints of the facts of the case and the resources that can be devoted to it. The attorney constantly assesses the case and the client, and communicates honestly his or her evaluation of the strengths and weaknesses of the case. The attorney reviews all relevant documents, assesses the strength of the case, identifies weaknesses, develops overall strategy, seeks out necessary clarifying information, communicates with the opposing attorney, engages in settlement negotiations, helps prepare the client for the hearing, prepares questions for use in direct and cross-examination, prepares memoranda of law, and prepares/presents an opening and closing argument.

The Paralegal

A good paralegal can make the difference between success and failure in many ways. The paralegal is the custodian of the process—logistics, communication with client and arbitration panel, scheduler, preparer of exhibits, supporter and cheerleader for the client, and observer of the nuances of the hearing. The paralegal is often the individual who keeps the client apprised of the progress of the case, if the attorney is in court or otherwise indisposed.

The paralegal handles dozens of details, any of which could derail the process or provide a major distraction if not managed properly. At the hearing, the paralegal ideally functions almost as an additional "associate" or "second chair," following the testimony, making notes of important points for later exploration on cross-examination, redirect, or in the closing argument.

I am fortunate in having continuously had Joan Herman as my paralegal since 1999. Prior to working with Nixon, Peabody, LLP, Joan had an extremely distinguished paralegal career of more than 20 years. Joan worked on the MGM Grand case, which involved a balcony collapse in Las Vegas, in a reinsurance capacity. Over a seven-year period, she worked on all three aspects (criminal trial, civil trial, Coast Guard hearings) of the Exxon *Valdez* case. Joan's insight, many talents, and strong character are an indispensable part of my legal work.

The Arbitrator(s)

The arbitrator or arbitration panel plays the role of "judge and jury" in NASD arbitration. The NASD has 7,000 individuals who have been certified as arbitrators. Each has been selected due to their relevant background in public arbitration or in the securities industry. Each has passed a written exam and received NASD arbitration training. As described by the NASD, arbitrators are "people from all walks of life and all parts of the country. ... Some arbitrators work in the securities industry; others may be teachers, homemakers, investors, businesspeople, medical professionals or lawyers."

The diversity of the backgrounds of NASD arbitrators presents a challenge for both sides of the dispute. The NASD provides background information on arbitrators, and there are additional commercial research tools available. Despite this, the temperament, background, and style of an NASD arbitrator often represent an unknown for both sides of the dispute.

The Broker-Dealer Firm

The broker-dealer firm plays an important role in the process. The broker-dealer firm has a stake in the outcome of the case. A settlement or award negatively impacts the reputation of not only the rep, but also, indirectly, the broker-dealer firm.

A firm is only as successful as its registered representatives, so anything that could damage the ability of a rep to secure, retain, and serve clients is undesirable to the firm. The larger the settlement amount, the greater the negative impact on future errors-and-omissions insurance rates. Although any increases are generally passed on to the registered representatives, it is conceivable that with a large enough record of awards and settlements, a broker-dealer firm might have to consider self-insuring against future losses. Broker-dealer firms are particularly concerned about the outcome of large-dollar claimant cases, which could damage the firm's long-term insurability and provide negative press coverage that could impact reps nationally.

Large-dollar, highly publicized settlements against a broker-dealer firm's representative(s) become negative publicity for the firm, with a wide range of negative consequences, including the ability to attract new representatives and creating a more difficult environment for the firm's representatives to conduct business. Investors may believe that "where there is smoke, there is fire," and have skepticism about working with a registered representative from a broker-dealer firm with a negative record of settlements. A large, highly publicized case encourages complainant attorneys to target the reps from that firm, and may encourage investors on their own to decide to file.

For these reasons, broker-dealer firms are usually very cooperative in working with the attorney who is trying the case for the representatives. The attorney, as a matter of practice, keeps the firm informed of developments and his or her assessment as the case moves forward.

The Errors-and-Omissions Carrier

The errors-and-omissions (E&O) carrier hires and pays for the attorney and the legal services that are required, as well as the costs of any covered settlements or awards (minus the registered representative's deductible) up to the upper limit of the coverage. Most E&O policies do not cover fraud. Fraud is frequently one of the allegations listed in a Statement of Claim. However, the standards for proving fraud are very high. It is often either dismissed by agreement of the parties prior to an arbitrator decision, or dismissed by the arbitrators as having not been proven. In those cases in which arbitrators agree that fraud was proven by the claimant, it is almost always one of several allegations listed in the decision. Carriers generally regard the decision as a single entity and simply pay the claim in its entirety. Therefore, provisions that exclude reps from being covered by the carrier for fraud rarely result in reps being liable for covering awards on claims of fraud.

While fraud is often one of the allegations listed in a Statement of Claim, it is relatively rarely identified as being the direct cause of an award, so for practical purposes this provision does not affect the majority of NASD arbitration cases. The E&O carrier can be thought of as a silent partner to the proceedings. The attorney communicates with the carrier throughout the process, including informing the carrier of any formal settlement offers the complainant's attorney may make.

Initiating a Claim against a Registered Representative

There are three ways in which an investor who believes that he or she has a claim against a registered representative can attempt to recover monetary damages: a letter of demand, mediation, or arbitration. Disputes are sometimes initiated by a claimant's contacting an attorney, who prepares a letter of demand, outlining a complaint against a registered representative, specifying a certain level of damages, and asking for money to settle the claim.

A second approach is through NASD mediation. As described by the NASD, mediation is "an informal process in which a trained and impartial mediator facilitates negotiations between disputing parties, helping them to find their own mutually acceptable resolution. What distinguishes mediation from other forms of dispute resolution—principally, arbitration and litigation—is that the mediator does not impose the solution, but rather, makes it possible for you and the other party to form and accept a resolution yourselves." From 2002 to 2005, 13 percent of the total arbitration cases filed with the NASD were resolved through mediation (4,045 out of 31,078).

In the area of securities arbitration, the NASD handles the vast majority of claims, but not all. The new account forms of all securities offered through NASD-designated registered representatives contain the provision that any dispute will be handled through NASD mediation or arbitration. In some cases, investors are allowed to select a venue. The New York Stock Exchange (NYSE), the National Futures Association (NFA), and the American Arbitration Association (AAA) also handle securities arbitration cases.

To initiate NASD arbitration, an investor, typically through an attorney, will file a Statement of Claim. The NASD tells investors that the Statement of Claim is a "description of what happened, written in your own words. You should tell the story clearly, concisely, accurately, completely, and in sufficient detail so that someone reading it will understand what happened, what monetary damages you are seeking, and why you feel that you are entitled to receive a favorable decision" (NASD.com web site). Often, however, the Statement of Claim is prepared by a claimant's attorney.

The Statement of Claim

The Statement of Claim is filed with the NASD, which notifies the current broker-dealer firm of the registered representative. The broker-dealer firm then contacts the E&O carrier, who then selects an attorney. Upon being selected as the attorney for the case, the first order of business is to review the Statement of Claim and understand what is being alleged. Claimants are alleging that one or more improprieties in the management of their assets resulted in monetary damages to them. Almost all NASD arbitration cases involve actual losses—an investor had the value of their assets decline during the period in which they worked with a registered representative. It is rare to find a case in which there were no actual losses. Tom's case was an example of this rare occurrence.

The Statement of Claim will present, in legal language, the "narrative" under which an investor believes he or she is owed monetary damages. It will also include allegations of impropriety on the part of the registered representative, which are also known as "controversies." Many of these controversies are sales practices (including churning, suitability, unauthorized trading, and misrepresentation). Statements of Claim almost always include multiple controversies (see Table 15.1).

A review of the NASD statistics for 2002 through 2005 shows that breach of fiduciary duty is by far the most common controversy. Negligence, unsuitability, and failure to supervise (a

TABLE 15.1   Controversies Involved in NASD Arbritration Cases

	2002	2003	2004	2005	Total
Margin calls	366	244	168	78	856
Churning	824	665	449	315	2,253
Unauthorized trading	930	789	520	395	2,634
Failure to supervise	2,633	3,230	2,743	1,828	10,434
Negligence	2,522	3,500	3,398	2,225	11,645
Omission of facts	1,178	1,949	2,195	1,123	6,445
Breach of contract	1,958	2,328	2,723	1,987	8,996
Breach of fiduciary duty	4,236	5,565	5,426	3,514	18,741
Unsuitability	2,644	3,198	2,697	1,926	10,465

Source: NASD.com. Reprinted with permission.

claim against the broker-dealer firm rather than the rep) are also cited in a large number of cases. The three least cited controversies are unauthorized trading, churning, and margin calls.

Although a complainant and his or her attorney can amend the document, adding additional charges throughout the arbitration process, the Statement of Claim can be thought of as the "founding document" of an NASD arbitration case. It is the starting point for the attorney and the client.

Responding to the Statement of Claim

Once introductions have been made, the attorney and client begin their work together by preparing a response to the statement of claim, in the form of a memorandum entitled Response to the Statement of Claim. This is due within 20 days after the service of the Statement of Claim for claims less than $25,000 and 45 day for claims more than $25,000, barring an extension of time (which are typically given).

It is incumbent upon the defense to make a detailed and very strong response to the Statement of Claim. The Statement of Claim and the response to it are the first documents that the arbitrators read about the dispute. They may be the only documents they read prior to the hearing date, setting the stage for what will follow. The attorney and the client agree on the wording of the response before it is sent.

Honest Self-Evaluation Is Vital

With regard to preparation, reps should be fearless, unbiased, and thorough in their examination of the facts. It pays to be brutally honest, especially about those aspects of the case that pride may make you want to gloss over. It is natural that in the review of the client relationship, there will be some topic(s) a rep doesn't want to face, or about which there are some guilt feelings. It might be something like not having great documentation on client meetings or something much more serious.

Whatever it is, it is absolutely essential that the rep and the attorney have a full and frank discussion about the downside aspect of the case. A client who withholds important information from his or her attorney is a disaster waiting to happen. It is a safe assumption that whatever weaknesses exist in a case will be exploited to the maximum by other side.

Assessing the Strength of the Case

As a result of the process of thoroughly reviewing the Statement of Claim, examining all the relevant facts and documents, and preparing the Response to the Statement of Claim, the attorney arrives at an initial assessment of the strength of the case. This assessment is communicated to the E&O carrier and becomes an important consideration in making strategic and tactical decisions as the case proceeds. A simple way to understand this is to think of it as an attempt to understand the facts of the case as an arbitrator might view them. Some of the factors are discussed next.

Claimant's Background

Points of interest in checking the claimant's background include age, educational level, professional history, and investing history. In Tom's case, we had an investor who was college educated, was a senior vice president of sales for a corporation, had been investing in the market for more than 20 years, had included his accountant during a portfolio review with Tom, and had a wife who sold real estate and was an investor of many years. Virtually all of these facts were favorable to our contention that the complainant had a strong basis for understanding the risks involved.

The claimant's background is always a large factor in how arbitrators view a case. Imagine the same factual set of circumstances as we had in Tom's case. Substitute a different complainant—a woman in her 80s who had been widowed just prior to working with Tom, had no education beyond high school, who had never invested before, who in testimony would appear to lack energy and mental clarity, and who had no other sources of information for her investments other than the rep. The very same set of facts could be perceived in a significantly different light by an arbitration panel.

The Size of the Loss

In the vast majority of NASD arbitration cases, there are significant, actual, provable losses in portfolio value, which are central to the claim of damages. In Tom's case, the client started with a portfolio of approximately $800,000, which rose to just over $1 million and then went back down to approximately $800,000. While the complainant viewed his "loss" at $200,000, a panel generally would look at this as having no real losses. It is rare for an investor to file for arbitration when there were no actual losses in portfolio value. By contrast, there have been arbitration cases in which the losses were enormous, sometimes reducing a seven-figure portfolio by 80 percent or more. Attorneys for claimants, especially in larger-dollar claims, often utilize sophisticated forensic accounting analysis in determining and justifying the damages they claim. Arbitrators pay attention to the size of the claimed loss as one factor.

Critical Issues

Statements of Claim typically contain multiple alleged controversies. It is often the case that many of these can be relatively easily handled. In Tom's case, from his initial narrative of the case and related supporting documentation I was able to virtually eliminate concern about many of the items alleged in the Statement of Claim, including "churning," "fraud," and "violation of securities law." We were able to spend a lot of our time preparing for what ended up being the core of the case—asset allocation and suitability.

The Quality of the Registered Representative's Documentation

This is a huge factor. It may well be that the rep is innocent of what has been alleged in the Statement of Claim. But to prevail, it is necessary to substantiate that viewpoint under the intense pressure of an adversarial proceeding. With poor, conflicting, or incomplete documentation, a skilled complainant's attorney can take an ambiguous factual set of circumstances and make the rep appear guilty to an arbitration panel.

In Tom's case, we had exceptional documentation—some of the best I have ever seen. Nonetheless, there were moments where the information he didn't have seemed more important than the information he did have. I was worried throughout the course of the proceedings that his level of documentation was so excellent, it almost made it seem sinister in the few cases in which he didn't have every answer to every question.

The Quality of the Representative as a Potential Witness

If the case goes to a hearing, the representative will testify under oath in two ways. In direct testimony, he or she will respond to a series of questions asked by the attorney, which will have the effect of laying out their side of the case and getting important facts on the record. In cross-examination, he or she will be questioned by the claimant's attorney, who will try to tear apart these facts and get the rep to lose his or her composure.

As an attorney works with the representative in understanding and preparing for a case, he or she is constantly evaluating the rep as a potential witness. The rep is being examined not only for how solid his or her case is, and the extent to which it can be supported through documentation, but also for how the attorney believes the rep will come across to an arbitration panel.

Some reps might be excellent at organizing their material, but poor in presentation. Some may be very knowledgeable and confident, but risk appearing arrogant to the panel. This is a very crucial and ongoing assessment. If a rep performs poorly under oath in testimony, it will negatively affect the attorney's assessment of the case at that stage, and may be a factor in deciding to settle as opposed to continuing to try the case.

The Responsiveness of the Representative to Requests

It is perhaps surprising to read this, but some reps do not put a lot of effort into their own defense. If an attorney is working with a rep who is slow to respond to requests for information and does not seem to be actively engaged in the process of his or her own defense, the attorney's assessment of the strength of the case will be negatively affected as it goes forward. The attorney may fear that the rep will not be able or willing to give a full effort in dealing with the nearly inevitable surprises and crises that characterize adversarial proceedings.

Settlement

It is a statistical fact that the majority of NASD arbitration cases settle prior to a hearing (see Table 15.2).

Over the period of the calendar years 2002 through 2005, 38 percent of the total cases were settled by arbitrators. The remaining 62 percent were settled between the parties, in most cases between the legal representation of the parties or by mediators. This particular chart is of all disputes handled by the NASD, which includes disputes between reps and their broker-dealer. The issue of settlement is a constant factor at each stage of every arbitration case. Settlements can take place relatively soon after a Statement of Claim has been filed, or literally on the courthouse steps—just prior to the beginning of a hearing.

Complainants and their attorneys have a strong bias to settle prior to a hearing, as it avoids the time and expense of additional preparation time, trial time, and, in many cases, hiring expert witnesses. It also avoids the risk that the complainant will not be effective in testimony and cross-examination.

Attorneys for registered representatives in NASD arbitration can at any time (prior to a hearing or while a case is being tried

TABLE 15.2 How NASD Arbitration Cases Close

Cases Decided by Arbitrators	2002	2003	2004	2005	Total	%
After hearing	1,463	1,764	1,915	1,767		
After review of documents	443	313	508	355		
Total	1,906	2,077	2,423	2,122	8,561	38

Cases Resolved by Other Means	2002	2003	2004	2005		
Direct settlement by parties	2,204	2,616	3,700	3,940		
Settled via mediation	752	1,182	1,201	910		
Withdrawn	547	647	677	806		
All others	489	679	1,073	1,127		
Total	3,992	5,124	6,651	6,783	22,621	62

Source NASD.com. Reprinted with permission.

before arbitrators) be approached by the opposing counsel to discuss the possibility of settlement. Because such an approach represents an unstated admission of some weakness in their case, these approaches are often made in a less than direct manner. Rather than making contact and directly asking for a settlement amount ("What do you say we agree on 75 percent of our claim?"), the claimant's attorney may instead float the settlement idea in conversation and see what the response is ("I have spoken to my client, and he would be amenable to a possible settlement").

It is the obligation of the attorney to listen to any settlement discussions, convey them to the client, formulate a response, and communicate the response to the opposing counsel. The registered representative's attorney is also obligated to convey any formal settlement offer to the E&O carrier. The attorney should advise the rep, based on the attorney's evaluation of the case to date, utilizing the best judgment to assess what is an uncertain and fluid process.

It is here that the multiparty aspect of the NASD arbitration process can create potential conflict among the rep, the attorney, and the E&O carrier. The investor's suit is first and foremost filed against the rep (and his or her office of supervisory jurisdiction [OSJ] or branch manager), and secondarily the broker-dealer firm, which is utilizing its E&O insurance to fund the effort. The rep has already paid the insurance deductible. Assuming there is coverage for all claims, the legal fees, and the amount of any award or settlement (up to the limit of the coverage) will be paid by the carrier.

What happens if the carrier, taking into account the attorney's assessment of the strength of the case, believes it is in its best interests to settle, even if the rep is strongly against such a course of action? Many E&O policies contain the provision that a carrier has the prerogative to instruct the representative's attorney to accept a settlement that has been offered. It is here that the carrier's interests may diverge with the client's. It would be unusual for a representative at this point to be willing to self-fund further legal defense efforts and accept liability for a later settlement or award. It is here that the judgment of the representative's attorney becomes potentially decisive. If the attorney believes there is a good chance to prevail in a hearing, the carrier will often allow the case to proceed.

There are anecdotal reports of reps feeling pressured to agree to a settlement in circumstances such as this. The strength of the rep's position is determined by the facts of the case, the quality of the documentation, his or her ability to present the case in testimony, and the desire he or she has to see the case through to completion. A rep who is well prepared, with strong documentation, can make a persuasive case to continue. It is my experience that in dilemmas such as this, the desire of the rep to continue to a full hearing (or the conclusion of the existing hearing) can be a determining factor.

Selection of Arbitrators

The NASD uses the Neutral List Selection System. There are approximately 7,000 individuals on that list nationally. Attorneys from both parties in the dispute receive a computer-generated list of 15 potential arbitrators from their general geographic area. Of these, 10 are "public" arbitrators (experts in arbitration) and 5 are "industry" (experts in the securities industry).

Backgrounds of each potential arbitrator are made available, including their academic background, professional experience, and a list of NASD arbitration matters that have resulted in awards. Attorneys are allowed to strike any potential arbitrators from the initial list of 15 without giving cause. A strike from either legal team eliminates the individual from the list. Each attorney can submit a rank order list of the remaining arbitrators. If only one party submits a list, that becomes the controlling list. The NASD reviews the two lists and, if there are enough names that neither side has eliminated, selects an arbitrator or a three-person arbitration panel.

After eliminating the arbitrators that each side has struck out, if there are not enough names remaining, the NASD will generate a second list. On the second list, attorneys for each side can strike potential arbitrators only for cause. This will require the demonstration of a potential conflict of interest based on the individual's background or prior rulings.

Civil and criminal law in the past several years has seen the rise to prominence of systematic and often extremely expensive "jury" consultants, who help each side screen out jurors who are theoretically unfavorable to their side and end up with jurors who might be favorably disposed to the kinds of arguments that will be advanced during the trial. This is, at best, an extremely inexact process.

In reviewing potential arbitrators on behalf of my clients, my preference is for attorneys who either have experience deciding the matters that comprise the heart of the case or significant business law experience. With a relatively strong factual case, I want attorneys who I believe are more likely to rule on the basis of the law as opposed to arbitrators who I believe might be more prone to balancing the perceived equities in a case. I like to review the award records of potential arbitrators, including whether or not they have had cases in which punitive damages were awarded. However, caution is appropriate in overinterpreting this information, as one does not know the underlying facts of the cases.

Scheduling

Once the arbitration panel has been selected, panel members receive copies of the Statement of Claim and the response. The next order of business is to coordinate the schedules of all parties involved (the arbitrators, the complainant, the rep, and the legal teams) to set hearing dates. Each side is asked to provide an estimate of how many days of hearings will be required. If the case will involve more than one day of hearings, the NASD tries to schedule at least the first two days consecutively. The paralegal is key to the scheduling process. In terms of juggling the conflicting schedules of counsel, reps, and witnesses, scheduling is, in many cases, a very dynamic process. Schedule conflicts arise, dates get changed, the process is often extended, and each side simply has to adjust.

Once a case has been scheduled for hearing, preparation shifts into another level of seriousness. Hearing dates are often set several months into the future, giving both sides an opportunity to prepare. There is also an ongoing chance to negotiate a settlement during this period. As the time draws closer to the hearing date, it becomes more and more likely that the hearing will take place, necessitating both sides to intensify their preparations.

During this period, the attorney, paralegal, and rep can begin to put special attention on those issues that appear to be the most critical in the case. Once the basic facts of the case have been reviewed, the attorney and the rep begin to drill down and focus on details that impact the issues they anticipate will be most prominent in the case. Although in theory reps have a record-keeping system that allows them to gather all necessary information in one effort, the reality is that over time additional information is found, recollections sharpen, and little twists and turns begin to appear that either help or hurt the rep's cause.

One of the most useful things a rep can do throughout the preparation process is to, where appropriate, educate the attorney on fine points of the securities business. The attorney knows securities from a legal standpoint. The rep knows the securities business in many other areas—products, marketing, sales, operations, and customer service. By taking the time to explain appropriate fine points to the attorney during preparation, the rep is helping the attorney to come across in the hearing as an expert. This can be critical to how a case is perceived by arbitrators.

Organizing Exhibits

The attorney and the paralegal begin to assemble the documents that will become exhibits. Most, if not all, of these exhibits will be entered into evidence at the hearing, with the agreement of the opposing legal team on the first day of the hearing. The paralegal plays an extremely important role in working with the attorney to devise a system of organizing and cataloging the exhibits so that they are easily accessible during the hearing.

There is often a natural way of categorizing the exhibits, by witness and by topic. Not all exhibits are of equal weight. It is not uncommon to have hundreds, even more than 1,000, pages of exhibits. However, it is often the case that a small number will prove to be the hinge upon which the case turns.

Exhibits need to be thoroughly reviewed for their value in helping advance the rep's case as well as the potential that they may be used by the other side to damage the case. It is important to prepare the exhibits and, ideally, have the attorney, paralegal, and rep completely familiar not only with exhibits themselves but also where they are filed within the system, which is usually comprised of multiple large three-ring binders.

As part of the process of organizing exhibits, the attorney may request information about the claimant through his or her attorney. Both sides have the power of subpoena, which can be utilized. This might include a request for information on the individual's financial holdings or his or her investment pattern subsequent to the time period in question.

During this phase of preparation, and in fact throughout the entire process, an attorney and a fully engaged rep will be communicating back and forth on a variety of issues. E-mail is a wonderful technology tool in this regard.

Key Trial Memoranda

An important part of an attorney's preparation is to organize a series of important memoranda:

- An outline of the direct examination of the rep.
- An outline for cross-examination of the complainant and any other witnesses for their side.
- An outline of the closing argument.
- An outline of the questions to be asked of the rep's expert witness(es).
- An outline of the questions to be asked of the opposing sides expert witness(es).

The memos for examination usually are broken into categories, including background, employment history, a chronology of the client relationship, and specific areas to address the critical issues. These memoranda can be prepared in a "bulleted" manner or in any other way the attorney believes most effective.

The memo on the closing argument is one of the most important documents in the entire case. The first draft will include each of the categories of controversy mentioned in the Statement of Claim. As the attorney and client prepare and refine their case, each of these documents is upgraded and refined.

The thoroughness with which the attorney and client have prepared is reflected in the clarity, organization, and quality of these documents. As in all aspects of the case, preparation really pays off during the hearing. It is impossible for the legal team to be "too organized." There is a natural amount of give and take during a hearing and improvisation by both attorneys as they respond to developments in the testimony. But the greater the degree of organization, the more thorough and systematic the preparation, the stronger the foundation on which the team stands.

Prehearing Preparation

Parties are required to abide by the 20-day exchange rule, providing agreed-upon materials to the other side no less than 20 days prior to the hearing date. The attorney reviews this information, with an eye toward anything new that might impact how the case will be tried. One of the items of particular interest is the background and credentials of the other side's expert witness(es), if any. Within three to five days of the hearing date, both sides exchange the exhibits they plan to use and enter into evidence. This can provide significant additional insight into the core of the complainant's case.

Expert witnesses are to be expected in an arbitration hearing of any claim size ($50,000 or more). They represent a type of wild card in the arbitration contest. It is conventional wisdom that any point can be "proven" through the selective use of statistics. Similarly, it should be expected that the adversaries in an arbitration case will be able to find an expert who will testify in a way that supports their case. The rep's attorney needs to carefully consider, screen, interview, and select an expert witness(es) to counteract the effect of the claimant's expert witness presentation.

The attorney and the rep should have an extended face-to-face meeting within two to three weeks of the hearing date. At this meeting, all of the exhibits should be reviewed. In addition, the attorney should help prepare the rep for testifying under oath. For many reps, an NASD arbitration hearing is the first time they have been sworn in to a legal proceeding and offered testimony that can be challenged by an aggressive cross-examination.

While there are differing philosophies on this point, I do not believe in a high degree of "coaching" of the rep. There is some value in this type of session to have a dry run of what it would be like to do some direct examination and some cross-examination—a series of questions on direct and some on cross-examination. The purpose of this is to get a feel for the format and its flow, not to try and write a detailed screenplay to follow during the actual hearing.

It is not effective for a rep and the attorney to try and script out dozens of word-for-word questions and answers. Testimony should simply be the truth, and not something that is a strain for the rep to remember. It is unlikely that when the heat of the moment comes, either will be able to reproduce the words they had agreed to in a prep session. Coached testimony has a way of sounding like coached testimony.

Expect Surprises

It is an axiom of the practice of law that preparation determines 80 percent of the outcome. If one believes that, then it stands to reason that the other 20 percent consists of properly reacting to the challenges that take place over the course of a case. The claimant and his or her legal representation present their case in whatever manner they choose. They may wish to begin by asking the attorney to conduct direct examination of the rep, followed by cross-examination, or call the rep immediately as an adverse witness. The legal team should be prepared for this possibility. However, it is far more typical for the other side to begin with the claimant's direct testimony.

NASD proceedings are recorded with audio equipment and also transcribed. Despite this, during the entire hearing all members of the legal team should make every effort to follow the testimony closely, making notes of issues that can be used later in the process. The taping technology is not 100 percent reliable, and even if it were, there simply is not the time in most arbitration cases to assign someone to listen to the recording and take notes from it. Similarly, transcription is helpful, but it is even more useful if the team has zeroed in on a discrete number of moments in the testimony that they can use later in the trial— in cross-examination or closing argument.

Anyone who has been in an adversarial judicial proceeding knows that these events take on a life of their own. Facts that may have appeared to have one connotation when looked at in the comfort of an office can take on a different light in live testimony. Personal conviction, emotion, body language, and voice inflection all work together to create an impression.

A claimant who might have been expected to struggle as a witness in testimony could turn out to be a star. A rep who was expected to do well might melt down under cross-examination. Developments in the case may require that the team conduct a rapid research effort for information to rebut expert testimony, as happened in Tom's case. The result of all of this is a sense of direction and momentum that each case has, which can pivot with no prior notice. It is here that the quality of preparation and the ability of the legal team to function as a team, each individual performing their role properly, is tested.

Opening Comments

At the beginning of an NASD arbitration, each attorney is given the opportunity to make opening comments. These are relatively brief, thematic previews of their views of the case, of the evidence that will be presented, and what they believe the evidence will demonstrate. The claimant's attorney will often restate the highlights of the Statement of Claim, plus any additional points that he or she wishes, including a preview of the expert witness testimony. The rep's attorney can use the outline for the closing argument in preparing this brief, tone-setting statement.

Claimant and Expert Witness Direct Testimony

Witnesses are examined alternately by each side of the dispute. In direct examination, an attorney is asking questions of his or her client. It is a "friendly" examination. Cases often begin by having the claimant under direct examination by his or her attorney. They often will cover biography and the history of the relationship with the rep. It is a standard practice for the attorney and the claimant to use this part of the testimony to demonstrate the claimant's relative lack of financial sophistication and his or her reliance on the rep for advice. In covering the relationship with the rep, they are presenting their point of view, their narrative of what happened.

Reps watching this testimony often get upset at how the relationship is being portrayed. They often believe that the claimant's self-presentation is bogus, bordering on fraudulent. They may feel as though their former client is out-and-out lying in the way some of the facts of the relationship are presented. Similarly, when the other side's expert witness testifies, the rep may find his or her line of reasoning to be flawed, even outrageous. It is understandable that with so much at stake, a rep will want to correct what he or she believes to be inaccuracies or outright falsehoods.

However, it is important that the rep not get carried away emotionally with this, but instead channel his or her energy into taking notes that the attorney can use in cross-examining the claimant and/or expert witness, and also perhaps in making certain points during the representative's direct examination. It is even more helpful if the rep can, from his or her own memory or with the assistance of a paralegal, make reference to an exhibit that will back up these points. The paralegal is also observing this testimony and using his or her years of experience and knowledge of the case to also come up with helpful information to use. This is the legal team in action.

It is in the crucible of a hearing that the bond of trust that has been built up between the rep and his or her attorney becomes evident. The rep gives the attorney the information and puts the case in the attorney's hands. It is part of the magic of the rule of law that this battle between adversaries takes place, with truth and justice, hopefully, emerging.

At any point in the proceedings, arbitrators may choose, without warning, to interrupt any witness testimony and ask a question or a series of questions. It is particularly interesting to note what types of questions are being asked and how the witness responds. Questions are often asked for the purposes of clarification. Their questions may indicate skepticism in how the attorney is shaping the testimony. The witness's response to these questions, and the resulting interaction, may provide an insight to the observant attorney, paralegal, or client, which can be used later in the hearing.

Cross-Examination of the Claimant

Once a claimant has completed direct testimony, his or her case will have theoretically hit a peak. The claimant has had the un-fettered opportunity to present his or her view of the facts, with minimal, if any, interruption from the opponents. In NASD arbitration, it is relatively rare for opposing attorneys to object frequently or strenuously to the manner in which the opposing attorney is conducting questioning. NASD arbitration has, relative to civil or criminal litigation, relatively lax standards for rules of evidence and procedure. The arbitrators have significant leeway to allow testimony to come in (sometimes including documents with minimal foundation) and to permit the other side to pursue lines of questioning. It is understood that the arbitrators will evaluate all the evidence presented in the way they believe appropriate.

The cross-examination of any witness is a critically important phase of a hearing. Through intelligent, directed, precise questioning, a different side of the story emerges, one more favorable to the respondent. The attorney works from the memorandum that has been prepared for this purpose, as well as any additional notes from direct testimony.

There are many approaches to and styles of cross-examination. An attorney may begin with an aggressive, confrontational question or series of questions. He or she may begin in a gentle, friendly way, disarming and relaxing the witness before leading into more productive areas of inquiry.

In cross-examination, it is not productive to try and rehash every aspect of testimony. The attorney must cover those areas from his memorandum and hearing notes that will have the most positive impact on the arbitrators. The attorney may sometimes ask a question in a few different ways, as each arbitrator may hear each answer a little differently. Leading questions, which give the witness the opportunity to answer only "yes" or "no," are a staple of cross-examination. An attorney may summarize a witness's testimony, and then ask, "Isn't that right?" Phrases such as "You would agree, would you not ...," "You are aware, are you not ...," and "Is it fair to say ...?" can be sprinkled into the questioning.

Cross-examination is a combination of art and science. It is a blending of preparation, experience, natural ability, and intuition. One of the more commonly cited principles of cross-examination is to never ask a question to which you don't know the answer. That may have a certain ring to it, and there are many examples of attorneys who asked questions on cross that they later wish they hadn't. However, actual practice dictates that there are moments when a flash of intuition is acted upon, a potentially risky question is asked, and it turns out to be a great decision.

When done properly, one of the aspects of effective cross-examination is that the attorney is, through the witness, testifying to the panel. Through effective preparation, focused questioning, proper voice inflection, a respectful tone, and the integration of little tidbits of expert knowledge by the attorney into the questioning, the attorney is presenting him- or herself as highly credible to the panel. This is a process that takes place over the course of the entire hearing, which may take several days over a period of many months. By doing this, the attorney is building up a reservoir of goodwill and reliability that will be drawn on in closing argument, when fighting for the best interests of the client.

Direct Testimony of the Representative

In civil and criminal trials, testimony is expected to be precise and narrowly focused. Witnesses are to answer the question asked of them and no more. There is no editorializing allowed. Attorneys are restricted to lines of questioning that have foundation either in evidence or in prior testimony. Judges and opposing attorneys are often quite aggressive in enforcing these practices, which can result in frequent and contentious skirmishes throughout the course of a proceeding.

Direct examination of the registered representative gives the rep, under questioning by his or her attorney, the opportunity to explain what happened from his or her own perspective. Under direct examination, a rep should be as expansive as possible. Under cross-examination, a rep should be careful and circumspect.

Testimony in NASD arbitration is conducted under a much more relaxed standard. This can work to a rep's disadvantage in that hearsay testimony, which would be permitted in civil or criminal trials only under certain strict exceptions, is frequently allowed. However, the rep and the attorney can and should use the more relaxed standards of testimony to their advantage. Arbitrators will allow a witness in direct examination to expand an answer to include the "why" behind it. If there is an objection to this, the attorney can get in the habit of simply asking "Why did you do this?" after a "yes or no" question.

For example, an attorney might ask, "Did you have portfolio reviews with this client?," then ask, "What would you cover in one of these sessions?," then ask "Why would you do that?" The rep is explaining how he or she does business, the standards of service, and the client education component of the business. The attorney may have the rep explain in detail the safeguards within a firm against clients not understanding what is offered, or how investment recommendations are arrived at.

In doing this, the rep is testifying in a combined educational and "sales" mode, with the arbitrators as the audience. He or she is explaining issues with calmness and clarity, much like they might be explained to a prospective or current client. The rep is engaging in an extended conversation with the arbitrators, hopefully coming across as extremely credible—sincere, well-informed, polite, and thoughtful.

It is important in direct and cross-examination that a rep properly handle any question an arbitrator may ask. Questions are opportunities to explain and to clarify. Even if arbitrators seem to be asking what appears to be the same question sever-al times, the rep should never show annoyance or irritation. Every question from an arbitrator needs to be answered clearly and directly.

Redirect Examination

After the opposing attorney completes cross-examination, an attorney has the opportunity to ask "redirect" questions. When a cross-examination has been particularly effective, redirect is an important effort to rehabilitate the energy and credibility of the witness's testimony. It is often difficult to develop a large number of questions on redirect. Sometimes attorneys will choose to make redirect efforts very brief. The back-and-forth questioning by each side continues until each side has completed its examination of a witness, who may be called later in the hearing.

The Use of Expert Witnesses

The higher the size of the claim in an arbitration hearing, the more certain it is that one or more expert witnesses will be used. Expert testimony represents a significant challenge. If the expert has impressive credentials and a persuasive manner, his or her testimony can have a significant impact on arbitrators. Expert witnesses are often testifying about what may appear to be relatively abstract or technical aspects of evidence. However, if their testimony is not refuted through effective cross-examination and a competing expert testimony, their testimony may be convincing to arbitrators. It is nearly essential to respond to a claimant's expert witness by using an expert witness who can effectively rebut their testimony.

When an expert witness is testifying for the complainant, the registered representative needs to pay extremely close attention to the details of his or her testimony. The rep should provide the attorney with the knowledge necessary to refute what the witness has said or put it into a context that is most useful to the rep's side of the case. Similarly, the rep should play an active role in working with whatever expert witness(es) his or her attorney has selected. At worst, it is important to at least neutralize the effect of the claimant's expert witness testimony. Ideally, it can be refuted through an examination of the credentials of the witness and the testimony that he or she has given.

Daily Review/Analysis/Strategizing

At the end of each day the attorney, the rep, and other members of the legal team (if any) will spend time reviewing the key developments of the day. If a case takes more than a full day of hearings, there is virtually always "homework" for everyone on the team. There may be additional direct testimony or cross-examination to prepare for. Exhibits may need to be combed to try and secure a needed bit of information. Additional documentary evidence may need to be secured. If the case requires hearing time additional to what was originally scheduled, there is usually some legal research and preparation of memoranda for the arbitrators. No matter what the obstacles, the team needs to be organized and in a high state of readiness for the next challenge.

Closing Argument

When all direct testimony, cross-examination, and redirect testimony is completed, each side presents a closing argument. This is the last opportunity to appeal to the arbitrator(s) and represents a synopsis of the case from each side's viewpoint.

Attorneys who believe in the importance of a good closing argument begin working on it almost as soon as the case is initiated, but they must be prepared to address new matters that have arisen during the course of the hearing. Whatever happens during the trial, attorneys keep their mind's eye on the fact that, at the end, all of the key testimony from both sides needs to be tied together in a clear narrative that leads to a conclusion favorable to the client.

An attorney will have an evolving outline of the closing argument and continually revise it as the trial goes on. Tidbits of testimony should be used throughout the closing argument. These can be provided by the rep and the paralegal during breaks throughout the hearing. At the closing argument, the attorney draws on every reserve available to make the best argument possible on behalf of the client.

One approach that is often effective is to review for the arbitrator(s) the uncontested facts of the case. Presented in a crafted, sequential manner, they can have significant weight as part of a closing argument. Another useful tool is to limit the universe of what is at issue, focusing on the truly critical aspects on which the decision will hinge, and presenting clear and convincing information and arguments on those points. Quotes from testimony and visual presentations are often very helpful.

Summary

NASD arbitration proceedings are a major challenge for everyone involved. The results can impact a registered representative for the rest of his or her life. By treating every aspect of the process with the highest level of seriousness and working cooperatively as a member of a cohesive legal team, the chances for a successful outcome are maximized.

How to Prepare for NASD Arbitration

A Marathon, Not a Sprint

One of the most useful ways for the registered representative to envision the process is to realize that it is a marathon and not a sprint. The NASD has an objective to have arbitration proceedings closed within a year of their initiation. However, this is not always accomplished. The case detailed in the first part of this book went on for more than 21 months.

NASD arbitrations do not happen at warp speed, but rather unfold over time. In the days just leading up to and during the actual hearings, the intensity is phenomenally high. However, there are often prolonged periods of time when the case seems to be lying dormant and requires little actual budgeted weekly time.

If you have received either a letter of demand or a Statement of Claim, one of the most useful actions you can take is to read and re-read the previous chapter. It contains a significant amount of very useful information which will help you understand and prepare for what is about to take place.

The purpose of this chapter is not to review every point in the previous chapter. It is to expand on some of those points and to provide additional information, from the rep's perspective, which will be useful in responding to an investor complaint.

What to Do First

When you receive either a letter of demand or a Statement of Claim, among the first reactions may be shock, followed by anger and indignation. These documents typically are written in a bold, flamboyant style, often using colorful, if not inflammatory, language in describing the representative's behavior. This is coming from someone whose interests you genuinely tried to serve. Your professional behavior is being described in a legal document with phrases such as "contumacious disregard," "wild and frenzied trading pattern," and "seized control of the investment portfolio," among others.

There are four actions that you must take immediately:

1. Inform the relevant broker-dealer firm's compliance department.
2. Inform the relevant office of supervisory jurisdiction (OSJ) or branch manager
2. Notify the errors-and-omissions (E&O) carrier.
3. Begin a file that documents every development and every action taken.

Cases can be filed up to six years after the time period in question. By the time you receive either a demand letter or Statement of Claim, there may be multiple broker-dealer firms involved.

The primary firm will be the firm you were with during the period described. This firm's E&O insurer will fund the legal effort. In the event you have been with multiple broker-dealer firms, it is prudent to inform any that might be affected.

If a letter of demand was received, the broker-dealer firm will usually inform you that it will handle the issue until further notice and instruct you not to communicate further with the client. This is almost always the correct course of action. However, there are some examples in which reps believed that they knew the client well enough to be able to defuse the situation by calling them directly. In some cases, this has resulted in demands being dropped. However, it is clearly a risky course of action.

It is a prudent course of action to communicate on a regular basis with the compliance department to track the progress of the case. This could be monthly for the first few months, then bimonthly, until it has been resolved or elevated into an arbitration case.

If a Statement of Claim is received, the broker-dealer firm usually will have been notified by the NASD in the same manner as you have been notified—by mail. In this case, the broker-dealer firm will contact the E&O carrier, who will select legal representation.

A Must: Contact the E&O Carrier

Whether it is a letter of demand or Statement of Claim, it is important self-protective action to personally contact the E&O carrier and inform them of what has happened. If a Statement of Claim has been received, this action will duplicate the effort of the accountable broker-dealer firm's compliance department, which is fine.

If a letter of demand has been received, contacting the E&O carrier may be the action that saves the rep tens or even hundreds of thousands of dollars of legal expenses and exposure. E&O policies contain numerous provisions, which are written in a legalistic language and often glanced over, at the most, by many reps. Some of these provisions relate to the timeliness of informing the carrier of a claim or potential claim. If the carrier is not notified within a certain time period of the claim, or potential claim, coverage may not apply, and the rep will be exposed for the costs of the legal defense and any award or settlement. One such case is detailed in Chapter 11.

Organization and Documentation

The third important action is to begin a filing system for the case and fastidiously document every development and action taken. You are on a war footing and at a high level of preparedness regarding this issue until it is resolved. In an arbitration hearing, every little step that is taken can have far-reaching consequences.

Documentation is the lifeblood of the process. Document the calls you made and what was communicated. Follow up with e-mails as appropriate. For really important information, it is a good idea to take the next step and actually prepare a written letter and mail it to the appropriate parties. This is especially true with regard to the communications—with the broker-dealer firm and the E&O carrier.

If organization and detail has never been your strength, now is the time to be more organized, more diligent, more detailed, more fanatical than ever before. This is like tax audit time. Let the shock of the proceedings and the negative possible consequences motivate you to perform at your absolute best, starting with the first moment and continuing through the resolution of the case.

Organizing the Facts of the Case

It is surprising to realize that not all broker-dealer firms have a formal, written procedure for reps on how to prepare the case files for their attorney. It is arguable that the items are common sense, but it is worth listing them here.

- All documents involving the client. This will include a number of signed documents, including prospectus receipts and new account forms.
- Any hard copy notes that involve this client.
- Printouts of all trades and confirms conducted on behalf of the client.
- Printouts of any electronic files involving this client. This may include records and notes of calls that were taken by the staff or the rep. If you print out anything from an electronic file that does not contain a date, you should date stamp it.
- Any documentation or printouts of electronic files that might have been supplied to you by your broker-dealer.
- Client account statements (monthly or quarterly) from relevant statements.

The other two steps that come in early in the process are:

- Signing the Uniform Submission Agreement, which binds both parties to the process and in which they agree to abide by the decision.
- Paying the E&O insurer for the deductible of your coverage in a timely manner.

For writing your narrative, this information should be copied at least twice, three-hole punched, and put into a large three-ring binder. At this point, the best organization is chronological. So, this binder would start off with the initial documentation, likely including an investor questionnaire, followed by new account forms. It is helpful to use tabs to separate the documentation, likely by time periods.

You will find it helpful and calming to put the material together in this sequence.

You will want to speak with your attorney as you perform this due diligence. Offer to write the attorney a memorandum that explains the relationship between you and the client at a fairly high level of detail. Virtually any attorney would be very pleased that you offered to do this. Most representatives who are in securities arbitrations do not. You are immediately separating yourself out as a client who is focused, determined, innocent, and willing to do whatever is necessary to provide your attorney with everything he or she needs to provide you an outstanding defense.

Assuming your attorney would like you to do this, approach this exercise with the utmost seriousness. Unless a better scheme suggests itself, write it in chronological sequence. Include any information or insight that will help the attorney better understand what happened. Going back over the records is like watching a movie of your relationship with this client. With the wisdom of perspective, you will undoubtedly be able to provide details, insight, and little bits of information that will paint a vivid picture. Did your client have some important family issues that might have impacted his or her actions? Did the client experience any significant personal changes or challenges during the time you worked with him or her? What is the client's personality? By providing this type of information, you are not only giving your attorney the best information to assess the case, you are also starting him or her off in preparing to cross-examine your former client.

Self-Examination—Brutal Honesty

One of the points that attorney Jim Weller made in the previous chapter as essential is that you be brutally honest with your attorney. Even if you are basically innocent of the charges, it is unrealistic to expect that subjecting any professional relationship to this level of scrutiny will result in a "fairy tale" story of perfection. There will inevitably be some gray areas. You discover a note or file or form that you realize the other side can use against you. You recall moments where you took actions about which you had little more than 51 percent conviction. With the wisdom of 20/20 hindsight, there are a few things you would have done different.

It is extremely important, for both yourself and your attorney, that you scrutinize the client relationship very intensely, with an eye toward anything that might be construed as supportive of the claimant's case and damaging to yours. This is especially challenging when you consider that there may come a point at which your attorney may literally hold your fate in this case in his or her hands. In most cases, your attorney will be required to communicate any settlement offers to the E&O carrier, who may have the option (under the terms of the coverage) to accept the offer. If that moment comes, and your attorney believes in your case and your chances to prevail in a hearing, he or she may be able to convince the carrier to refuse the offer and allow the case to go forward.

It may be tempting to think that it might be a good idea to either ignore or gloss over any deficiencies that you might have, in order that your attorney will be favorably impressed. This is a formula for a total disaster. It is a near certainty that whatever you are trying to hide will come up at some point, either from your own attorney's questioning of you or during the hearing. If, at any point in time, your attorney gets the feeling that you have been anything less than totally forthcoming, you have damaged your relationship with him or her and set your case back, perhaps irreparably.

An Extra Attorney

If you are an extremely cautious professional and want to do everything possible to maximize your outcome, one extra step that can be taken is to research and select an additional attorney to advise you through the process. You will be assigned an attorney by the carrier, and most of your work will be with that individual.

This will involve some additional expense on your part, and

you have to assess whether the extra few thousand dollars are worth it to receive an incremental level of support and advice. There are four specific and potentially very useful functions an additional attorney can serve:

1. Shadow the work of the primary attorney in case preparation and evaluation.
2. Provide a second opinion in the event that your primary attorney is encouraging you to settle, even though you feel you have a good case.
3. Help prepare you for direct and cross-examination.
4. Be prepared to step into the case if for any reason the primary attorney does not work with you through to closure.

If you decide to utilize this tool, you want to be sure to select the right attorney. The most important criterion is an attorney with experience in arbitration, including multiple cases that have gone through the full hearing process. Many attorneys may have experience working up a case and playing a part in a settlement negotiation process, but you want someone who has been through the entire process, ideally one who has had more than one case in which they completed the hearing and the claimant received no award. An external attorney can be added at any point in the process but will be most useful to you if you bring him or her in at the beginning.

The Statement of Claim Is Your Guide

You will be assigned an attorney by your E&O carrier. Typically, this is done fairly expeditiously. However, it is not necessary to wait for this to happen to get into action. The immediate order of business is to begin researching the facts of the case. If you are not a rep whose strong suit is personal organization, now is the time to become a fanatic about organization, detail, and self-discipline. Research and organize your case as if the entire outcome is riding on it, because it is.

Before you begin, review the Statement of Claim. Make a copy of it. With a highlighter, highlight those aspects that will need to be refuted in order for you to win your case. The statement will probably have several charges involving "sales practices" (e.g., asset allocation/suitability, churning, omission of facts) as well as additional charges that have a legal meaning (e.g., fraud, breach of fiduciary duty). It is not necessary to be an expert in these terms to begin work. You want to start with a basic familiarity of the charges. These become a lens through which you conduct your research.

Getting Started on the Right Foot with the Attorney

You will be notified that you have been assigned an attorney. This individual will immediately, and for as long as you work together, become an extremely important individual in your life. Treat the attorney with that level of respect—with the same level of responsiveness and care as if he or she were your most important client, which in many ways is true.

After you have assembled the documents and electronic files that describe the contours of the case history, discuss with your attorney how you can be most helpful to him or her. It is important to have this discussion with the attorney before beginning to compose your narrative because of the concept of attorney-client privilege. Once you have discussed the subject with your attorney, then all of your work falls under the umbrella of attorney-client privilege. If you wrote the narrative on your own before discussing the subject with an attorney, your writing might have to be turned over to the claimant and his or her legal representative as part of the discovery process. After having this discussion, and agreeing on what should be included, take the time and energy to write a clear and detailed narrative of the case history for your attorney.

Although the writing of a detailed narrative is a good idea, one that most attorneys would desire from their clients, this step is rarely done by reps. Many of them feel as though it is the lawyer's job to represent them, and all they have to do is to bundle up the relevant documents, send them along, and "outsource" the effort of the legal preparation almost entirely to the attorney.

This is not the right attitude—not the white-belt attitude. The proper approach is to take on, in your mind, full responsibility for doing anything and everything that will help your attorney represent you. It is imperative to get a fast start to this process and perform every aspect of it to the very best of your ability.

Look at the Numbers—Can You Get to an Arbitration Hearing?

Although every case is different, if you look at the NASD arbitration statistics, you will find some interesting things. The statistics reviewed by attorney Weller in the previous chapter show that over a three-year period approximately 62 percent of cases were resolved prior to a hearing. Of those that went to a hearing, approximately 50 percent resulted in a monetary award for the claimant. Using rough numbers, this means that of all NASD arbitration cases filed, approximately 75 to 80 percent result in an award for the claimant. This should give you an idea why cases are filed. If you walked into a casino knowing that you had an 80 percent chance of walking out a winner, how often would you go?

Next, take a look at the pattern of what happens for those cases that do reach a hearing. Table 16.1 shows the pattern of NASD arbitration cases that went to a hearing.

These numbers could suggest that the system is "working" in getting cases that should settle to settle, and taking to hearing only those cases in which there is a real dispute as to whether the rep did anything wrong. Another way to look at it is that if you can get your case before an arbitration panel, you do so knowing that historically 50 percent or more of them will result in no

TABLE 16.1   Results of Customer Claimant Arbitration Award Cases

Year Decided	All Customer Claimant Cases Decided (Hearings and Paper)	All Customer Claimant Cases Where Customer Awarded Damages	Percentage of Customer Award Cases*
2000	1,196	635	53%
2001	1,172	637	54%
2002	1,330	702	53%
2003	1,513	742	49%
2004	1,894	888	47%
2005	1,610	687	43%

*Percentage of customer claimant award cases has been recalculated to reflect only instances in which investors as claimants recovered monetary damages or nonmonetary relief.

award, with those statistics increasing year to year over the past few years.

This means that the work you do between the time you initially receive the demand letter or Statement of Claim and your first meeting with your attorney is important. You want to work hard first to organize the information that will demonstrate that and, second, to convince your attorney that you will be an enthusiastic, committed client and an effective witness while testifying under oath. Getting your attorney's support is a major success.

Incentives for the Claimant's Legal Representation

A lot of drama takes place between the receipt of the Statement of Claim and the scheduling of a hearing. Look at it from the other side. Estimates are that it costs a law firm between $5,000 and $7,500 to "work up" a case and file a Statement of Claim. However, to go through a complete hearing, estimates are an average between $50,000 and $75,000 per case, with some cases in the hundreds of thousands or even higher.

Law firms working on a contingency basis know these numbers. There is, using the numbers in the previous chapter, approximately a 60 percent settlement rate prior to a hearing, for cases that average $5,000 to $7,500 to work up. There is a 50 percent or more chance that they will complete a hearing and receive no award at all after investing an average of $50,000 to $75,000 per case. Doesn't it make sense that they will use every tool they have to get a rep to settle?

The incentives built into this system drive all sorts of behavior by the plaintiff's attorneys. Here are two examples:

1. **Loading up the Statement of Claim.** There is research that suggests, unsurprisingly, that the more sales practices alleged in the Statement of Claim, the greater chances of an award. This leads to attorneys loading up Statements of Claim, including a number of categories in which they don't really expect to prevail. By doing so, they force the rep and his or her attorney to prepare responses to what may be baseless charges. And by presenting an entire laundry list of items, there is the hope that the sheer force of the overall presentation might sway an arbitrator to assume that with enough smoke, there must be fire.

2. **Playing games with the hearing schedule.** There are many examples in which a plaintiff's attorney will submit a lowball estimate of the time the case will require. The attorney tells the NASD that he or she expects it is a "two-day case," knowing that it is probably a four-day case. The break after two days gives an automatic time to talk settlement with the rep's attorney. A settlement avoids additional costs of more legal preparation and trial time. Also, additional hearing dates will require the coordination of the schedules of multiple people. These schedules can change, and the hearing gets put off and put off into the future. This creates a pressure to the rep to settle, to get rid of the aggravation and get on with his or her life.

Errors-and-Omissions Carrier Realities

On the E&O side of the equation, they also know these numbers. If it costs them $5,000 to $7,500 on average to work up a case, they realize that it will cost an additional amount, up to an average of $50,000 to $75,000 to go to a hearing. If an award is given, then that will also be paid by the carrier, up to the limits of the coverage. Even with the success rate of hearings, you can see how tempting it would be for a carrier to want to settle if a claimant and his or her attorney is willing to settle for an amount in the $50,000 range. These are the twin pressures you are dealing with.

What this tells you is that the early stages of the case, and your relationship with your attorney, are enormously important. Your attorney's solemn and sworn ethical obligation is to provide for you the best possible representation. But he or she does so in the context of the economic realities of the entire system

Meeting Your Attorney Face to Face

A big moment in the life cycle of your case comes when you go to meet your attorney face to face to discuss the case in detail. It is important, first of all, that this meeting take place. Astonishingly, some reps never meet their attorney until the first day of the hearings. This is a huge mistake.

Think of that meeting as your first live "audition" of your case. It could be considered to be, up to that point in time, the most important presentation of your career. Think of it as a dress rehearsal for an actual hearing. Get your exhibits organized. Be prepared to present the overview of your case. Be prepared to answer any questions your attorney has for you.

This approach may seem a bit formal. But it recognizes one vitally important reality. You are selling yourself and your case to the attorney, just as surely as you will if you go to a hearing. You want to be knowledgeable, easy to understand, highly credible, and immersed in the details of the exhibits. It can be stated in a number of ways, but the truth of the matter is that your attorney is your first judge and jury. By convincing him or her, you have overcome a first, but extremely important, hurdle.

Your attorney has an excellent idea of how you and the facts you present would be perceived in live testimony. While you talk, he or she is imagining you under oath at a hearing. Prove yourself to have a good case, and be a good witness on your own behalf, and you have made an important step on the road to success.

How Your Attorney Assesses Your Case

As attorney Jim Weller explained in some detail in the previous chapter, one of the ongoing activities of the attorney during the hearing is to assess the strength of the case. That assessment can vary, positively or negatively, as information becomes available in the discovery process, as he or she meets you, and all throughout the hearing process. Every attorney has his or her own way of evaluating the strength of a case, but the seven Weller criteria are a good place to start:

1. The claimant's background.
2. The size of the loss.
3. The facts of the case.
4. The quality and quantity of documentation.
5. Critical issues.
6. The strength of the rep as a potential witness.
7. The responsiveness of the rep to requests.

Your attorney should be able to provide you with an honest assessment of the strength of your case at that meeting. Hopefully, he or she believes in you and in your case and believes that you stand a reasonable chance to convince an arbitrator or panel of your innocence. However, in the event that after all of your best efforts, he or she believes that you have significant, proven vulnerabilities and might want to settle, you have to take that assessment very seriously.

Extra Effort

In the period between the scheduling of the hearing and the hearing itself, there are a few things to do. Keep in touch with your attorney and/or his or her paralegal for any developments in the case. Some clients find that they develop a healthy, regular e-mail relationship with their attorney, in which they go back and forth about some of the particulars, how to deal with the critical issues they have identified, and so on. This is a good sign.

Another thing you can do is a little extra credit research on the claimant. There are two case examples in this book in which claimants neglected to mention in their disclosures prior to the hearing significant financial assets that increased their net worth. You might want to hire someone to check local government records to see if any additional stones can be turned in this regard. One of the classic legal moves is to discredit a witness, undermining their credibility by uncovering in testimony some damaging information. This is known as "impeaching the witness." Whatever you can provide for your attorney in this regard can be very helpful.

The third important thing to do is to keep studying those exhibit books. At this point, the attorney and/or the paralegal will be organizing the exhibit books for the hearing. You want an exact duplicate of whatever will be used. It should have a clear index of all documents. On a regular basis, you should look through these. You don't have to read every one of the hundreds of pages. Many of them, such as prospectuses, you can just glance over. But be very familiar with where the critical documents are, both those you believe are the crux of your case and those you believe can be used by the other side to attack you and/or present their case.

Ideally, you will have another meeting with the attorney within a few weeks of the hearing date. Your attorney should have received documentation from the opposing side within 20 days of your hearing date. You will want to be sure and understand what new information, if any, this has provided you and what you will need to do as a result.

At this meeting, there is often some kind of preparation for testifying, on both direct and cross-examination. Each attorney has his or her own philosophy or approach about this. Some feel that they want to create as realistic a situation as possible, and actually role-play both direct and cross. Others will want to go over with you the areas they plan to cover and general tips about how to testify. This is a time at which, if you have hired an additional attorney, helping prepare you for this could be very helpful.

Finally, as the hearing date approaches, you want to control the logistics and details. Leave yourself some buffer room so that you arrive at the hearing with your mind clear, as rested as possible, with the right clothes and a great attitude. Make yourself as unavailable as possible to the outer world, taking special care to block out any professional obligations. The last thing you want to be doing is running in and out of a hearing room making cell phone calls to clients or your staff handling emergencies—not a formula for success.

Preparing to Testify and Managing Your Case to Conclusion

The Challenge of Cross-Examination

Of all aspects of preparing for an NASD hearing, none is more important than the preparation you do for cross-examination. If you have never testified under oath when being subjected to hostile cross-examination, there is no other experience quite like it.

To try and get an idea of what it is like, go through your records and find the name of a client with whom you worked two, three, or four years ago and with whom you have had little contact since. If you have a paper file on him or her, it is even better. Pull out that file and find any piece of paper in it. If you can, go back through your electronic scheduling notes and try and find the time frame at which that form would have been filled out. Now, imagine yourself on the stand being asked these questions:

Q: "Did you fill out this form, or did the client fill it out?"

A: "The client filled it out."

Q: "Do you remember the meeting at which the client filled out this form?"

A: "I have a record of the meeting, so I am sure it took place."

Q: "I did not ask if you are sure if it took place. Please answer the question. Do you remember the actual meeting?"

A: "No, not specifically."

Q: "Then why did you testify that the client filled out this particular form?"

A: "It is my habit and practice to have the client's fill out forms like this at our meeting in my office."

Q: "I am not asking you to testify about your habit or practice. I am asking you if you remember the client actually filling out this form?

A: "No, I do not."

Q: "Look at the handwriting on the form. Does it appear to you that there are two different types of handwriting?"

A: "I am not sure, but I don't think there are."

Q: "Is it possible that either you or someone on your staff might have filled out part of this form?"

A: "I don't believe they did. It was not our practice to do that."

Q: "I did not ask you about your practice. Please just answer the question I ask you. Is it possible that either you or someone on your staff might have filled out part of this form?"

A: "It is possible, but I believe it is very unlikely."

Q: "Does it appear to you from this copy that there might have been two different types of ink used in filling this form out?

A: "I don't believe so."

Q: "Do you see the different level of intensity in this section versus this section?"

A: "Yes, I see it, but I don't know if it means that two different types of ink were used."

Q: "Is it possible that someone might have added some information onto this form after your client filled it out and signed it?"

A: "No, that is not possible."

Q: "Please reconsider your answer. We can subpoena the actual document and bring it in here for examination. Are you 100 percent sure that someone did not add some information onto this form after your client filled it out and signed it?"

A: "I can't say 100 percent, but I would be shocked to find out if that was the case."

Q: "Is it possible that this form could have been filled out at the client's home?"

A: "Yes. Sometimes we send the clients prospectus receipts at their homes and they fill them out and send them back."

Q: "Do you have any records that would indicate whether this particular form was filled out at your office or at the client's home?"

A: "No."

This is a slightly stylized example of what actual cross-examination can be like. This little exchange on what was probably a very innocent document took slightly less than three minutes. The attorney, through use of aggressive questions, was able to suggest a sinister twist to what was in all likelihood a simple document with nothing whatsoever sinister about it.

Actual cross-examination can go on for hours without a break. Skilled attorneys move from subject to subject, and then back to a previous subject. They exhaust you with a series of questions about something like this, which may not be a key point, and then switch subjects to something they believe is a key point. They get you thrown off balance, doubting yourself. They don't let you explain your answers. They often interrupt you when you are trying to do so. Demeanor is very important in any adversarial judicial proceeding. You may be completely innocent, but if you are rattled, become confused, or get argumentative under cross-examination, you undermine your case.

Have you ever been pulled over by a police officer while driving? Do you know the feeling of having adrenaline racing through you, with your mouth going dry? Have you experienced what it feels like when the policeman starts asking you questions, and it seems from his questions that you are guilty of something? This is somewhat analogous to what it is like to be cross-examined.

Preparing for Cross-Examination

The truth is that virtually everything you do in working on your NASD arbitration case is, in some way, preparation for cross-examination. From the moment you begin assembling the facts of the case through every phase of prehearing preparation, it is all done with a mind's eye toward going under oath and being cross-examined.

There is duality at play here as well. You definitely want to look at this as a unique event, one that requires high preparation. However, it is not like you have never been grilled before, either. You do have a baseline of ability to conduct one-to-one conversational combat, and a lot more experience with this than an individual who has no sales background.

The approach that a rep takes to an NASD hearing is quite similar to that of an athlete preparing for a championship event, an actor or actress preparing for the biggest moment of his or her career, or an individual getting ready for a job interview for a position what would be the opportunity of a lifetime. You have had big moments in your career before—moments that at the time seemed to you to be "make or break." This is just another one of those moments. You have evolved your own system to prepare for these big events. Draw on all of that in preparing for your arbitration hearing. The three fundamentals of preparation are: becoming an expert at the documents and exhibits; communicating with and meeting your attorney; and your own rehearsal.

Communicate continuously with the attorney and/or his or

her paralegal as the exhibit books get organized. You need to be ridiculously familiar with them. Something will come up in the hearing and you want to be able, while under a lot of pressure, to know just where the document is in the exhibit which will prove your point. This is an example of acting as if the entire case is riding on you. This is the difference between a good and great client. This may be the difference between victory and an award. Think and act as if every little edge will be the determining one—because you can never tell if it might be.

Let your attorney advise you regarding the pace and activities of preparation for testifying. He or she may have a system or approach they would like you to follow. Ask for his or her advice in terms of getting extra practice being cross-examined, in the event you have hired another attorney. Keep asking, "What else can I do?"

You can do some very useful practice on your own, without paying someone's hourly rate. This is a system that was originally developed for executives preparing for job interviews. It is a combination of mental, physical, and emotional preparation combined into one exercise.

Take regular time away from your work, your family, and other responsibilities—off in a room by yourself. Go through some of the questions you know you will be asked by the other side. Say them out loud. Then give your answer out loud. Listen to the words you say. Stop. Ask the question again, and improve the answer.

Keep going back and forth, asking and answering, improving your answers until you really like them. As you get into this roleplay, become animated. Walk around the room. Gesture with your hands. Warm up your voice until it has the ring of full conviction. As you warm up, ask tougher and tougher questions of yourself. The point of this is not to memorize word-for-word answers to any questions. It is to condition yourself for the combat of cross-examination, to get your voice warmed up, and to get your blood flowing. You are getting, as motivational guru Anthony Robbins would say, "in state." A few of these sessions can be a fantastic supplement to working with your attorneys.

Think of it this way. If you were a football player preparing for the Super Bowl, a golfer preparing for the final round of the Masters, an actor or actress preparing for the biggest audition of your career, or a major party presidential nominee preparing for a nationally televised debate, how would you prepare? You would have a clear picture of the stage, the time, the people involved. You would visualize what it would be like, cognitively and emotionally. You would get your blood flowing and in an emotionally high, but controlled, state. You would do everything you could to make sure that when the time came, you were rested and totally ready to go. Put that level of preparation into this, and you are maximizing your chances for success.

One final thought: What is your picture of a successful outcome? It is easy to say to yourself, "Well, that's easy, winning the case—getting the arbitrators to declare no award for the claimant." That may be the ultimate result you want, but it is not the proper mental picture for your testimony. The truth is that the arbitrators' decision will not come until weeks have passed since the final day of hearings. In addition, the case may hinge on factors about which you have little control.

So, the proper image, the success picture you want to have is that of completing your testimony with the arbitrators completely convinced that you were telling them the truth. It is authenticity that is the goal. You want to not only be right, but to appear in the right as well—through controlled confidence, respectful demeanor, the ability to answer all the questions put to you, and by successfully withstanding hostile questioning without losing your cool. The picture you have in your mind is that when you are done testifying, the arbitrator(s) say to themselves, "That person was telling the truth."

As part of the mental rehearsal for the event, you learn what martial artists learn through belt testing. Prepare for all the things you could anticipate, and then also prepare for the un-expected. What does this mean? It means that you literally run through your mind all of the possibilities that you can think of, and make sure you are mentally ready for them, and then you also prepare for the unknown—the possibility you couldn't anticipate.

You tell yourself, "If I am the first one to testify, that's fine. If I don't testify for the entire day, that's fine. If the arbitrators let me explain my answers to my attorney's questions, that's fine. If they interrupt me, that's fine. If I like the setting, that's fine. If I am very uncomfortable in the setting, that's fine. If I feel I am connecting with the arbitrator(s), that's fine. If I get no reaction at all or even a feeling of hostility from the arbitrator(s), that's fine. If the claimant sits there and starts flat-out lying through his teeth, that's fine. If my attorney destroys him on cross-examination, I don't get overconfident." You literally say things like this to yourself, picturing them, and predetermining your own emotionally controlled, professional response.

Then you add in the "X factor" by telling yourself, "I am ready for some surprise that I can't even anticipate." When you have gone through all that, you are ready for the hearings to begin.

After all of the preliminaries are done, there is actually something quite satisfying about having your NASD arbitration hearing begin. You have prepared yourself thoroughly. You did all of the research, wrote the detailed initial narrative, worked with your attorney, received an assessment of the strength of your case, learned about the process, tried your own case against yourself, and continued to dig deep for more ideas, more perspectives. Now it is time to have your day in "NASD court." You never want to be the slightest bit overconfident, but you also have to keep in mind that approximately 50 percent of the reps who complete a hearing walk away with no award against them. At this point, the claimant and his or her representative have, in many respects, nearly as much to be worried about as you do.

So you arrive on the day of the hearing, as rested as possible, with your business handled by others, unavailable by cell phone, mind clear and looking good, but probably not "too good" (follow your attorney's lead on dress etiquette, but if the dollar value of your clothes and jewelry is three times as large as anyone else in the room, it is not considered a good thing). When you walk into the hearing room, you will know that you have prepared properly if you have a combination of a state of anticipation/anxiety and a sense of calm. You feel centered and peaceful in your depths. You are ready to begin.

Opening Comments

After some introductory, procedural matters have been completed, both attorneys give their opening arguments. As you listen to the claimant's attorney, to the extent that you can, separate yourself emotionally from what is being said. It will sound to you like fiction, character assassination, and outrageous fabrication. It is natural to let it grip you and want to fight back.

Try and be more clinical, more detached. Watch the attorney in action. Listen to his or her cadence. Watch for mannerisms and body language. You have spent thousands of hours in your career sizing people up. Because of your profession, you have a lot of experience in reading nonverbal cues. You are building your mental file on the individual who will be cross-examining you at some point in the hearing.

Listening to the Claimant's Direct Testimony

Hearings will typically start with the claimant under direct examination by his or her attorney. You have already gotten a preview of what this will be like with the Statement of Claim. You know the story that they are trying to tell. If there are features in the claimant's background that can be brought into a light to make him or her a sympathetic character to the arbitrators, it will be done. In many arbitration cases, the attorney and the claimant will paint a picture of the claimant as an unsophisticated, even naïve investor who depended on you, the rep, to help guide him or her.

The claimant and the attorney are playing softball. The attorney is lobbing easy questions and the claimant is hitting singles, doubles, triples, and home runs. They get some momentum. From your experience, you can just feel that this is having an effect. Again, rather than get emotional about this, be functional. Take notes. Write down actual phrases of what they say and on break give your attorney the ammunition to contradict this. Make more notes if something is said that reminds you of a little detail you hadn't covered, which can be brought up on your direct examination. Realize that however good this all sounds, your attorney will have a chance to shed an entirely different light on this testimony. Take comfort in the fact that you are getting to sit and watch this and get the rhythm of the proceedings before testifying.

Duality—What Are the Arbitrators Thinking?

Duality is an extremely important principle to keep in mind throughout the NASD arbitration process. Learn to listen to testimony through two filters: first, from an advocacy point of view (how can this best be presented to reflect well on me in my case?), and second, from a hypothetically neutral third-party perspective (how are the arbitrators looking at this?). Early in a hearing process, if you have the time, ask your attorney to explain how the arbitrators are processing this information.

When you hear the claimant tell his or her story, it is almost certain you will say to yourself, "These are lies!! I never did or said that!!" While the claimant may be shading or shaping the truth, especially as you see it, it is far more typical that, at least in his own mind, he is giving honest testimony. The claimant's recollections of the events in question can be tainted by imperfect memory, anger, and a sense of injustice he may have if he lost a significant amount of money, or the very natural and human desire to want to prevail in a dispute.

In Tom's arbitration case, the complainant repeatedly referred to Tom having, in essence, "guaranteed" him a minimum 10 percent annual rate of return. Led by the questions of his attorney, he said this in several different ways. He testified that Tom said that "10 percent was no problem" and "10 percent, that was the minimum" and "10 percent, that was the base." In his mind, he honestly believed, in retrospect, that Tom had "guaranteed" him a minimum 10 percent annual rate of return.

As Tom explained under cross-examination, the truth was a bit more complicated, more nuanced. Tom testified that he shows virtually every potential investor the Ibbotson chart that demonstrates that the United States equity markets historically average an 8 to 10 percent rate of return, over a long time horizon. Like any good rep, having talked about this with hundreds of other clients and potential clients, there is no doubt that Tom explained this correctly, and was careful in his wording. But in recollection, and in the heat of an adversarial setting, this became, in the claimant's mind, a "guaranteed rate of return."

Consider how these competing claims would be evaluated by an arbitrator in the role of an unbiased observer. You have two opposing recollections of the same set of circumstances. There is no audio or video record of what actually took place. How do you evaluate the issue? This is up to the individual arbitrator, but it is not hard to understand how a neutral third party could give at least some weight to each side of this little dispute, of which there are dozens within each case—a classic gray area.

The problem with this "he said–she said" back and forth is that it often works to the advantage of the claimant. If a registered representative wants to prevail completely, and emerge with no settlement or award, he or she cannot afford a great deal of "gray area." Even the most fastidious rep will have some imperfections in documentation. A skilled complainant's attorney can make significant use of this gray area to argue on behalf of his or her client.

Use Your Time Wisely

Time and energy are at a real premium during hearing days. After being through one, you will understand why litigators charge such a high premium for days in court. It is very intense, and a lot of action is packed into every half hour of the proceedings.

Use your time wisely. Have a sense of your priorities. You may not understand something that is going on, so by all means ask your attorney or, if he or she has one, the paralegal, to explain it to you. You want to understand the process as it unfolds.

But it may be far more important to use the precious break time you have strategizing with your attorney, providing information, teeing up the cross-examination to come.

Watching Cross-Examination

Avoid the temptation to feel as though you are at an athletic contest. When you see your attorney cross-examine the claimant, there will likely be times when you will want to stand up and cheer. That is not what this is for. Again, pay attention to little details, phrases of answers to questions, points that can be brought up either later by your attorney on cross-examination or through your own direct examination. Your attorney is up there performing, in the moment. You need to be his or her eyes, ears, and second mind. This is what it means to be a good member of a legal team.

You will see that when your attorney is cross-examining a witness, he or she is actually testifying to the arbitrator(s). His grasp of the facts of the case will be quite high. If you can enhance that with your own little value-added points and bits of knowledge, the total effect can be quite persuasive. It is a great sign, for example, if your attorney is so well prepared, partly with information you have provided, that in cross-examining the other side's expert witness(es), the attorney appears to the arbitrator(s) to be more of an expert than the witness! If that happens, you have both done very well.

Use Your Expertise—Educate Your Attorney and the Arbitrators

A critical point to be aware of when the other side is in direct examination of the claimant, expert witness, or any other witness is the shaping or fudging of technical information regarding the securities industry. This is especially important during the testimony of the expert witness. The claimant's attorney has developed a theory of the case. He or she has figured out what has to be proven to the arbitrator(s) to prevail. Then he or she finds an expert witness who, armed with some type of credentials (which might be impressive or weak), will testify to some theory and set of supporting facts that will arrive at the desired answer.

This is where you as the rep must put your industry expertise to work. If you have a three-person panel, two of them are "public" arbitrators and may have little or no knowledge of securities concepts or terminology. In Tom's trial, one of the public arbitrators interrupted the proceedings and said, "I have no idea what a corporate bond is—or any of these terms you just mentioned." Public arbitrators are very closely attuned to the process, but may not be knowledgeable about the subject matter.

If that is the case, it becomes a matter of highest urgency that you make sure your attorney has the knowledge and the factual backup to counter the argument. This can be partly accomplished through your own direct testimony. It can be bolstered by an expert witness. But if it is left hanging unanswered or partially answered, chances are good that you will lose your case, even if the theory was so bogus the person delivering it would have been laughed out of a room full of registered representatives.

Your attorney may understand the nuances of these types of issues very well, but you should not assume that this is the case. Your attorney's profession is law. Yours is investment advice. Take charge as appropriate and educate your attorney and the arbitrators about technical issues, which are certain to be discussed.

Testifying Under Direct Examination

If you have watched some direct testimony already, you have a pretty good idea of what it is like. It is friendly fire—a chance to get your set of facts on the table. You have at least some idea of the personalities of the arbitrator(s). Do they tend to listen or interrupt? Do they allow long answers, or do they want short ones? This is all filed in your subconscious mind. You relax and concentrate entirely on what your attorney asks you.

You and your attorney will have prepared, at least to an extent. He or she will have a rhythm and you follow along. You are dance partners. Let the attorney lead. Then do your part. Use a similar style in terms of eye contact and vocal cadence to what you would use in making a small group presentation in a sales or training setting. You are using your verbal and nonverbal ability to communicate to connect with the arbitrators, not just cognitively, but emotionally as well.

Make no mistake about it—you are selling your story of what happened. There is, however, a very delicate balance. Tone is extremely important. At no time do you want to come across as egotistical, overbearing, or flamboyant. Even if you use humor in your normal pattern of persuasive communication, a hearing is not the place to try and inject humor. All of your communication is extremely respectful, and your words are calm and measured. In direct examination, you want to use the right number of words—not too few, and not too many.

One of the minor but important points in testimony is that, unlike most of your other communication venues, you cannot expect significant verbal or nonverbal feedback on "how you are doing." Arbitrators maintain an even keel and exhibit a judicial temperament. They do not intentionally want to signal to you if they are buying what you are saying. So, you need the discipline to keep testifying in a good rhythm, but not being thrown off by a lack of a feedback loop.

Arbitrators will ask you questions. They may interrupt something you were saying. Welcome those questions. Those questions are fantastic. They are asking you about something that is not clear to them. They have detected an inconsistency and they want to resolve it. Never show the slightest bit of annoyance, even if they bore in on some subject and seem to almost be advocating for your opponent.

Answer each question as best you can. You do not have to win every battle to win the war. You may end up with some answers that don't seem favorable to you. Forget and move on. If you are not sure about something, say so. All of this works together to create in the minds of the arbitrators your credibility. They will be impressed if you admit to things not favorable to you, and don't seem bothered or stressed by them. The overall impression that you want to give is an individual on the stand telling the truth, down to the finest detail. If you do that, you have succeeded.

Being Cross-Examined

At its worst, being cross-examined can be a devastating experience. At its best, performing well in cross-examination can be a triumphant experience. In either case, cross-examination is an extremely intense and emotionally draining experience.

But the payoff is potentially huge. It is in cross-examination that, if your case is solid, your preparation is strong, and your execution is excellent, you can go a long way to destroying the core of the claimant's case.

In cross-examination you will be facing an attorney whose job it is to make you look bad. He or she has also prepared well and does this for a living. Your cross-examination may be the highlight of the hearing process. If you end up prevailing, you can then relate to Winston Churchill's famous statement, "There is nothing more exhilarating than being shot at without result."

As with martial artists preparing for a belt test, it is in cross-examination that your fundamentals need to be their strongest. This means your awareness level, mental clarity, emotional energy level, and ability to think under pressure. If you are well prepared, cross-examination will seem very demanding, but at a certain level you will really enjoy it. This is what all of your preparation was for.

Here are some suggestions for surviving and succeeding at cross-examination:

- Listen very carefully to the wording of each question.
- If you want the attorney to repeat the question, ask him or her to do it. For very tense moments, it is an excellent way to get some breathing space to gather yourself for a particularly tough question. But don't do that every other question.
- Answer the question that was asked, not the question you might have wish was asked.
- Answer the question briefly and directly. If you can summarize yourself so that you seem as if you stop half a sentence before you were going to, you probably gave a good, concise answer.
- Don't try to be fancy. Your attorney will try your case. Your job for now is to simply answer the questions asked of you.
- If you are asked a question that involves a document, take the time to read the document carefully before answering. Good cross-examiners can trick you into believing something is on a document that is not.
- The more the process heats up, the more you slow yourself down. Breathe deeply. A little pause between question and response is appropriate. If the arbitrators see that you are being careful and complete in your answers, it is to your advantage.
- Don't check your watch, metaphorically or in actuality. President Bush checked his in the middle of a presidential debate in 1992, and observers believe it may have cost him the election. There is no rush. It will take as long as it takes.

Settlement Offers

You and your attorney will discuss how the hearing is progressing. There is absolutely no way to know for sure how a case will be decided. But both of you will probably have a shared view of your progress.

With regard to settlement offers, know where you stand at all times. If settlement is the right thing, don't be afraid to do it. There are times when, due to the flow of the case, the additional time and aggravation further hearings will cost you simply won't be worth it. Some reps have caved and settled, and then really regretted it.

However, it may be that a formal offer was made, and conveyed, as required, by the attorney to the E&O carrier. If the carrier decides it would like to accept the offer, typically the only factor that could prevent them from doing so is your attorney's belief that you stand a good chance to prevail. If that is not the case, you probably need to recognize that going on your own at that point (funding a further defense and opening yourself up to the liability of an award) is probably not prudent.

But it is a big decision—one that should not be made as a result of a feeling of pressure or helplessness. If you are on the verge of deciding to settle, then "decide in theory," and give it 24 hours, if circumstances warrant it, to see how the decision feels to you. Keep in mind that some industry experts believe that 80 percent of all filings are baseless, and historically 50 percent of the hearings end in no award for the claimant.

Conclusion

Your NASD arbitration case will be one of the pivotal experiences of your professional life. Make sure that when it is over, you have no regrets that had you prepared a little better or been more aware of what to do, the result might have been different.

APPENDICES

APPENDICES

NASD ARBITRATION CASE FLOW

We would like to present the NASD arbitration case flow from two perspectives. The first is the flow as described by the NASD on its web site. It describes the stages of NASD arbitration and the fees that apply at the various stages. On NASD.com, an in-depth description of each stage is available (see Figure A.1).

The Sequence of NASD Arbitration

Claim Initiation

1. Claimant, usually through an attorney files a Statement of Claim with the NASD.

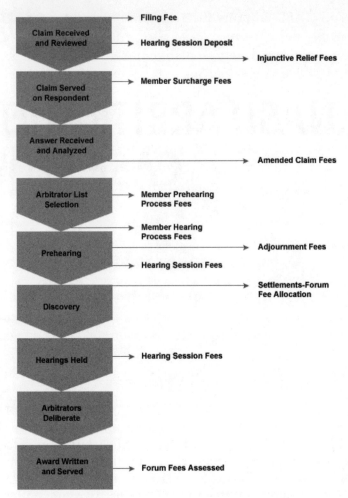

Figure A.1 NASD Dispute Resolution Flowchart
Source: NASD.com. Reprinted with permission.

2. The NASD informs the registered representative and the broker-dealer firm.
3. The registered representative receives the Statement of Claim. He or she informs the broker-dealer firm(s) and the errors-and-omissions (E&O) carrier. It should be noted, as discussed in Appendix C, that often the broker-dealer procures the E&O coverage for all of its registered representatives on a group basis and charges back the cost of the coverage to each registered representative. This does not relieve the registered representative from the obligation to notify the E&O carrier in the event of a claim. If the notice requirement in the E&O policy is not complied with, the E&O carrier is entitled to, and most certainly will, disclaim liability, leaving the registered representative without insurance.
4. The registered representative researches the case and organizes all relevant documents. The broker-dealer firm prepares whatever documentation it may have and sends it to the registered representative and the attorney.
5. The E&O carrier assigns the case to an attorney and informs the registered representative and the broker-dealer firm.
6. The attorney makes initial contact with the registered representative.

Initial Case Study/Assessment

1. The registered representative prepares a document that summarizes the facts of the case, responding to all issues identified in the Statement of Claim. He transmits this, along with copies of all relevant documentation, to the attorney.
2. The registered representative and the attorney meet to discuss the case (or have one or more extensive telephone conversations).
3. The attorney assesses the case and the registered representative as a potential witness and communicates this assessment

to the registered representative and the E&O carrier. This may include a discussion of settlement, if the facts warrant.

4. The attorney prepares a response to the Statement of Claim and reviews it with the registered representative. Upon finalization, this document is sent to the complainant's attorney, the registered representative, and the NASD.

Selection of Arbitrators

1. The attorney reviews a computer-generated list of possible arbitrators.

2. The attorney studies the available information about the potential arbitrators, that includes a listing of the cases that the arbitrator heard that resulted in awards, as well as the amount of the awards.

3. The attorney strikes out as unacceptable any potential arbitrators who, in the opinion of the attorney, would not be appropriate.

4. The attorney presents the NASD with a list of preferred arbitrators.

5. If necessary, the NASD will generate a second list, in which arbitrators can be challenged only for cause.

Prehearing Preparation

1. The attorney is informed by the NASD of the arbitrators who have been assigned to the case. The paralegal, if one is assigned to the case, coordinates with the registered representative, the opposing council, and the arbitrators to arrive at a mutually agreeable process of finding acceptable dates for the hearing.

2. The attorney and the client continue to review the facts of the case, anticipating issues that will come up and discussing how these issues should be addressed. The attorney and the registered representative meet in person or have one or more

telephone discussions to help prepare the registered representative for direct examination and cross-examination.

3. The attorney begins the process of preparing for the direct examination of the registered representative, the cross-examination of the claimant and any additional witnesses (including expert witnesses), cross-examination of any additional opposing witnesses (including expert witnesses), and closing argument. These documents are constantly reviewed, revised, and updated throughout the entire process.

4. The attorney reviews opposing counsel's communication, which includes a list of potential witnesses (including expert witnesses). The attorney and the registered representative decide on the use of additional witnesses, including expert witnesses. The attorney, the paralegal, and the registered representative help prepare additional witnesses, if any.

5. The attorney may communicate (or receive communication from) the clamaint's counsel and have discussions about settlement. Any offers are communicated to the registered representative, discussed, and decided upon (outright refusal or counteroffer).

6. The paralegal, if one is assigned to the case, prepares and indexes all exhibits. The paralegal coordinates all logistical issues, including schedule changes, preparation and distribution of documents to all parties, making sufficient copies of all documents, and transportation.

7. An offer to settle can be received and evaluated at any stage of the process.

Hearing

1. The opposing counsel selects the order in which the claimant's case will be presented. Normally, this will begin with the direct examination of the claimant. However, the registered representative should be fully prepared to testify at any time, including being the first witness.

2. While the opposing counsel conducts direct examination, the attorney, paralegal, and registered representative carefully observe what is being said, and take notes on points that can be covered in direct or cross-examination. This information is used to prepare for the rest of the hearing and to utilize in the closing argument.

3. The attorney, paralegal, and registered representative meet at the end of each day of the hearing to evaluate the day's testimony and organize a game plan on how to proceed going forward.

4. The attorney cross-examines the claimant and any other witnesses.

5. The attorney conducts direct examination of the registered representative and any other witnesses, including expert witnesses.

6. The registered representative is cross-examined by the claimant's attorney. The registered representative's attorney may then conduct redirect questioning.

7. The attorney and the client continue to evaluate the case and, as appropriate, discuss settlement.

8. The attorney prepares memoranda of law, as necessary (at various points in the hearing—e.g., if there is a break).

9. The attorney continues to revise and refine the closing argument, utilizing testimony from the hearing.

10. The attorney makes closing argument, and prepares any memoranda of law.

Decision

The arbitration panel renders its decision, which includes an award amount (if any). The decision may include the panel's reasoning.

NASD ARBITRATION TRENDS

This is a brief overview and analysis of NASD arbitration statistics. The intention is not to provide an in-depth analytical review, but rather to demonstrate general trends that might be of interest to the registered representative. All figures and tables in this section are from the NASD.com web site, and are reprinted with the permission of the NASD.

Caseload

Figure B.1 has statistics that include all NASD arbitration cases. The trend is obvious and easy to understand. The boom market of the late 1990s was followed by the market "correction" of the early part of this decade. There was a spike in cases being filed,

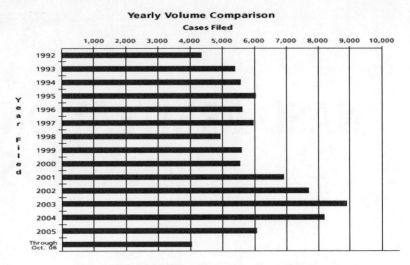

Figure B.1   NASD Arbitration Case Filings
Source: NASD.com. Reprinted with permission.

as investors attempted to recover some of the value of their portfolio losses.

The high point in caseload was 2003, with 8,945 cases. It decreased each of the next two years—to 8,201 in 2004 and 6,074 in
2005. Through October 2006, 4,057 cases were filed, projecting to
approximately 4,800 cases for the year.

These statistics viewed in the short term provide some comfort for representatives, but also a warning. While it may stand
to reason that continued rise in the equities markets may result
in fewer filings, there are two additional key points.

First, for those reps who become involved in arbitration, the
challenge is just as severe in a "down" year for case filings as in
a year in which filings were on the rise. Second, today's market
increase historically has preceded, at some point, another correction. When and if that happens, as it nearly surely will, these
statistics suggest that an increase in filings is also likely.

Table B.1 How NASD Arbitration Cases Close

Cases Decided by Arbitrators	2002	% of Cases	2003	% of Cases	2004	% of Cases	2005	% of Cases	%	Total
After Hearing	1,463	25%	1,764	24%	1,915	21%	1,767	20%		
After Review of Documents	443	8%	313	4%	508	6%	355	4%		
Total	1,906	32%	2,077	29%	2,423	27%	2,122	24%	38	8,561

Cases Resolved by Other Means	2002	% of Cases	2003	% of Cases	2004	% of Cases	2005	% of Cases		
Direct Settlement by Parties	2,204	37%	2,616	36%	3,700	41%	3,940	44%		
Settled via Mediation	752	13%	1,182	16%	1,201	13%	910	10%		
Withdrawn	547	9%	647	9%	677	7%	806	9%		
All Others	489	8%	679	9%	1,073	12%	1,127	13%		
Total	3,992	68%	5,124	71%	6,651	73%	6,783	76%	62	22,621

Source: NASD.com. Reprinted with permission.

How Cases Are Decided

Over the four-year period of 2002 to 2005, 38 percent of the NASD arbitration cases were decided by arbitrators, and 62 percent were decided by other means. These cases include all NASD arbitration disputes. As a general overview, approximately 10 percent of the cases were withdrawn. Thus, approximately 52 percent of all cases filed resulted in a settlement prior to a hearing (see Table B.1).

Results of Customer Claimant Arbitration Award Cases

This is a particularly fascinating table for registered representatives to consider. It focuses exclusively on customer claimant cases, which are investor claims against registered representatives. It demonstrates a consistent decreasing trend of awards to claimants. In 2005, claimants received awards in 43 percent of the cases, meaning that no awards were given for 57 percent of the cases. This suggests that registered representatives who are successful in bringing their case to hearing prevail more than half the time, with no award against them (see Table B.2).

Table B.2   Results of Customer Claimant NASD Award Cases

Year Decided	All Customer Claimant Cases Decided (Hearings & Paper)	All Customer Claimant Cases Where Customer Awarded Damages	Percentage of Customer Award Cases*
2000	1,196	635	53%
2001	1,172	637	54%
2002	1,330	702	53%
2003	1,513	742	49%
2004	1,894	888	47%
2005	1,610	687	43%

*Percentage of customer claimant award cases has been recalculated to reflect only instances in which investors as claimants recovered monetary damages or nonmonetary relief.
Source: NASD.com. Reprinted with permission.

ERRORS-AND-OMISSIONS INSURANCE

Financial advisers are required "observe high standards of commercial honor and just and equitable principles of trade." Investment adviser regulation and securities laws in many states stipulate that financial advisers owe a fiduciary responsibility to their clients. When financial advisers' actions are contrary to these principles, investors may incur damages, which in turn may result in restitution by the advisers' employer and/or the adviser through settlements, awards, and/or regulatory actions.

For advisers who handle hundreds of clients' accounts with total assets of millions of dollars, it is not uncommon for one or two legitimate complaints to surface over a career of 30 or more years. Often, the claim comes about due to an oversight, administrative error, or simple misunderstanding. These types of claims are the primary reason that advisers buy E&O insurance—just as other professionals such as doctors and lawyers buy professional liability insurance.

Put another way, Scott Hoyt, senior vice president and general counsel at Securities America, Inc., writes, "Maybe once or twice in their careers, securities reps will have to defend themselves against an action brought against them by a client seeking damages in connection with some purchase or series of transactions. They have two kinds of potential losses: the indemnity loss—or the amount of an award that might be used against them—and defense costs. ... Having E&O insurance is like having car insurance; you are protecting yourself against the chance of having a bad accident (Laurie Kulikowski, "Scott Hoyt, senior vice president and general counsel at Securities America in Omaha, Neb., discusses the state of E&O insurance." *Financial Planning*, September 1, 2003).

This brings to light an often overlooked aspect of E&O insurance for independent financial advisers who pay for "group E&O coverage" provided through their employers. These employers often require their financial advisers to pay for coverage that, while covering activities of the financial advisers, primarily provides coverage for the employer as the first insured. The policies then extend coverage to current financial advisers of the firm when the following conditions apply:

1. The alleged activities occurred while the financial adviser was employed by the current employer.
2. The financial adviser is still employed by the employer when the claim is received by the employer. Once a financial adviser leaves an employer, his E&O coverage usually terminates. Financial advisers are sometimes able to purchase "tail coverage" to continue coverage for their actions conducted at the former employer. But it is often offered only for periods of one or two years and has significant limitations. When a financial adviser joins a new employer, the group E&O coverage offered through that employer typically excludes

activities conducted at prior employers. So when no tail coverage is in effect, claims involving activities from a former employer can represent a significant liability for financial advisers.

3. The alleged damages did not involve activities excluded by the policy. Today's financial advisers often offer a broader array of products and services than in the past. However, it is important to ensure that each activity is covered by the financial adviser's E&O policy. In addition, a claim of fraud against a registered representative is typically excluded by E&O carriers.

4. The alleged activities occurred during the policy coverage periods.

5. The client complaint is received and reported to the insurer during the policy period.

6. The policy's aggregate limits have not been reached. E&O policies have two types of limits: a limit per claim and an aggregate limit. Once an insurer pays out the aggregate limit for all claims during a policy period, further claims will no longer be paid. So if an employer reaches the aggregate limits on the E&O policy before a financial adviser's complaint is received, there may not be coverage for his complaint.

In summary, E&O insurance is an area that registered representatives overlook at their potential peril. The most important thing to realize is that when coverage is provided through an employer, even though the cost of that coverage is passed on to the rep, the policy is written to protect the employer first and the rep second. It is prudent for a registered representative to review his or her E&O coverage, on at least an annual basis. Any questions regarding the coverage should be researched to the rep's satisfaction, even if it might involve paying a legal fee.

This report was prepared with substantial assistance by Christopher Gryzen, vice president of compliance at BancWest Investment Services and special faculty member at Creighton University.

TECHNOLOGY TOOLS

There are many fantastic technology tools available to registered representatives. We feature two of them in this section.

Copytalk

www.copytalk.com   (866) 267-9825

Copytalk is a mobile scribe service used by many financial services professionals. Through its use, registered representatives can dictate anytime, anywhere, from any phone. The dictation is received by transcriptionists, with all identifiable information stripped out (customer's name, company, area code, phone number), for confidentiality reasons. Each transcription can be up to four minutes in length.

The transcription is typed into a file and e-mailed to the customer. This can then be modified, as desired, and used either as the basis for follow-up communication with the client (e-mail or letter), or as action items for the registered representative or a staff member. The business was designed specifically for the unique privacy and security needs of the financial services industry. There are a number of additional precautions that are put into place to ensure the security of the data. As of this writing in March 2007 there are no set-up fees, turnaround is same-day, and the customer has an unlimited number of monthly dictations for a flat rate.

Tom Hine has used Copytalk as a regular aspect of his process for four years. Following are his tips for optimal use:

- There is a learning curve. There is a tendency at first to dictate more information than is necessary. For a client review, there is no need to mention that the client needed a Kleenex halfway through the meeting. I try to keep them brief—one and a half typed pages maximum.
- Cover the highlights of the event. If it was a client meeting, break the dictation into two main sections: "Meeting Summary" and "Action Items."
- Train a staff member to take the e-mails and clean them up. As you get better at dictation, this is less and less necessary. The staff member puts the meeting summary points into letter form. The letter is then sent to me for review, modification, and send-out.
- All letters should include some type of language that asks for a response if the summary does not meet with the client's recollection, such as "If anything in this letter does not meet with your recollection, please let me know." If there is no response, you have a solid piece of documentation as part of the relationship. If there is a response, you have another action item.
- There is a danger in overpromising in a summary letter. In the

event you promise to do something that is not done, you have created a vulnerability for yourself. You need to have a system by which your letters are reviewed to see that action items have been taken care of.

Securities Arbitration Commentator

www.sacarbitration.com   (973) 761-5880

This web site offers a variety of informational products and services relating to securities arbitration. Access to the company's arbitration awards library is available on a "point and click" basis from the "Arbitration and Mediation" section of the NASD.com web site. Exact replicas of the arbitrators' awards are available in pdf format.

Beyond this service, sacarbitation.com offers a variety of more sophisticated services, which involve querying their database to retrieve information of interest to parties on either side of a securities arbitration. The records of individual arbitrators can be searched to determine how many awards each has made, either as an individual arbitrator or as a member of a panel.

Claimants and respondents have made use of the company's database products in a number of other ways. Data is available by a large number of fields, including by broker, broker-dealer firm, type of dispute, record of awards in cases with similar characteristics, and trends involving punitive damages.

The *Securities Arbitration Commentator* is a monthly newsletter. As of this writing in March 2007, the company claims that it is the only periodical that focuses exclusively on the practice and processes of securities/commodities arbitration.

As the entire arbitration process becomes more sophisticated, registered representatives should realize that informational tools such as those available on this site can be incorporated into defense strategy and may be part of the claimant's strategy.

INDEX

A

Account control, 93, 94
Account minimums, 160–162
Adapting versus adopting, 143, 144
Admitting fallibility, 149, 150
Admitting mistakes, 152
Alcoholics Anonymous
    and 12 steps, 136
Allocation models
    actual, 47–51, 76, 77
    mythical, 42–46, 66
Appearance
    awareness of your, 179
Arbitration
    and setting goals, 18
Arbitrators
    defined, 224, 225
    selection of, 236, 237
    in Tom Hine's case, 28, 29
Asset allocation
    breakdown of, 96, 97, 99–101
    and cross-examination of Tom Hine,
        97–102
    as crux of claimant's case, 83–85
    and the 80 percent level, 85–88
    and testimony of claimant in Tom
        Hine's case, 38

Asset allocation meeting, 183
Attorney
    extra, 257, 258
    initial meeting with, 12–15, 263, 264
    and NASD arbitration hearing,
        219–250
    preparing for initial meeting with,
        6–12, 259, 261
    in Tom Hine's case, 10, 11
Attorney's duties
    assessing the documentation, 232
    assessing the responsiveness of the
        respondent, 233, 234
    assessing the size of the loss, 231, 232
    assessing the strength of the case,
        230–234, 264
    checking the claimant's background,
        231
    cross-examining the claimant, 245,
        246
    daily
        reviewing/analyzing/strategizing,
        249
    expecting surprises, 242, 243
    identifying critical issues, 232
    organizing exhibits, 239
    organizing key trial memoranda, 240

Attorney's duties (*continued*)
    performing redirect examination, 248
    preparing closing argument, 249, 250
    preparing for prehearing, 241, 242
    preparing opening statements, 243
    questioning the respondent, 247, 248
    scrutinizing the suitability of the
      respondent as a witness, 233
Awareness of the industry, 186
Awareness principle
    and going against the grain, 186, 187
    and martial arts, 89, 90
    and protecting and growing your
      financial services practice, 134, 135,
      137, 177–187

B
Bach, David
    and Strategic Coach, 195
Balanced Wealth Process, 181–183
Beginner's mind, 20
Besser, Albert G.
    as arbitration chairperson in Tom
      Hine's case, 28, 29
Broker-dealer firm
    and informing them about receipt of
      Statement of Claim, 252
    in NASD arbitration hearing, 6, 225,
      226
Broker versus fiduciary, 65
Buffett, Warren
    and qualities of character, 157, 158
Building a practice
    and duality, 172, 173

C
Carnegie, Dale
    and *How to Win Friends and Influence
      People*, 148, 149
Carson, Ron
    and PEAK Productions, 183, 185, 193
    and *Tested in the Trenches*, 141–143, 161
Churchill, Winston
    and courage, 191
Civil litigation
    versus arbitration, 219, 220
Claimant
    checking background of, 231

cross-examination described, 245, 246
and cross-examination in Tom Hine's
    case, 34–39,110
defined, 220, 221
and ensuing investment pattern, 106,
    109, 110
identified as growth investor, 92, 93,
    102
legal representation of, 221, 222
listening to testimony of, 274, 275
testimony described, 243–245
and testimony in Tom Hine's case,
    30–34
in Tom Hine's case, 6–8
and undisclosed real estate holdings,
    21, 35
wife of, 70
Claimant awards, 260–262
Clarification with clients, 151, 152,
    170–172
Client-centric business, 179–181
Clients
    clarification with, 151, 152, 170–172
    and duality, 167–169
    and signs that a portfolio change may
      be indicated, 169, 170
    support and activities for, 184, 185
    your appearance to, 179
Closing arguments
    described, 249, 250
    in Tom Hine's case, 105–127
Covey, Stephen
    and *The Seven Habits of Highly Effective
      People*, 136, 149, 167
Cross-examination
    challenges of, 267–270, 280, 281
    preparing for, 270–274, 280, 281
    surviving and succeeding at, 281
    watching, 277
Cycle of life, 131–139

D
Damages
    of claimant in Tom Hine's case, 5, 78,
      117, 118
    of respondent, 205
Dancing in the gray zone, 169
Decision-making meeting, 183–184

Dedication principle
and martial arts, 107, 108
and protecting and growing your
financial services practice, 134, 135,
137, 189–196
Deming, W. Edwards
and quality management, 190
Dismissal of claims, 118
Doctrine of Overwhelming
Documentation, 11, 12
Documentation, 11, 12, 74, 75, 171, 172,
183, 232, 252, 254
after receiving Statement of Claim,
252, 254
Duality
and building a practice, 172, 173
and clients, 167–169
and entrepreneurs, 172, 173
and humor, 166, 167
and listening to testimony, 275, 276
and martial arts, 67, 68
and wanting it both ways, 173–175
Duality principle
and protecting and growing your
financial services practice, 134, 135,
137, 165–175
and yin and yang, 67, 68, 137, 165–175
Dubas, Mary
on arbitration panel in Tom Hine's
case, 29

E
Edison, Thomas
and persistence, 191
Emotional stress
of NASD arbitration hearing, 202
Entrepreneurs
and duality, 172, 173
Errors-and-omissions insurance
and carrier incentive to settle, 262,
263
carriers, 6, 8, 226, 227
deductible, 201
and informing the carrier about
receipt of Statement of Claim,
252–254
Exhibits
organization of, 239

Expert witness
and closing remarks, 112, 113
credentials of, 40, 57
and cross-examination in Tom Hine's
case, 56, 57
testimony described, 243–245
and testimony in Tom Hine's case,
40–44
unmasking of, 53–80
use of, 248, 249
Extra efforts
in preparing for the arbitration
hearing, 21, 22, 47–51, 57, 58, 62, 106,
107, 200, 264–266

F
Fact finding meeting, 181–183
Financial fact-finding questionnaire, 17
5 percent theory, 41, 42
Franklin, Benjamin
and 13 virtues, 135, 136
Fung, Dennis
and the O.J. Simpson trial, 82, 83

G
Gehrig, Lou
and humility, 148
Goodwin, Doris Kearns
and *A Team of Rivals*, 147, 148
Google.com, 192
Gratitude
and humility, 154, 155
Growth investor
identifying claimant as, 92, 93, 102

H
"The hard way," 164
Hearing day 1, 25–51
Hearing day 2, 53–80
Hearing day 3, 81–104
Hearing day 4, 105–127
Heightened supervision
and NASD arbitration hearing, 203
Herman, Joan
as paralegal in Tom Hine's case, 26,
39
Humility
and gratitude, 154, 155

Humility principle
and its application in NASD
arbitration, 20–22
and martial arts, 18–20
and protecting and growing your
financial services practice, 133, 135,
137, 147, 155
Humor
and the duality principle, 166, 167
and Stockholm syndrome, 108

I
"I could be wrong," 149, 150
Integrity principle
and martial arts, 48, 49
and protecting and growing your
financial services practice, 133, 135,
137, 157–164
Investor scorecard, 16, 72, 73, 84

K
Kaizen, 107, 108, 189–196
"Know your client," 163, 169, 179, 185,
186
yin and yang of, 185, 186

L
Lehman Brothers Aggregate Bond Index,
54, 55
Lennon, John
and "Imagine," 191, 192
"Let me clarify," 151, 152
Letter of demand, 5, 252, 253
Life insurance policy
surrender of, 55, 56, 66, 67
Lincoln, Abraham
and humility, 147, 148

M
Martial arts
and the awareness principle, 89, 90
and the dedication principle, 107,
108
etiquette of, 9
and the humility principle, 18–20
and the integrity principle, 48–49
positive life impact of, 8, 9
and the principle of duality, 67, 68
Monetary costs
of NASD arbitration hearing, 201, 202

N
NASD arbitration hearing
and added staff time, 200
and additional client time, 200, 201
and assessing the strength of the case,
230–234
from the attorney's perspective,
219–250
and being brutally honest with your
attorney, 256, 257
case studies, 207–217
versus civil litigation, 219, 220
and client and prospect relationships,
202
costs of, 199–205
emotional stress of, 202
and errors-and-omissions insurance
deductible, 201
and "extra credit" research projects,
21, 22, 47–51, 57, 58, 62, 106, 107,
200, 264–266
and heightened supervision, 203
how to prepare for, 251–266
how to prevail in, 124–126, 197–282
monetary costs of, 201, 202
and NASD filing fees, 201
and opportunity cost, 202
organization and documentation
prior to, 254–256
NASD arbitration hearing (continued)
and outside business dealings, 204
patient approach to, 159, 160, 251, 252
and preparing the case with the
attorney, 10–18, 200
and professional services, 201, 257,
258
and proportion resulting in claimant
awards, 260, 261
and prospecting, sales, and recruiting
staff members, 204, 205
and researching the case and
preparing a summary for the
attorney, 6–8, 199, 200
and restricted broker-dealer
movement, 203
scheduling of, 237–239
and self-evaluation, 230, 256
and side settlement, 201
and slow-down of new product
appointments, 203, 204

and staff overtime, 201
time considerations of, 199–201
of Tom Hine, 1–127
and travel costs, 201
and trial time, 79, 80, 200
using time wisely during, 277
and using your expertise to educate
attorney and arbitrators, 278, 279
and viral contagion, 205
NASD filing fees
and arbitration hearing, 201
"Never say never," 150
New account form, 59, 60

O
Oerter, Al
and awareness during Olympic
Games, 177, 178
Office of supervisory jurisdiction
and informing them about receipt of
Statement of Claim, 252
Opening statements, 243, 274
in Tom Hine's case, 29, 30
Opening your mind, 167
Opportunity cost
and NASD arbitration hearing, 202
Outside business dealings
and NASD arbitration hearing, 204

P
Paralegal
defined, 224
in Tom Hine's case, 26, 39
PEAK Productions
and Ron Carson, 183, 185, 193
and Strategic Coach, 194, 195
Peters, Tom
and *In Search of Excellence*, 179
Poisoning the well
and claimant's undisclosed real estate
holdings, 35
Portfolio adjustments, 169–172
and major changes, 172
signs indicating the need for, 169, 170
Portfolio decrease in value, 8
Practicing in slow motion, 159, 160
Prehearing preparation, 10, 22, 241, 242
Professional services
and NASD arbitration hearing, 201,
257, 258

Protecting and growing your financial
services practice
using five black-belt principles,
129–196

Q
Quest for Excellence Coaching Program,
160, 193

R
Rate of return
and testimony of claimant in Tom
Hine's case, 31, 32
and testimony of expert witness in
Tom Hine's case, 60
Redirect examination
described, 248
in Tom Hine's case, 39, 67
Registered representative
initiating a claim against, 5, 227,
228
Registered representatives
functions of, 91, 92
Respondent
and credentials of Tom Hine, 69
cross-examination of, 267–270, 280,
281
and cross-examination of Tom Hine,
97–102
defined, 222, 223
and direct examination of Tom Hine,
90–95
direct testimony described, 247, 248
legal representation of, 223, 224
and responsiveness to attorney's
requests, 233, 234
and suitability as a witness, 233
and testimony of Tom Hine, 68–80
and testimony under direct
examination, 279, 280
Restricted broker-dealer movement
and NASD arbitration hearing, 203
Risk
calculating, 86–88
Robbins, Anthony
and unreasonableness, 191
Rose, Pete
and the white-belt attitude, 153
Rule 2310, 163, 169, 179, 185
Russell 3000 Index, 54, 55, 95

S

Sanders, Harlan
  and integrity, 164
Sanduski, Steve
  and *Tested in the Trenches*, 141
Scheduling
  and incentive to settle, 262
  of NASD arbitration hearing, 237–239
Self-evaluation
  and NASD arbitration hearing, 230,
  256
Settlements, 18, 62, 63, 122, 123, 201,
  234–236, 260–263, 282
Slow-down of new product
  appointments
  and NASD arbitration hearing, 203,
  204
Statement of Claim
  defined, 228, 229
  documentation after receiving, 252,
  254
  first steps after receiving, 252–260
  loading up, 262
  responding to, 229, 230
  in Tom Hine's case, 5
  as your guide, 258, 259
Stockholm syndrome, 108, 109
Strategic Coach
  and PEAK Productions, 194, 195
Support and activities for clients, 184, 185
Sweat of perfection, 19

T

Taylor, Frederick
  and manufacturing efficiency, 190
Technology fund purchase, 46, 47, 75, 94,
  95, 101, 120, 121
1035 exchange, 55, 56, 66, 67
Tested in the Trenches
  and Ron Carson, 141–143, 161
Testimony
  under direct examination, 279, 280

  dueling, 81, 82
  preparing for, 267–282
  by telephone, 57, 58, 62, 63
  yin and yang of, 67, 68
The third eye, 177–187
Three-meeting rule, 181–184
Time considerations
  of NASD arbitration hearing, 199–201
"To be fair," 163
Tough phone calls, 162
Travel costs
  of NASD arbitration hearing, 201
Trial time
  of NASD arbitration hearing, 79, 80,
  200

U

U-4 issues, 18, 122, 123, 202, 205
Uncontested facts, 114, 115
Uniform Submission Agreement, 255

V

Vindication, 123–126
Viral contagion
  and NASD arbitration hearing, 205

W

Walking away from a sale, 163, 164
Weisman, Barbara
  on arbitration panel in Tom Hine's
  case, 29
Weller, Jim
  as Tom Hine's defense attorney, 10,
  12–18, 26–123
White-belt attitude, 20, 147–155
  power of the, 153, 154

Y

Yin and yang
  and the duality principle, 67, 68, 137,
  165–175

ABOUT THE AUTHORS

Thomas J. Hine, CFP®, CFS, MBA

Tom Hine is the managing member of Capital Wealth Management, LLC, and has more than 17 years of experience in the financial services industry. Throughout those years, Tom has been devoted to maintaining high ethical standards while developing sound financial planning ideas. Over the past 10 years, Tom has been a speaker at seminars given to major Connecticut corporations and more than 150 seminars given to the public.

Tom received a bachelor of science in business administration degree from the University of Connecticut in 1983, graduating cum laude. He also received a master of business administration degree from the University of Connecticut in 1986.

Tom earned his Certified Financial Planner (CFP®) designation through the College for Financial Planning in Denver, Colorado, and his Certified Funds Specialist (CFS) designation through the Institute of Business and Finance in La Jolla, California.

In 2003, Tom became what is known in the industry as a million-dollar producer. This means that his practice generates gross revenue in excess of $1 million. He has increased his practice over the intervening years. Tom was nominated by *Boomer* magazine as its Broker of the Year for 2005. In addition, he was interviewed or featured in three industry publications in 2006.

Tom Hine holds a fourth-degree black belt in Shotokan karate, awarded to him by the Japan Karate Association, an international school headquartered in Tokyo, Japan, which has millions of students worldwide. Tom began training with the Japan Karate Association in September 1980 at the University of Connecticut Karate Club under Sensei Robert Jacobs. Since 1992, Tom has served as an assistant instructor under the guidance of Sensei Jacobs at the University of Connecticut Karate Club.

There are many schools throughout the Northeast that meet for special training camps and competitions. All are under the leadership of Sensei Masataka Mori, who, at the age of 75, holds an eighth-degree black belt and is one of the original JKA instructors since the association was formed in the 1950s. Tom Hine has passed both the intensive two-year B class instructor course and the A class instructor training course under Sensei Mori. Tom has competed regionally, nationally, and internationally. In 1992, he traveled to Tokyo, Japan, to compete on the U.S. team in the International Shoto Cup Competition.

Tom and his family make their home in Glastonbury, Connecticut.

John K. Brubaker

John Brubaker has been a full-time writer since 1985, having written, edited, and produced more than 30,000 pages of final copy during that time. He graduated from Yale University with a bachelor of science degree in administrative sciences in 1976. For a period of seven years, John pursued a career in sales, sales management, and sales training with the Southwestern Company, a subsidiary of the Los Angeles Times Mirror Corporation. He was recognized as the company's Sales Manager of the Year in 1981. In 1983, he served as Northeast regional training manager, overseeing the training of 800 student salespeople.

In 1985, he co-authored *The AIDS Epidemic: How You Can Protect Yourself and Your Family—Why You Must* with National Institutes of Health Medical Investigator Dr. James Slaff. The book was published in five languages, endorsed by the American Red Cross and distributed worldwide, with 350,000 copies in print.

As part of the book's promotion, John made more than 60 appearances on radio and television.

Since 1989, John has created and managed two writing and consulting businesses.

Professional Resume Plus, LLC, a resume writing and outplacement service, has served more than 5,000 clients in 40 states and six foreign countries. The firm has helped clients secure placement with virtually every major employer in central Connecticut.

Brubaker and Associates, LLC, a multifaceted marketing/communications and business consulting firm, develops strategy and creates marketing material, press releases, business plans, and corporate speeches for small business and corporate clients. In 1995, the firm collaborated in the creation and promotion of *Yankee Fishing,* the first television series on northeastern fishing ever to achieve national syndication. The firm's clients include Fleet Bank/Bank of America, Sheraton, Nutrasweet, Heublein, Sony, and Volvo.

John has written business plans and marketing material for a wide range of industries, including manufacturing, retail, information technology, and e-commerce. As a freelance writer, his work has appeared in *Executive Edge* and *American Fitness* magazines as well as the *Hartford Courant* and *USA Today* newspapers.

While at Yale, John earned five varsity letters in track and field and was recognized as a member of the All-Ivy track and field team. He has continued his athletics as an adult, earning a first-degree black belt in martial arts, earning dual certification in tae kwon do and dae han mu doo in 2004. John has competed in masters track and field for the past several years, twice earning bronze medals in national competitions. He completed his first decathlon in the fall of 2005.

James W. Weller, Esq.
Nixon Peabody, LLP
Contributing Author

James Weller's legal career spans all aspects of commercial litigation. He has litigated numerous cases in the state and federal courts throughout New York, at the trial and appellate level. He has tried cases through verdict in the New York state courts, and has argued motions in jurisdictions throughout the United States and in the United States Supreme Court. Mr. Weller has extensive experience representing registered representatives in NASD arbitration. Mr. Weller has written and lectured widely. He taught constitutional law at the State University of New York at Stony Brook. Nixon, Peabody, LLP, is one of the largest law firms in the country, with more than 600 attorneys in 15 practice areas. The firm was recognized by *Fortune* magazine as one of the "100 Best Companies to Work For" in 2006.